Displaced

A MEMOIR OF SURVIVAL & STARTING

OVER AFTER HURRICANE KATRINA

LIVE WRITE PUBLISH | HOUSTON

Copyright © 2025 by Jocelyn Kerr.

All rights reserved. No part of this publication may be reproduced, distributed or transmitted in any form or by any means, including photocopying, recording, or other electronic or mechanical methods, without the prior written permission of the publisher, except in the case of brief quotations embodied in critical reviews and certain other noncommercial uses permitted by copyright law. For permission requests, write to the author at the website below.

Jocelyn Kerr/Live Write Publish www.jocelynkerr.com

Book Layout ©2025 www.LiveWritePublish.com

Book cover design by Rebekka Minar

Displaced: A memoir of survival and starting over after Hurricane Katrina / Jocelyn Kerr. —1st ed. ISBN 978-1-7327623-8-1

Ebook ISBN 978-1-7327623-9-8

Library of Congress Call Number 2025945522

*I will bring you through the fire and make you pure as silver
and refined as gold.*
- Zechariah 13:9

Prologue

There's a sound, like a wooden heart beating, and it's beating perfectly in time—ba-bommm (two, three, four) ba-bommm (two, three, four).

At first, I think I'm dreaming. Swimming in that space between wake and sleep. But my eyes open just a crack—I'm on the cold asbestos floor of the church fellowship hall, and I look up toward the stage where a piano sits. I see the heavy wooden doors on either side of the stage slowly creak open just an inch and ba-bommm they shutter closed in unison.

A thought, like a whisper, moves through my mind: *We're inside God's beating heart.*

I turn over to face the frosted windows where gray overcast light is flooding into the empty room, and I hear the wind howling against the windowpanes.

Eliot is sitting like a Buddha facing the windows, his back to me. He's perfectly still.

"What's with the doors?" I ask.

"Air pressure," he says. "The upstairs windows blew in around 3:00. We put boards up."

He pauses.

"Don't go up there; there's a lot of glass."

He doesn't turn. Doesn't move a muscle. I notice there's a blue plastic bucket to his right and I hear a steady drop-drop-drop of water falling into it. I look up to the ceiling and see a large tan wet spot in the acoustic tile.

"How long has it been going?" I ask.

"A little while. Everything's fine, go back to sleep."

A memory—like a dream, or a flood—can come on suddenly, disorient you, and take you places you never wanted to go.

One: Living in a Kind of Daydream

The Devil Lives Down in NOLA

I folded and unfolded a printed map—carefully creasing and bending back the folds as I looked out the Greyhound bus window at the miles of empty Texas land that seemed to stretch out for an eternity.

The bus would soon be crossing into Louisiana, the final leg of my journey. The road to New Orleans. A 24-hour, overnight ride from New Mexico, and California before that. A long way from where I started in Los Angeles.

Printed on the waxy paper was the image of a crescent-shaped river cutting through the city like an upturned horseshoe. I had never been to New Orleans, but I'd studied the map. Every bend of the crescent river. The streets that began at the Riverfront and crawled up toward an apex at Lake Pontchartrain. Everything about the place seemed foreign to me, even the name of that lake north of the city: PON-cha-train. Hard to pronounce. Harder to spell.

I fidgeted with the edges of the frayed map, then tucked it back into the hard-covered notebook that was my companion on this trip. The girl sitting next to me had fallen asleep. The bus was full, and we were both traveling alone—young women in our early 20s. Naturally, we sat together. We had spotted each other waiting in line to board in Amarillo and gravitated to each other. It was better than sitting with a weirdo or pervert.

Displaced

Before I left Los Angeles, people gave me near-endless lists of places to visit and things to see in New Orleans. People who had been there before told me I would know in the first five minutes whether the city was going to love me or grind me into the ground. There are only two ways to experience New Orleans, they said: The city will shower you with blessings or you'll wish you never went.

The city had that reputation, even back then—late November of 2001. She was The City That Care Forgot, in every sense of the phrase.

The girl sitting next to me stirred. During our hours of small talk, she told me she lived in New Orleans and was coming home from a vacation. She offered to give me a ride to my hotel when we arrived. I took that as a sign the city would love me—I had already been gifted a ride from the bus station to the hotel. What more would I need?

The bus crossed into Louisiana. The cold barren fields of Texas shifted from brown winter to a lush green landscape that absorbed us. The trees grew choked together in wild green brush. It started to rain, and the sky was blanketed with flapping white sheets of water. Each electric boom of thunder sounded as if God was calling out across the land. In the little towns we passed through, among cracked facades and crumbling brick houses, I saw churches on every corner—so many crosses—until I lost count. We plowed our way through hundreds of miles of wet, green land and tiny clusters of buildings dotting the quiet highway.

I thought, this is a place that needs God in abundance.

My seat mate woke up with the thunder. "Dang, we got some weather."

"Yeah, it's pretty bad."

"Nah, this ain't nothing," she said and pulled her sweater tight around her.

"What time do you think we'll get in?"

The Devil Lives Down in NOLA

"Aw, I don't know, maybe one in the morning? Traffic won't be bad. We should be able to sail through Baton Rouge," she patted my arm. "I got your back, don't worry. I wouldn't leave you in the station at night," she curled up in her seat and went back to sleep.

A snowstorm in Amarillo had put us behind schedule. We were supposed to arrive in late afternoon, but it was going to be well after midnight by the time we passed through Baton Rouge. From there it was another 45-minute drive into New Orleans.

I opened my notebook and jotted some notes about the scenery. The snowstorm. The girl sitting next to me. I'd had about 18 hours on the road to get excited for this adventure. It wasn't the first time I'd traveled alone, but it was the first time I'd ever been this far from home by myself. I'd broken an engagement. I felt like I was on the run—or running toward a new life. Going somewhere I had never been before. On a quest to become someone new. I wanted to be Tennessee Williams— or Truman Capote—or preferably, both. I scribbled everything I could into the blank pages of that notebook.

My seat mate was correct; we sailed through Baton Rouge just after midnight. That night was the first time I ever rode along the long concrete bridge that crossed the Bonnet Carre spillway and Lake Pontchartrain—two massive bodies of water that went on for miles. As we crossed this seemingly unending bridge over water, there was a brief pause in the rain that pelted us all day.

The sky and the water were so purely black that the horizon line had been erased across the water. I pressed my face to the cold glass of the window to look down at the road—the bus cast a small pool of yellow-white light beneath us. We were carried along this dark highway in a little bubble—our little oval of light.

In the distance, I struggled to find a horizon. The blue-black of the water bled so seamlessly into the blue-black of the sky that I marveled at the illusion—we were perfectly enclosed in this black womb. Somewhere in the distance, a sharp tendril of white lightning shot far and fast across the sky—like a vein shooting through with blinding light. In that brief second, everything was illuminated. I could see the water, and it seemed to go on forever around us. I shuddered and looked at my seat mate to ask if she'd seen it—she was sound asleep.

I turned on the reading light above my seat and pulled out the map. We were driving over miles of swampland and water. No matter which direction you arrive from, the descent into New Orleans occurs over water. From the west, where we were riding, Interstate 10 is a long, low bridge over the spillway and Lake Pontchartrain. From the east, you cross the Mississippi River over the Crescent City Connection bridge, or you cross the Industrial Canal. To the north, there's nothing but the lake. The south has the river. It's all water, everywhere.

I'd memorized the map.

As we finally rode into the light of the suburbs, my heart pounded in my ears with excitement. I was here. I took in every tattered billboard and ragged strip mall that lined the freeway. At that time, the above-ground cemeteries were still visible from Interstate 10. We drove past sprawling cities of the dead—their low stone walls butting up against the freeway. Mausoleums towering into the sky.

The city was smiling on me that night. We were deep into the witching hour when the bus pulled into the station, but I knew the city was smiling. The girl on the bus was groggy and half-asleep, but she gave me a ride to The Pontchartrain Hotel as she promised. She disappeared into the night, leaving me a little bit terrified, but ready to see where this would go.

If the trip went well, I would move here. If it didn't...I had no other plan. I'd sold off all my belongings, given up my old apartment and relationship, and the little bit of money I'd saved was used to take this trip. If it all went south, there was no fallback plan. I had nowhere to return to; I'd burned all my ships. I prayed the city would smile and open the door to a new life.

The Devil Lives Down in NOLA

The night clerk at the hotel showed me to a musty, closet-sized room with no windows. There was only enough space for an old wooden bed frame and a door to a small bathroom. I collapsed onto the threadbare flowered comforter, felt the mattresses' hard springs dig into me, and fell into a deep sleep.

* * *

Everyone starts their first trip at the French Quarter. I stood near Jackson Square, midday, my first day in the city, camera in hand. The St. Louis Cathedral towered above me and provided shade from the blinding sun. I wandered among the tourists in khaki shorts, and parents pushing strollers into the gated grassy yard of Jackson Square. Painters hung their wares on the black wrought iron fence that enclosed the square. Tarot and palm readers were stationed in front of the painters; they burned thick incense at their card tables, which were draped with purple and blue cloths.

A quartet of musicians belted out jazz standards from a park bench that served as a stage—a tuba player loomed as large as his instrument, a good looking young singer stood on the bench and carried a trombone in one hand and riled the crowd with the other, a wiry guy played an upright base with a hoodie pulled tight around his head to protect his fair skin from the sun, and a gray-haired trombone player stood behind them and fluidly moved his slide up and down the scale.

People stopped to dance and drop coins and dollars into a large white bucket at the tuba player's feet. I ducked around the dancers and kneeled on the steps of the cathedral to snap a few shots of the players and the people as they passed.

In those days I carried an old 1970s Canon camera that leaked light and ate film. The rest of the world was going digital in 2001, but I stuck to my old black and white stock. I stood and crossed to get a shot of the fountain in the square, but the camera jammed, and I couldn't advance the film. I spotted a doorway where I could open the camera and adjust the film. It was tucked away in the shadows, protected from the sun, so I slipped into the darkness, hoping it would limit the damage to my earlier pictures.

I opened the camera and put the film back on the sprockets. As I snapped it shut, a large leathery-faced man with a wild gray-blonde mane blocked my way out. "You a photographer?" His voice was gravelly.

"Sometimes." I focused on advancing my film a few frames and angled past him, back toward the crowds between the square and the cathedral.

He followed and stood next to me while I resumed shooting the tourists watching the band. "Photographers love me, they always seem to find me," he said. I didn't respond, so he continued, "I do street theater. Life is theater, you know what I'm saying? I'm the broom man!" He pumped his hands in the air.

I finally looked at him and his eyes brightened. "I've been written about in seven cities. Watch."

He strutted to a nearby tarot card table and grabbed an old wooden broom off the ground. He let out a tribal yell and began to pump the broom in the air, dancing in circles through the crowd like some kind of reincarnated Apache doing a war dance. His movements were made more dramatic by the stark contrast of his broom dance to his tourist-style orange Hawaiian shirt and khaki cargo shorts. His Santa belly shook as he pumped that broom in the air. He looked like an old tourist grandpa, except wielding this broom like a primitive weapon as he tore through the crowd.

People stood back to give him room. Some stared, some looked amused, some seemed frightened and looked away as they raced past. It was certainly something.

I watched but didn't photograph him. It was too performative. Too loud. Something about him made me feel uncomfortable and intrigued in equal measure.

He danced back to me, stopped and bowed before tossing the broom back toward the table. He pulled a handkerchief from his back pocket and wiped sweat from his brow.

"Did you see their faces? They had no idea what to do," he cackled and sighed.

When he smiled, he had the same sharp facial features as Jack Nicholson. The handkerchief was stuffed back in his pocket.

"That's life, you know what I'm saying?" He said the word "life" with contempt. "Come on, let me show you my book."

I followed him to the card table where the broom had landed. A purple tablecloth covered it and hung to the ground. There were two folding lawn chairs, one on either side. He sat in one and pulled a 3-ring binder from under the table. He motioned to the other chair, so I sat opposite him.

He handed me the binder. It had maybe 10 or 15 newspaper clippings taped to sheets of white paper. Each was held in a plastic sheet protector. All the clippings featured photographs of him dancing through crowds with the broom. Newspapers from St. Petersburg, Florida to San Francisco had done little news features on him.

The afternoon sun reflected off the paper and made me squint, so I only halfway skimmed the articles. They were all the same: local character performs amusing tricks.

"As you can see, I'm a good story," he said as I handed the book back. "People love a good story, don't they? When I'm in New Orleans I'm El Diablo. The Devil."

He lifted a laminated sheet of paper from where it was pinned to the tablecloth. It was a line drawing of his face, Jack Nicholson-style with a devilish smile and eyes glowing red, and two massive ram horns extending from the front of his head. Above his face it said, "Tarot Readings by" and below the face, in a spectacularly flaming font, it said, "El Diablo."

I nodded, and he dropped the sign.

"I'm mulatto," he continued.

"My mother's white and my father's a black panther—and I don't mean the political group. I mean my mother lived in Kenya and was raped by a black panther—the cat. When I was born, I had horns and they said I wasn't entirely human," he pulled his hair back to expose his hairline and sure enough, there appeared to be two faint scars on either side of his skull, right at the hairline, where horns theoretically could have been. "My mother had them removed when I was a child. You can feel the holes if you want."

"No, that's okay."

He let go of his hairline. "Let me do your reading, then. You have $40?"

"Sorry."

"How about $20?"

"I don't think I have $20 either." I knew very well I had about $100 in various small bills in the front pocket of my shorts.

"Well, what do you have? Special for you, I'll do it for whatever you've got."

I reached into my pocket and prayed to God I'd pull out a small bill. Please God, let it be a five or a one, I prayed. I rummaged around in my pocket and slid out a single bill: it was a ten. Whew! Okay, ten wasn't bad. I could afford to lose a ten.

I tried not to show my relief as I handed him the money.

He pulled a huge wad of cash from his own pocket and layered it in with the tens. There was at least a cool grand in that stack, probably more.

His Jack Nicholson smile returned.

"You know what? I'm going to read your palms and your cards. You got quite a deal, little sister. My usual price is $75 for a private reading like this. What a steal."

I knew from his excitement this was going to be a good show. He took each of my hands individually and traced the lines of my palms with his index finger. He clasped my wrists in his calloused hands and turned them over a few times: front and back, front and back. He examined the sides of my fingers and rubbed each of my palms with his thumbs. Each hand was raised close to his eyes while he made "hmm" sounds.

Finally, he spoke, "You recently came out of a relationship. It was amicable...."

He looked to me for confirmation, but I kept my face still. I knew plenty of "light healers" back home, and I knew about cold reading. From the time I could walk, my grandmother had taken me to *curanderas*—old Mexican ladies selling potions and spells and telling your fortune in the back room of crowded apartments. I could sniff out psychic pretenders, and I was on the fence about his skills.

Something about him was captivating, though. I admired his style. I could see he was fully committed to giving a good show.

"You're looking for a husband..." he continued, looking back at my hands. "You want to have a daughter."

I looked at him blankly. It didn't take a fortune teller to make those statements about any young woman. I was 24 at the time, and looked younger, wandering alone in the Quarter. Anyone could see I was single, and what young woman isn't looking for love? My façade stayed intact.

El Diablo scanned my face and said, "hm."

He dropped my hands and leaned down to pull a tarot deck from under the table. He spread them face-down in front of me. "Pick ten cards."

Tarot wasn't new to me. I had been reading tarot since middle school when my friends and I went through an occult phase. Astrology, astral traveling, tarot, crystals—we did it all. In fact, I still used the tarot deck I bought when I was twelve. It's not that I didn't believe in messages from beyond or *curanderas* or spirit healing—I did, very much. But I also knew a good hustle when I saw one, and I was curious where this reading would land.

My stomach fluttered as I pulled cards, giddy to see where things would go. Would he say something useful—give me a sign? Would he see something about moving here? Would I walk away knowing for sure that I was meant to be here?

I was dying to know. I kept my face calm and slid ten cards toward him. He pushed the rest to the side and placed the ten in a classic tarot spread: the Celtic cross.

So far, we were on the same page.

As he laid them out, I thought the cards I chose seemed inconsequential. There was no message there for me. Not a message I could see, anyway. No epiphany. But he stared at them as if he were reading the Rosetta Stone.

"You're hoping to find something here. You want to live here. You're on a search. For a man, maybe." He looked up for a reaction, but I held my gaze steady.

His brow tightened, and he looked back to the cards, "...not entirely. No. It's not a man. You're looking for something else...." He looked up, and I was stone.

His eyes narrowed as he stared into me, "What you're looking for is here. But be careful what you find."

I cracked a smile and cocked my head.

"You're not impressed." He was irritated; I could tell. He roughly gathered the cards back together.

"It was a little generic, right?" I was giving feedback on his performance as much as the quality of his reading.

"You don't have to believe me." There was a sharp edge to his voice as he put the cards under the table. "But you know what I'm saying is true."

"Everything's true and everything's false. Life is a theater, right?" I hoped he'd appreciate I was joking with him, trying to lighten the mood. I felt a little bad I'd rained on the show.

"That it is!" He coughed out a loud, hardy laugh. "Listen, I feel bad about taking your money, kid. Not bad enough to give it back," he laughed again, "but let me buy you a coffee. I'll make it up to you."

"Okay," I laughed.

The Devil Lives Down in NOLA

Now that we'd gotten past the hustle, I wanted to talk with him. I was dying to know how he ended up doing this dog and pony show.

"Come on, help me pack up this stuff," he said. "I'll leave it with my friend on Decatur."

I folded the chairs while he folded the tablecloth. He stacked two plastic bins of gear onto a small folding dolly. We carried everything down the stone walkway toward Decatur Street, past the other tarot tables and the artists stationed at the black iron fence. The walkway was shaded by the overhang of old oaks. As we passed, a few of the languishing readers called out and waved to Diablo from behind their incense clouds.

"They're all jealous of me," he leaned in and whispered to me. "I make more money than all of them combined. I try to tell them how it's done, how to talk to people, but they don't understand human nature. They don't know how to give people a show, you know what I'm saying?"

"I think so."

"Yeah, you know what I'm saying." There was a caustic tone to his voice.

We got to the end of the path where the buggy tour guides parked their donkeys and horses. A couple of people were standing around a table at the end of the walkway. A tall, gaunt guy stood against the iron fence in a long black cape and top hat. It was late November, but I imagined how hot it must be under that thick fabric. The rest of us were in shorts and t-shirts. Diablo stacked his things behind the table.

"Hey, I'm going to leave this stuff while we get some coffee. This is my friend..." he looked to me for my name.

"Jocelyn," I said.

"This is my friend Jocelyn, she's new in town," he finished.

They all smiled and said hello. We walked across the street to Café du Monde and found a seat at one of the retro 1950s tables and chairs in the outdoor patio. Everything was green: green overhang, green chairs, green signage announcing prices for café au lait and beignets. A young server in a white uniform came over and took our order: two coffees, black.

"You read tarot?" he asked.

"I can."

"You could make some money here...if you get in with the right people."

"The right people like who?" I sensed another hustle coming.

"It's all a racket. I could set you up with everything you need: permits, table, everything. I'd help you bring in a crowd...for a cut. A small cut. I've got several girls working for me already."

"You're like a tarot pimp."

He laughed. "A tarot pimp. I like that."

Our coffees came and he rolled a few bills from his wad and handed them over. "Keep the change."

To me he said, "I've got a little artist community going, you should think about joining. We move between Vegas, here, and Florida depending on the season. Got a lot of poets working for me—you a poet?"

"Not so much."

"You can be. Performance art. Busking. Put a few cups out; you can make some decent cash. I can show you how."

"How many people are in your 'community'?"

"Right now? Eight or nine, it changes. All women, mind you. Only women. You're surrounded by sisters with me. We believe in living the artist's life. Free love, you know what I'm saying?" He delivered the last line with a raise of his eyebrow and took a drink of his coffee.

"Of course."

"So, what do you think? You ready to live the artist's life? We're meeting tonight, you can meet the other girls."

I sighed and took a long sip of coffee. I watched pigeons flap from empty table to empty table. They pecked at mounds of powdered sugar that covered the tables and floor. I wasn't considering his offer. I was absorbing the scene. In Los Angeles, guys like this with "offers" are a dime a dozen. It didn't interest me. But I was enjoying the moment we found ourselves in.

I put my cup down. "Nah, I don't think that's for me."

"You're not an artist?" he asked testily.

"I'm not into communal living," I tried to joke.

"You'll never make it here," he snarled.

I was surprised by the shift in his tone, but I covered my expression by taking another drink of coffee. The energy had shifted, he was leaning toward me, and I realized I should leave—slowly, without causing a scene.

I tried to sound lighthearted, "Why do you say that?"

"You're not evil enough." He stared at me with slit-like eyes.

"You don't think so?" I tried to laugh and put my cup down between us.

With lightning speed, his hand snapped across the table and grabbed my wrist. He bared his teeth and growled, "This city will eat you alive, little girl. It'll send you running home to mama if you don't have protection."

I saw wells open in his sharp black eyes, and they were filled with malice. I looked at his hand and twisted my wrist toward the ground, breaking his grip.

As I broke free, he pulled his arm back and looked away. Picked up his coffee and took a drink. His face was calm as if nothing had happened.

I looked out toward Jackson Square across the street. My blood was pounding through my body as the scene around us drifted serenely. Like an animal, I knew I needed to back away—carefully. The sky was sliding into a gold-hazed purple as night threatened to arrive. My lungs felt constricted in my chest.

"It's getting late." I slid my chair back and stood. "Thanks for the coffee."

He hauled himself up to stand next to me, his warmth and jolly expression had returned. "We're meeting tonight at Jackson

Square around midnight. You coming? The other girls would love to meet you."

"I don't think so. Don't wait for me." I adjusted my camera strap across my chest.

He put out his hand to shake and I took it out of habit. He gripped my hand tight and bared his teeth in an animal smile, "Run home to mama, little sister. God can't save you here."

I pulled my hand back and turned to leave as he called after me, "You know where to find me when you're ready."

I didn't turn back.

My heart raced as I walked to the streetcar. Every vein pumped with adrenaline, but I wasn't consciously scared. If anything, I felt relieved. I felt alive. I felt something closer to excitement. I caught the streetcar to the bar next to my hotel and drank until the world slowed down. Half passed out, I stumbled to my room at the Pontchartrain and took a hot shower with a sickly-sweet peach almond hotel soap. I fell into the old bed and slipped into a dream:

I was split in two. The physical me laid in my bed, while the spirit me floated just above. I was both simultaneously, looking at myself. I kissed myself, inhaled my spirit, and became one.

I sat up with a jolt—fully awake and gasping for breath. I was about to vomit everything inside me.

I raced to the bathroom just in time to projectile vomit into the tub until I'd wretched up every orange, nasty substance in my stomach. Irrationally, I was convinced it was the devil's doing—he'd put a curse on me for not showing up that night.

The devil wasn't going to keep me out of New Orleans, though. If anything, I was determined to prove I was evil enough to handle this little old city in the South. I would capture every ounce of its essence and turn myself into someone new.

Life is a Carnival

I took a second trip in the spring to find an apartment. The rents were a fraction of L.A. prices—I could afford to live on my own—but rentals ran the gamut from expensive Warehouse District lofts to hole-in-the-wall dingy rooms where it looked like crime scene investigations were still underway.

My mom drove out with a few boxes of things I'd kept—some clothes, mostly books, and a few dishes. She drove me from one end of the city to the other, looking at (and rejecting) every place we saw.

Finally, we hit on a winner: a run-down, 15-story high rise that sat next to the freeway and St. Charles Avenue.

It was halfway between the Garden District and the French Quarter—far enough away from those hot spots that the rent was reasonable, yet close enough to walk to either. The streetcar stopped in front of the building.

I didn't have a car anymore, so it was perfect. The studio apartments were small, but the building had security and a gate, which gave the illusion of safety.

"You're in luck," the girl in the leasing office said. "We've got a corner apartment on the thirteenth floor that'll be ready in a few days. It's a little more expensive, but you'll have a great view of the bridge and the river."

"I'll take it."

The city had smiled on me again.

We spent the next few days in a motel near the airport, ordered a futon and dining table and bookshelf to be delivered to the apartment, and took in the sights until I could pick up the keys. I couldn't believe my good fortune. Every star had aligned. Every light had turned green. All systems were go. Even my mom, who didn't want me to move, had to admit it had gone smoothly. It seemed doable. The cost of living was low, she even paid my rent before she left to give me time to find a job.

Before I'd even unpacked, I met two ladies at the French Quarter Market who made t-shirts in their garage. We struck up a conversation and they offered me a job. It was only a few hours a week, but I'd have time to write and soak up the city's energy. I couldn't believe all these divine interventions. I decided New Orleans loved me. There was no other explanation.

Flushed with confidence, I settled in and started running at Audubon Park. I'd ride the streetcar up St. Charles, run a lap around the two-mile track, then head over to my little part-time job with the ladies or work on screenplays and short stories that I was trying to sell.

A few weeks into my new routine, the cracks started to form.

I had to ride two buses for an hour to get to the ladies' garage—it was all the way across town. They bickered with each other all day and "forgot" to pay me at the end of the week. Twice. The second time their check bounced.

I needed another job. Fast. I got to work applying for anything I could find—office jobs, retail jobs. Not food service, though. I had worked in restaurants before, and I wasn't going back to that.

Before I'd dropped out of college a few years prior, I worked in the library. I went to all the universities and applied for all the library jobs. There were two—Tulane and Loyola—right across the street from Audubon Park on the streetcar line. I prayed the city would come through with another bout of fortune before I ran out of cash.

In the interim between the two broke ladies and a new job, I spent a lot of time jogging at Audubon Park. I was there every morning at dawn, ready to hit the track. It was the only thing that helped me feel grounded.

I was only a couple of months into this adventure, and I was already terrified I'd made a mistake. No savings. No job. Constant anxiety.

But there was no way I'd let myself fail. No way I'd hang my head in shame and crawl back to California.

I belonged in New Orleans. I had never felt happier than jogging around that track. Never felt so alive as when I walked along the river. I was going figure out how to make it work here. I was *home*.

One morning on my jog I caught sight of a man in the distance. I noticed him from a long way off—maybe a quarter mile away—a tiny figure pounding toward me. He was one of many runners, but something about him caught my eye.

He was wearing bright yellow running shorts and a grey t-shirt. And he had perfect running form. I slowed to a walk to watch him approach, transfixed by his form: his back perfectly straight, shoulders broad and relaxed, and he was fast. His pace was so fast it only took a moment until he was close enough that I could really get a good look at him.

He had short dark hair, a thick neck, broad shoulders, a sharp nose and dark eyes. Olive skinned and muscular. He was a perfectly masculine form in full motion. His eyes closed as he approached, and I could hear him pant-cough-exhale every other stride.

Time slowed down, and I saw every part of him: the sweaty gray shirt that clung to his body, the sweat rolling down his forehead. The other runners disappeared. He opened his eyes and looked directly at me as he passed—something electric shot through me.

That's him.

An irrational thought; it made no sense, but it was as if I knew he was the reason I was supposed to be there that morning.

Displaced

After that first encounter, I kept running, and I looked forward to seeing him a few times a week. We'd stare at each other every time we crossed paths. We always ran toward each other. He gave me a look I couldn't interpret—dark, almost angry. I gave him the nickname Menacing and joked with friends that I was going to marry that man. It made no sense. I knew it was silly, but it passed the time.

It gave me something to fantasize about as I settled into a city where I didn't yet know anyone.

I would imagine a dreamy future where we'd buy a house and have a thousand kids and packs of dogs and one day we'd look back and laugh at how we met one day jogging in the park.

At that moment in my life, I needed a big dream to keep me going. I was running out of money and there was no way I could admit defeat that early.

Within a month, the city's love came through again. I found the holy grail of NOLA employment: a part-time job, 16 hours a week, that paid just above minimum wage (just barely). It was a nice, quiet job shelving books in a university library.

I wasn't going to have to work in a bar or flash my chest. I could work on my writing and explore the city and barely afford my rent. I wouldn't make enough money to buy groceries, but at least the rent would be paid. I could sort out the rest later.

On my first day, I walked through the sliding glass doors of the library looking for Miss Viv, the book sorting manager. I had been interviewed and hired by the head of the department—a lady I would never see again—so Miss Viv, my manager, was meeting me for the first time that day. And she didn't seem pleased. A lady was scowling at me as I approached the book sorting area.

"I'm here to see Viv?" I smiled, and her scowl intensified.

"That's me."

Miss Viv was a stout, post-menopausal lady who stood about five-foot tall with a caramel brown bob wig. She pulled a gold lipstick tube from her black polyester dress pants and applied a fresh coat of bright orange-red lipstick. It perfectly contrasted the deep tone of her skin, and I immediately loved her.

"You the new girl?" she said.

"Yes! I'm excited to start." Too excited, in fact.

"Mmhmm." She eyed me harder. "Where you from?"

"California."

"Mmhmm. You ever shelve books?"

"I had this same job when I was in college."

"Mmhmm. You know how call numbers work then."

"I do! Where do you want me to start?"

"You can go sort that bin," she motioned to a metal bin of returned books.

She didn't have patience for me and she let me know it, which made me love her even more. I had never been so happy to have a job—in a library! It was better than my wildest dreams. I stopped jogging so I could get to work early every day and read.

The whole first week I noticed Miss Viv glared and bristled every time I called her "Viv." Not being Southern, I was too ignorant to know I was being rude, and she was too polite to correct me. By the second week I caught on to the more appropriate "Miss Viv" that everyone else called her, and she bristled less.

By the third week, she softened enough to let me work alongside her and started sharing snippets of staff gossip. As we shelved books together, she filled me in on everyone's history and personal business.

There were only four people in their 20's working in our department—me, the I.T. guy, a student worker named James, and a newly minted librarian named Ginny.

Ginny was only 23, but she had just been promoted to run one of the small research archives. For now, she was helping our department while transitioning to her new role. We all suspected she and James were secretly dating.

A few weeks into the job, the department had a graduation party for him. James had been working in the library for all four years of his program, and Miss Viv was as proud as his mama when she brought in his cake. The week after the party, Ginny showed up wearing a ruby wedding ring—we all flocked to the front desk to get the scoop.

"We eloped! James and I got married," she beamed.

"Mmhmm. Baby, we knew you all were sneaking around!" Miss Viv hugged her. "We're all so happy for you, hear?"

"We didn't want anyone to know—but I'm sure everyone did," Ginny laughed.

I hadn't been there long enough to know them, but I was happy for them, too. They seemed like a sweet, good-natured, beautiful hipster couple.

Once we got a new student worker, and a new librarian came in to replace Ginny, I was no longer the new girl. I became part of the scenery, blending into the background, listening to Miss Viv and the book sorting ladies talk about church gossip, and who was sneaking around with whom, and all the plot lines of the latest Lifetime made-for-TV movies.

With everything settled in for real this time, I went back to jogging. There was no time to ride the streetcar all the way to Audubon Park twice a day—once for a run and once for work, so I'd need to find a new route.

With the crumpled city map I'd carried on my first trip, I plotted a new course—through the Garden District, down to Lafayette Cemetery No. 1 on Washington Street.

Every morning, as the sky turned a pink-tinged yellow, I'd breathe in the greasy chicken smell of the Popeye's next door and take off on a jog. Past the daiquiri shop that never closed—that was the only hour when the corner wasn't packed with a line. But even at dawn, one or two men would be leaning in the doorway or passed out on the sidewalk next to the blue clapboard façade.

Life is a Carnival

A few stray dogs would always be roaming the streets of the Lower Garden District. A shaggy black shepherd often chased me down the center of the street next to Coliseum Square. I learned not to be afraid when they chased me, and after a few weeks they ignored me altogether. I became part of the scenery.

The streets of the Lower Garden District had a strong stench of wet jasmine and tar-smelling asphalt where a few of the many potholes had been filled. Jackson Avenue marked the entrance to the Garden District—the beautiful grand homes tourists imagine when they think of a New Orleans neighborhood. The air would explode with a sweet olive-jasmine-magnolia smell, and it felt jogging through another world.

By the time I'd hit the Garden District, the sun would be high enough to burn off the haze and glints of white-yellow light would pierce my eyes from between branches of sweet olive and crepe myrtle trees.

This was my favorite stretch of the run, where I'd hit my stride, criss-crossing the potholed streets until finally reaching Commander's Palace restaurant and the tall white wall of Lafayette No. 1 Cemetery.

The kitchen staff at Commander's would be spraying down the rubber floor mats and loading in the day's supplies at that hour. The whole corner smelled of dishwater and garbage. It became my favorite smell—the sourness of the garbage mixed with the fragrant wet trees.

A right turn on Prytania put me back in the direction toward home. I'd sprint from the cemetery back to my building, grab a shower, and catch the streetcar to work. Life went on like this for months—until Carnival.

No one told me Carnival is a season. The party starts on Twelfth Night and doesn't end until Lent on Ash Wednesday. Not being Catholic, I thought Mardi Gras was a weekend event that took place on Bourbon Street. I had no idea how many parades would roll down my street in the weeks before Lent.

Displaced

For two weeks leading up to Mardi Gras our apartment building gave out color-coded wristbands for each of the major parades. You weren't allowed in the building without the proper-colored wristband. Forgot your wristband? Good luck. It was the only time of the year our security guards ever enforced the rules about coming in the gate.

Because we were on St. Charles, only a few blocks from the French Quarter, our building was besieged with tourists trying to get into the building to find a bathroom.

Bathrooms, apparently, were in very short supply. The bar down the street charged $5 just for bathroom privileges. Oh, did you think you could use the restroom if you bought a drink? No! Pony up $5 extra. The side streets and back alley around our building reeked of vomit and urine for two weeks straight.

Until Carnival rolled around, I had no idea how lucky I was to find a corner apartment on St. Charles. I could sit high above the parades and watch the world go by—with a private bathroom.

And forget about the streetcar. You needed a hope and a prayer to get anywhere. It unexpectedly stopped mid-day or ran a shortened route to make way for parades. It only got worse as Lundi Gras approached.

Lundi Gras, I learned, meant "Fat Monday." It was the big parade day before the Zulu and Rex parades closed out Carnival season on Fat Tuesday.

The whole city shut down on Lundi Gras, so I headed for the Moon Walk—a little park by the river in the French Quarter. On the way home, I underestimated the size of the crowds. Canal Street was blocked, and people were packed together in throngs waiting for the coming parade. Families had set up chairs that blocked the sidewalks, children ran and screamed with laughter through the blockades while adults sat around eating from large coolers and shouted at each other over the roar of the crowd.

Standing at the back of the crowd, wondering how on earth I'd swim through this sea to get home, police on horseback started clearing the road. The start of the parade was closely behind them.

Children screeched with excitement. Every inch of the street was packed at least five people deep. And further down, scaffolding blocked the sidewalk entirely. It looked impossible to get home. I must have looked worried as I scanned the crowd.

"Looks like we're stuck here for a while." A deep, friendly voice came over my shoulder and I turned to see an attractive man smiling down at me.

He had short clipped black hair and wore Malcom X-style glasses, a white dress shirt with the sleeves rolled up, and black slacks. In his hand he carried an instrument case.

I smiled and he continued, "Or we could cut down to Magazine. Follow me." He stepped in front of me and cut a line through the crowd for me to follow. I placed my hand on the small of his back and lightly pinched his shirt to keep from losing him in the jostling crowd.

We squeezed our way around the next corner and walked briskly through the crowd until it thinned. By then we were a block away at Magazine Street.

I let go of his shirt. "Thank you."

"Where you headed?" he asked. Our eyes met, and he smiled as he switched his case from one hand to the other.

"Uh," I looked around. I didn't know where we were. "Lee Circle. The other side of these buildings, I think?" We were still walking, and I felt disoriented.

He leaned in a little so I could hear him over the parade ruckus getting louder on the next block. I could faintly smell incense. "We'll have to cross the parade then. I'm going down to Jackson; I can show you the way."

He set off ahead of me—his pace was quick, and I struggled to keep up.

"Are you from New Orleans?" I shouted at him as a brass band got louder.

"Philly," he yelled back.

"Yeah, you walk fast!"

"Ha!" He slowed down a little so I could catch up. "Been here seven years but never got into the pace, you know what I'm saying? Too slow." I nodded and fell into step next to him. "So, you live here or just visiting?"

"Live here. First Mardi Gras. Or Lundi Gras, I guess."

"Ahhh, well, if I can give you some advice—don't get stuck downtown during a parade," he laughed.

I laughed, too. "I'm getting that. You coming from work?" I nodded at his case.

"Yeah, got another gig tonight."

"Why leave if you've just got to go back again?"

"Shower. Change. Tell you the truth, I don't like the Quarter much. I try to stay out of there."

We passed the next few blocks with small talk. His name was Thaddeus. We were both writing screenplays. He'd left an urban planning job in Philadelphia to follow his dream of being a jazz musician in New Orleans. So far, he was nailing it.

He said he was divorced with a daughter who lived in Philly with her mother.

We cut up Andrew Higgins Street to Lee Circle and the parade was going strong. Tractors pulled colorful floats and rows of teenage girls danced by in fringe-covered leotards doing a complex hip-hop dance formation.

It all stood between me and my apartment, and I wanted to get home. Large crowds gave me anxiety, and I was starting to hyperventilate. We surveyed the crowd to find a spot to cross through the parade. People covered every inch of sidewalk and spilled into the street eight to ten bodies deep. Some people were up on ladders catching beads, or "throws."

"This is going to be tricky," he said. "We might have to overshoot your building to get through the parade...unless you're free to get a beer?"

Life is a Carnival

I smiled, "I might be, yeah."

My anxiety lifted like the sun burning off a haze.

We wove through the crowd down to Jackson Avenue, dodging beads and plastic cups flying toward our heads and ducking around the grasping hands struggling to catch them. There was a brief lull in the parade just before Jackson and we darted between a line of dancing girls and a tractor pulling a float. We made it to Igor's bar. The same bar I went to when I stayed at the Pontchartrain Hotel.

"Hey! How you doin'?" A girl called to us. She wore a black apron and carried two beers to a couple of guys laughing at an outdoor table.

"Hey, baby," Thad called back. He motioned to a table, "This okay?"

I nodded and the girl came over to us. He introduced us and said she was a fellow writer. "What can I get you all?" she asked.

"Two Abitas?" Thad asked me.

I nodded again. She went inside to get the beers, and we turned our attention to the parade moving past us on St. Charles.

"So, this is your first Mardi Gras?" Thad asked.

"Yeah, but it's funny because I'm not much for parades."

"Me neither, but the business is good. More work than I can handle." The waitress came back with two frosty brown bottles, and we started to drink. "You seen the Wild Magnolias yet?"

"What's that, a group?"

"You've never heard of the Mardi Gras Indians?" He rumpled his eyebrows at me with concern. I shook my head. "Well then, you've got to come downtown tonight so I can show you. You've probably never even been to Frenchman Street."

"What's that?"

He guffawed.

"Girl, I know you didn't just say that. You need to meet me downtown tonight. I get off work at ten. We'll go to Rampart, and I'll show you the real New Orleans."

That night I went down to the café where Thad led a jazz trio six nights a week. There was a long wooden bar with a marble top along one side of the room and fine dining along the other. I pulled myself up to the bar at a quarter to ten and asked for a coffee. The band closed out their song and I waved to Thad. He smiled and raised a hand before starting the next song.

The bartender returned with my coffee.

"You a friend of Thad's?"

"Yeah," I rummaged through my bag for my wallet.

He waved his hand, "No charge." We exchanged a smile, and he went back to the other end of the bar.

When his set was over Thad packed up his saxophone and put a charcoal wool flat cap on his head. He motioned for me to follow him outside and we walked a few blocks down to Frenchman Street.

As soon as we turned the corner, the sights and sounds of Frenchman Street swelled up and burst out at us—red and blue and yellow neon lights spilled into the street from the doors and windows of two solid blocks of throbbing clubs. A cacophony of live music pounded through the open doors of disparate clubs and created a luscious wall of sound you could almost taste.

Thad took me on a tour of every room on the street. We sampled a song or two from each venue: The Dragon's Den, The Blue Nile, The Spotted Cat, Snug Harbor. I lost track of all the names before we were halfway down the street. Musicians lingered in doorways with cigarettes dangling from lips and conversations in full swing. Doormen hugged Thad as he passed, and they waved us inside every venue. People welcomed us with a "hey, baby" and a cocktail on the house as we stayed just long enough to down that drink and sample a song before moving further down the street.

The night was moving fast, so we made our way down to Rampart Street to Donna's to catch the Wild Magnolias. We arrived ahead of the crowd and slid into one of the few tables off the dance floor. Thad ordered fries and beer. Donna and her husband stopped by to say hello and ask Thad how business was coming. He was one of the few outside musicians to have a steady gig every week—most of the steady work was held by born and bred New Orleanians.

"It took seven years of door pounding to be taken seriously in this town," he told me when they left.

A brass band kicked up, and a crowd gathered at the door to pay the cover and file in. There wasn't an inch of room in the place, and I gorged myself on greasy fries and cold Abita.

The tempo slowed, and the most beautiful and elaborately costumed man I'd ever seen took the stage. The baby blue sequins on his traditional Mardi Gras Indian costume shimmered like the sun. A tall, feathered, cobra-like headdress made him appear seven-feet tall, or taller—larger than life, larger than anything I'd ever seen up close in person.

That singer belted out Mardi Gras standards as the horns blew wild sounds through that tiny dark room. The crowd was on fire—moving as one, like a beast in heat. My chest vibrated as fast and hard as my eardrums as the band worked that room into a frenzy.

I couldn't get enough of that headdress and leaned across the table to yell at Thad, "What's the deal with the Indian costume?"

He yelled back, "The Indians around here were part of the early slave revolts! They took in the escaped slaves and intermarried with them! Their descendants have a long tradition of second lining for Mardi Gras! You should check it out!"

I nodded and leaned back in my seat to revel in the rest of their show.

By the time we made our way out of Donna's my ears were ringing and felt stuffed with cotton. We made a quick stop at the Funky Butt, but the exhaustion had already set in. How do you top a performance like that? We decided it was too late, or too early in the morning, to keep going. Thad walked me home.

"Now if you really want to know Mardi Gras, you need to see Zulu," he said. "Come up to my place on Jackson in the morning. I've got a balcony where we toast the king—it starts rolling around 8."

"In the morning?" I laughed. "That's way too early for me." It was only a few hours away.

"Well, I've got lots of people coming by to barbecue. We'll be out front all day. Anytime you want is fine." He leaned in to kiss my cheek and I kissed his in return.

"Thanks. I might stay in and watch from my window."

He smiled and I watched him for a moment as he walked briskly down the street toward Jackson. He swung his saxophone case from one hand to the other—an incredibly handsome man. Thad was my first friend in New Orleans, and we often met up to talk about our screenplays at the Please U diner between our apartments.

I liked Thad, but I couldn't think about dating anyone. El Diablo had been correct: I *had* just gotten out of a relationship. It *was* amicable. I was taking time out to figure out what should come next. I was, in fact, looking for something. I just didn't know yet what would manifest.

In the back of my mind, although I never would have admitted this, I was also waiting for Menacing. Even though I hadn't seen him in months, I could feel it: We were going to meet again. He was *someone* to me.

On Mardi Gras morning, the parades started before I was awake. Thirteen stories up, I woke to the sound of brass bands and crowds roaring from below.

I went downstairs briefly for each of the two main parades: Zulu and Rex. I caught a few beads from each because I thought it was the right thing to do. When in Rome, and all that.

The float riders of Zulu wore blackface and straw skirts. The riders of Rex wore plastic masks and tall conical hats reminiscent of the Klan. All the riders seemed to be a mix of black, white, and all shades of brown, and both parade groups pelted the masses with handfuls of cheap plastic beads.

I knew there must be rich history and symbolism behind the costumes, but the parades disturbed something inside me. Maybe it was the Californian in me reacting to the visuals. I had been raised in a Chicano matriarchy—aware of the struggles my grandparents endured. One of my maternal great-grandmothers was indigenous Navajo. The other had worked in fruit packing warehouses from the time she dropped out of school at age 12. I was well-versed in the complexities of American history, and something about the imagery of these parades made me feel uneasy. After experiencing a few minutes of each parade, I watched mainly from my window 13 floors up.

From there, everything seemed ant-like. I could take in the whole picture: miniature floats and plastic bits and bobs flying across bodies crammed together ten-deep. As the parades passed, so did the crowds. By the end of the afternoon there was nothing left in the street but mounds of garbage, slick puddles of vomit, and piles of broken beads as far as the eye could see.

I slept with all the windows open that night to let the late winter breeze flow through the apartment. The next morning, I woke to the sound of power washers and street sweepers and the overwhelming smell of rancid vomit and stale beer that had drifted all the way up to my room. The smell was so powerful I couldn't even think about running in it.

This was the smell of Ash Wednesday, the first day of Lent. I got dressed for work and went downstairs to catch the streetcar.

Along the street, men in bright orange safety vests used long metal hooks to pull gobs of vomit-coated Mardi Gras beads out of the storm drains. They piled them up on the side of the road while a street sweeper rolled by noisily across the street.

As I walked past the Popeye's, I eyed a tower—taller than I was—leaning against a dumpster. It was a huge pile of mostly chicken bones and trashed dinner boxes. I fought my gag reflex.

The air was wet and hazy—heavy with the stench of grease and vomit. I crossed to the streetcar stop in the median and watched as a green wooden car rumbled closer, headed toward downtown. I was waiting for the opposite train, so I watched it approach with its cargo of downtown office workers.

As the car slowly trundled past, I saw it was packed with zombified faces in each open window—people in suits looking exhausted, pale, and half-asleep. They had all stopped for repentance before heading to work: Each forehead was smeared with a thick black ash cross.

The car rolled to a stop across from me, and they all seemed to turn and look at me in unison. It was like a scene from a horror movie. Black-ash zombified faces staring out at me. A chill shuddered down my spine.

A few minutes later the same streetcar had dropped off its cargo downtown and looped around to pick me up. I had been in New Orleans for almost a year and survived my first Mardi Gras. It was 2003, and I felt more alive than I'd ever been—living a life I had only dreamed of.

There was nowhere else I wanted to be.

Los Angeles, 2001

The sun felt especially bright that morning. It blinded my eyes. I pulled down the sun visor in the car, rubbed crust from my eye socket and applied a thin coat of lipstick. It was earlier than usual for us to be making the commute to Pasadena. My 1981 Tercel broke down again and was collecting dust in our apartment building's garage.

K.C. was scheduled for the early shift, and he had to drive out of his way to drop me off at the little Japanese imports shop where I worked. He sped along the winding uphill road toward Green Street. Sunlight spattered between the trees, and I flipped up the visor and closed my eyes.

"What do you want to do about dinner tonight?" He wasn't usually the one to ask that question, and I heard impatience in his voice.

"I don't know. Whatever you want."

"What time should I pick you up?"

I opened my eyes and looked out the window. Perfectly manicured lawns and beautiful mansions flew past my view.

"I close the shop at 5. I don't know. It doesn't take that long to count the drawer and lock up."

My car had been broken down for a couple of weeks, and I knew he was annoyed I hadn't gotten it fixed.

He turned on the radio, but instead of our usual KCRW morning grooves there was some kind of news report. People talking in serious tones. Chaos sounds in the background. K.C. turned up the volume.

"...towers appeared to be burning..." a woman's voice.

We pulled up at the shop before there was time to hear the rest. I leaned over to kiss his cheek before getting out of the car. "Let me know what happened."

"Will do."

I went through the ritual of opening the shop. Pulled open the heavy security gate and flipped the metal switches that flooded the industrial space with light. The ancient swamp cooler roared to life. I dragged a massive aloe plant outside and set up colorful folding chairs on the sidewalk. Hung bright orange paper lanterns along the storefront to draw attention to the otherwise bland brick exterior. Albert Einstein once had an office in this building when he worked at Caltech, but you would never know it in its current form: a Pilates studio, a framing shop, a high-end photographer. This boutique.

An old CD player was hooked up to a janky speaker system. It was the only technology in the shop. There wasn't even a point-of-sale machine. Every purchase was written on receipt paper with a pen.

The owner was always on me about forgetting to manually add the sales tax. Customers loved me for it.

I put in a Zap Mama CD and hit play.

An hour passed. Then two. No foot traffic. No customers.

I dusted the shelves and rearranged $80 iron teapots and stacks of UK Elle Decor. Where is everyone? What happened?

I stood in the doorway and looked up and down the tree-lined street. No cars. By lunchtime, the framing shop and the photographer still hadn't opened their doors.

Finally, the phone rang.

"Good morning. Yuzu."

"Hey, babe." It was K.C.

"Hey, what's going on? No one has come in today, everything's closed, it's crazy weird."

"The towers fell—two planes crashed into them."

Los Angeles, 2001

He said it so matter-of-factly it took me a minute to process what he said.

"You mean like...the tops of the towers? Planes hit the top floors? They can repair that." I envisioned a hole—a fire, even—but surely, he meant floors had collapsed. Maybe the top floors?

"No, the towers fell. They *fell*. They're not there anymore."

"That's not possible." I said it instinctually, reflexively. My mom's second husband was a civil engineer. I'd heard all my life that the safest place to be in an earthquake was a high-rise building. They're built to withstand everything.

I had faith in exactly two things in life: engineering and building codes.

He sighed. "They're gone."

I couldn't visualize it, but I wasn't going to argue about it. "Okay. I'll see you after work."

"Yep." The line went dead.

I spent the afternoon trying to conceptualize it. But I kept thinking, no, there must be something left.

The owner of the store called next. "Would you mind watching the shop another week on your own?"

"You want me to keep it open?"

"Would you mind? I know it's an imposition, but air travel's suspended and we're stuck in Japan."

"Oh, sure. Of course."

The owners had been on a buying trip and were trying to figure out how to get home. No one came in. No one else called. At 5:00 I closed the shop and K.C. drove me home. We rode home listening to the radio.

At home, our answering machine was full: my mother had seen the second plane hit live on TV and was in shock; my friend worked in a newsroom and was reading out bulletins that came in over the wire. Horrific details. A friend in Staten Island said he emailed K.C. photos of the whole thing.

K.C. opened his email and I turned on CNN.

33

Finally, I saw the footage for myself. I had to lie down on the couch. We didn't eat. I didn't sleep. I watched the towers fall all night, over and over, ad infinitum.

In the morning, I asked K.C. to drop me off at a market about a half mile from the shop. I bought a cup of coffee and the L.A. Times and sat outside at a black metal table. I breathed in the cool morning breeze. The sun was bright and golden. There was a movie poster hanging on a bus shelter at the corner: Robert Redford and James Gandolfini and an American flag flying upside-down—a sign of distress. I tried to imagine what this would mean for the world.

I walked to the shop and went through my opening ritual in a daze. A man came in and browsed but said nothing. A woman bought a pack of Buddha note cards.

"I'm going to send them to all my friends in New York," she said. "They could use a little Zen."

Sister, they need more than Zen.

In the following days, protests sprang up near our house. American flags waved. I couldn't tell what people were protesting, but war was in the air. A CNN reporter interviewed a family in Old Town Pasadena. They were at a restaurant I'd been to a hundred times, on a street where I'd spent many, many days.

A mother and father sat at a table with two adolescent kids. They were celebrating a birthday. The reporter asked, "Do you feel strange having a celebration right now?" The mother said enthusiastically, "No! If we change our lives, they win!" I watched the expressions on the two bewildered kids—they looked shell-shocked to me.

If we change our lives, they win.

It became the mantra everywhere. I didn't understand it. I wanted nothing more than change. I wanted a change for the better. I wanted to do all the things I'd ever dreamed of doing—right now. Immediately.

Los Angeles, 2001

By the end of the week, life around me seemed to go on exactly as it was before. The shop owners returned from Japan. People came in and shopped as usual. There wasn't much said about the incident on the other side of the flyover zone.

Maybe we were all in shock, but it felt to me like we were in a collective denial. We could pretend this wasn't happening.

If we change our lives, they win.

Talk of war was everywhere overnight. Life suddenly felt impossibly short.

I couldn't square how I was feeling—unaccomplished, drifting—with this sudden sense of danger and fear about the world. Before that day in September I don't think I was consciously unhappy. I just had no direction or purpose.

What should I do with the rest of my life? Why did I feel so alone in asking that question? How was I going to settle this unsettled feeling inside me?

At the end of September I asked K.C., "Why aren't people talking about what's going on? Why aren't we talking about what this means for our future?"

He kissed my forehead, "This is L.A., babe. Nothing real ever happens here."

He was joking, but he hit exactly how I felt.

Nothing real was happening. Nothing real would ever happen for me there. I lived in the land of make believe. I wanted a new life. I wanted things to write about, and New Orleans became an obsession. I wanted to be surrounded by a real creative pulse. I had always admired the great Southern writers. I wanted to walk the streets they'd walked.

"Would you ever want to live somewhere else—just for a while?" I asked K.C.

"Nope. I was born here. I'll die here. There is no other place to be."

I tried talking with my best friend. We were both only children, so we'd grown up like sisters. Even as adults, we lived only a few blocks from each other. We'd spent our middle and high school years trying to astral travel together, ditching classes, and getting into trouble. As adults, she was an actress, and I was a writer—we had big plans to make big films together.

"You're not really going to leave," she said. She was driving me home from our favorite coffee shop where we'd spent countless hours over the years dissecting scripts and auditions. "You'd come back in a month if you went anywhere."

"Of course I could leave," I was irritated she didn't get on board with my New Orleans dream when I announced it.

"This is the center of the world. It would be stupid to live anywhere else."

"You just spent two years in Taipei!"

"That's completely different. I have family there. You're just running from your life. You don't even know anyone there," she paused. "And I came back. So, I'm telling you how it is."

"Well, I'm going." I was angry she wasn't more supportive.

We pulled up to my apartment and she looked at me.

"I won't even say goodbye to you, because you'll be back in a month," she said. "You're going to get there and see there's nothing there that you can't get here."

We hugged across the car's center console, and I squeezed her shoulders tight. I knew I wasn't coming back, and I knew I'd miss her more than anyone else.

By the end of October, I'd given away or sold almost everything I owned. K.C. and I had been living together four years, even picked a date for a wedding, but we split everything evenly and cleaned out the apartment.

There was nothing to argue about. I wanted to leave and he wanted to stay.

On some level, I think we both knew that was the inevitable outcome between us.

On our last day, he gifted me a new laptop.

"You're going to need a way to write wherever you go."

Los Angeles, 2001

Looking at our empty apartment for the last time, I felt equally terrified and excited. I could no longer live in a place where nothing real ever happened.

Menacing Becomes the Bostonian

On the Wednesday before Easter, Lady NOLA was on my side again. Lent was almost over, and I left work at the library at one o'clock, as I always did Monday through Thursday. I caught the streetcar to head home, but for some reason, at Louisiana Avenue, I had a sudden urge to get off and walk to the grocery store. I needed bananas. I needed bread. It felt massively important that I stop, *now*, and walk down there.

There was a light breeze blowing through the streetcar, the heat wasn't unbearable. The eight or nine block walk home promised to be comfortable. I stepped off the streetcar and walked down to Magazine Street.

As I approached the corner, I saw him—*Menacing*. The jogger. He was there, coming out of the New Orleans Music Exchange across the street. I almost didn't recognize him out of his running gear. He was wearing regular clothes: a blue striped t-shirt and khaki shorts. We stood on either side of the street, staring at each other.

For a split second I lost track of my senses. Time froze.

A cab pulled up in front of him and he opened the back door—but we were still looking at each other. I found the muscles in my legs and turned left, walking toward the grocery. I heard the cab door slam shut and looked back over my shoulder. He was still standing there. The cab was driving away.

My feet slowed, but my heart raced. I felt every pulse of blood push and pull through every vessel in my body. I glanced around again; he was waiting for traffic to pass to cross the street toward me. I'd been waiting, thinking, plotting for months about what to say if I ever saw him again—and the moment was here. The air felt heavy and wet. I kept walking, but I knew he was right behind me. I wanted to walk faster, to run, to prolong the chase—but he was getting closer, and I would have to turn around.

So, I did.

I faced him. He was less than half a block away. Only a few quick steps. I took a breath and stepped toward him. We met in front of the Big Fisherman Seafood market, the smell of fresh spring crawfish surrounding us.

We were the same height, so I looked directly in his eyes, "You used to run at Audubon Park?"

He looked a little taken aback and said, "I still do. Where've you been?"

He knew who I was. I wanted to die in the worst possible 12-year-old crush way. "I started a new job. I run near my apartment now."

"Uh-huh. I was out of town for a while. Then I pulled a muscle..." he knelt and ran his hand up the back of my calf and dug his middle finger into the hollow behind my knee, "right here. It killed for weeks."

He looked up at me and I stopped breathing. His hand was cupped around my calf, and I could feel his strength. My head was stuffed with cotton, but I had the sense to thank God I'd shaved my legs and worn shorts that morning.

He stood up and introduced himself, offered his hand and I shook it. He spoke with an accent I'd never heard before. I couldn't place it.

"Where are you from?" I asked.

"Boston. But I've been here about 15 years."

"You must like it."

"Take it or leave it." He looked at me for a second. "Want to get some coffee?"

"Sure."

We walked a few blocks to a Community Coffee shop. It was immediately obvious we had nothing in common. We didn't like the same music or read the same books. But I felt as if I'd always known him, as if he were a rediscovered memory I desperately wanted to explore.

At CCs, I chose a table by the window while he chatted with people he knew in line. I fortified my bravado until he returned with our coffee.

"Do you like Splenda?" he asked. He was tapping a packet into his coffee.

"I don't use sugar substitute." I sipped my coffee, black.

"It's made of sugar. Here..." he took my hand, palm up, and tapped a packet in.

I dipped my tongue in and scrunched my nose. "I prefer the real thing."

He took my hand to his mouth and licked the rest off my palm. The texture of his tongue made me laugh as much as the absurdity of his move. It was ridiculous and silly. He laughed and I closed my hand. He pressed my fist to his lips. His mouth was warm. He kissed the side of my hand. His eyes never left mine; they burned through me with the same intensity I'd felt on our runs. I tried to calculate if we'd killed a respectable amount of time yet.

"What are your plans this afternoon?" I asked.

He released my hand. "It's my day off. You?"

I sipped my coffee. "I was on my way home."

He took a drink of his. "Can I walk you home?"

"I live by Lee Circle. It's a bit of a walk."

"I was going to the Quarter anyway. It's on my way."

"Then yes." I took another sip of my coffee. "Should we go?"

"Let's."

We threw our coffee away and left CCs, walked toward Sixth Street. As we turned the corner, he took my hand, and I laced my fingers between his. I was barely aware of my actions. I had entered the dream I'd been having for months.

I let him lead. We waded through the thick jasmine magnolia air, and I was already aware of a thin film of sweat covering my body. I felt his fingers tighten around mine as we ducked beneath a row of low-hanging crepe myrtle trees in hot pink bloom.

The uneven brick sidewalk was slick with green-brown moss and the uprooted bricks jutted out at dangerous angles.

"Watch yourself," he warned.

The wet air engulfed me; my lungs expanded with the balmy soil smells of the Garden District, and I willingly erased the line between dream and reality.

We came to the tall white wall of Lafayette No. 1 cemetery—my morning running route. The wall was fractured by nearby roots that erupted from the ground.

He stopped and I almost tripped over him. He turned to me, let go of my hand, and in a swift movement his arms were around me, he gripped my chest and put his mouth on mine before I could react. My hands found the slick skin of his neck, my tongue discovered the space behind his lips, and I felt, inexplicably, that I had always known him.

And then I woke up.

I pulled away, pushed his chest. "I don't do this."

"Of course." He took a step back, "I'm sorry."

"I'm not this person; this isn't who I am." I leaned forward as if I'd been running and put my hands on my knees. All the blood had rushed from my head. I searched for my senses.

"No, of course, of course. I'm sorry." He took another step back to put more distance between us.

Whoa, whoa, whoa...I started walking away and followed the cemetery wall to Prytania Street. Instinctually, I made the right turn toward home.

He walked behind me, keeping a slight distance. I argued with myself in my head: What the hell am I doing? What is this?

"Do you still want me to walk you home—are you okay?" he sounded both apologetic and concerned.

I stopped and faced him. "I'm not the kind of person who does this. I don't want you to have the wrong idea about me."

"No, of course not. I'm not usually like this either." We stood uncomfortably for a beat. "I'll just walk you home. Really. Nothing else. Maybe we can get together some other day."

I didn't want him to leave. "Yeah. Okay, yeah, that's fine."

He walked me home and we made small talk until we got to my building's front gate. I pulled a pen and a scrap of paper from my purse and wrote my phone number on it. I handed it to him. "Give me a call if you want to get together."

He folded it and put it in his wallet. "You sure you're not going to invite me up?"

I smiled. "I'm not that kind of girl."

"I think we established that." He was smiling, but his eyes were dark and burrowed into mine. The April heat embraced us, seemed to close the world around us. He leaned in and said, "it's not like I'm going to attack you."

I laughed. "If you have to say that, then you probably will."

He was close enough that I could smell his cologne or aftershave; it was woodsy, earthy. It made me think of the sticky flesh of summer, of soaked Spanish moss and flooded swamplands after white sheets of rain. I thought of watching his perfect form, his pace, circling Audubon Park. I looked over his broad shoulders. He had a runner's frame: muscular, but not too thin. He was olive skinned and tan, Italian maybe; I let my eyes linger on his biceps. I was training for a triathlon. We were the same height. If it came down to it, I was pretty sure I could take him in a fight.

Or at least, that's what I told myself.

I turned up a corner of my mouth, "Ordinarily I wouldn't do this, but you seem like such a nice man. I think I will invite you up." I opened the security gate and pulled him through. He looked as surprised as I felt. I knew I would talk myself out of this if I didn't hurry, so I rushed us through the lobby and into the elevator. I pushed 13.

"You live on the thirteenth floor?" he asked.

"Mmhm." I watched the numbers light up: two, three....

"I always thought they didn't make those."

"They do here."

"Isn't that something?" He asked rhetorically.

We didn't look at each other. We watched the numbers above the door: six, seven, eight.... I worried this would be a monumental mistake. Was he as terrified as I was? My knees shook. My hands felt like wet ice. The bell rang when we reached my floor.

I led him down the hall and opened the door to my corner apartment. He entered first and I locked the door behind us. He walked through the studio's short entry hall and went straight to the windows that lined both sides of the room.

"Great view," he said.

"I know. You want something to drink?" I followed him in.

"Water?"

I poured him a glass of water. "Ice?"

"No, thanks." He was standing at the center window looking toward the bridge over the river. I brought him the water and looked out with him. He took a sip. "I used to live in Algiers when I was in the Navy. I drove over that bridge every day for ten years."

"Interesting. You want to sit down?" I looked at the table and chairs next to us.

Menacing Becomes the Bostonian

He picked up a worn-out copy of the *Bhagavad Gita* that was sitting on the table. "What's this?"

"I just bought it. You know that used bookstore on Magazine? They went out of business, sold all their books for like a dollar."

He read the back cover. "Looks good, maybe you'll let me borrow it?"

"Yeah. Remind me."

"Uh-huh." He put the book back on the table and walked to the bookshelf. He sat down cross-legged on the carpet next to it. "Do you mind if I sit on the floor?"

"Not at all." I sat on the floor a couple of feet away and faced him. We were close, but not too close. I was nervous, and my stomach fluttered.

He looked around, glanced at the books on the shelf behind him. Writing books. "I like your apartment."

"Me, too."

We stared stupidly at each other.

"So, what do you do?" he asked.

"I work in a library."

"Not your day job. What do you *do*?" He emphasized the second "do."

"Oh. I write."

"A writer," he said. "I'm a musician."

"I think you told me."

"Uh-huh. So, what do you write?"

"Lots of things..."

"How old are you?" He asked suddenly.

"Why?"

"Because you look young."

I smiled, "I just turned 26."

I said it a little too proudly.

"I'm 39." He set his glass on the bookshelf behind him. "Is that a problem?"

"Is it for you?" I asked.

"I don't know yet."

In a fluid movement he got on his hands and knees and crawled over me, pressed me into the floor and covered my mouth with his. My legs instinctively wrapped around him. He moved back onto his knees to help me pull off my shirt.

"I thought you weren't going to attack me," I said.

"I lied. Can we move to the futon?"

We fumbled toward the futon on the other side of the room. As he pulled off his shirt he tripped on his unzipped shorts that were now tangled around his knees.

"Your pants are slowing you down, my friend. You should lose them," I joked.

He stopped and looked at me. "You have a sense of humor."

"You thought I didn't?"

"No." He kissed me. "But you're funny, I love it."

As day moved into night, the evening passed in a stream of staccato scenes: the exploration of hands and mouths, the moon slowly rising over the Crescent City Connection. Thirteen floors below us the streetcar rumble-popped down St. Charles Avenue; I listened to it endlessly make its rounds around Lee Circle, marking time. It cut through the ocean sound of the nearby interstate traffic that lapped against the uncovered windows. And when it was dark enough, I watched the orange freeway lights below cast sharp-angled shadows across my ceiling.

"Are you hungry?" I asked. "I might have something in the fridge."

"Don't bother yourself. Later. How do you sleep at night with all this noise?"

The futon had long since been unfolded and he stared up at the orange shapes with me. I rolled over onto my stomach, and he draped his arm lazily over my back. "Do you have a middle name?" he asked.

"Ellen."

"Can I call you Ellen?"

Menacing Becomes the Bostonian

He turned his head toward me and stroked the side of my face with the back of his hand.

"No," I smiled, "you can learn my first name."

He smiled back. "What's your family name?"

"Kerr."

"You're Scottish."

"I don't think so." As far as I knew, my father's people were British. I ran my hand through his chest hair and pressed my forehead into his shoulder.

"Kerr," he whispered. "It's a Scottish name." He folded me into his arms, and I rested my head on his chest. His heart pounded a steady cadence against my ear, and I closed my eyes.

"We'll go to the Irish Shop and find your tartan," he said. "I was the house drummer at O'Flaherty's years ago, used to play with a Scottish pipe and drum group and got into heraldry."

"Did you wear a kilt?"

"Of course. Black Watch tartan."

I felt his chest rise and fall. I was drifting off but tethered to his voice.

"My people were stone masons in the Abruzzi region of Italy." He shifted his weight toward me and rolled me onto my back. "My grandfathers came to work in the quarries outside Boston." His face was in my neck and his body pressed into mine. "You know the Scottish were also big stone masons?"

"Were they?" I was at the edge of sleep but adjusted to his movements.

"But actually," he whispered in my ear, "we came over to Italy from Catalan because of religious persecution in the 1600s." The weight of him suddenly grounded me, brought me back from the edge, and I was no longer tired. "Our family crest is three ships sailing across the sea from Spain...."

Night gave way to morning, and the pink sun rose to fill our space with a bright yellow light. He checked his watch on the table and jumped out of bed.

"I have to get to work." He rushed around the apartment, throwing on his clothes. I went to the bathroom and put on my robe. He was already at the front door when I came out. He had my *Bhagavad Gita* in his hand and shook it, "Thanks for this."

I stood at the open door with him, bewildered.

"I'll give you a call," he kissed me, twice, before turning for the elevator.

I closed the door behind him and watched him through the peephole. I watched him push the button, look up at the light above the elevator, thumb through the book.

Wait a minute. *Wait a minute.* I came to my senses.

That man just left with my book!

I opened the door and rushed out after him. He turned and looked surprised to see me.

"Don't take the book," I blurted out.

"What?"

"It's annotated, and it's out of print. I just bought it," I said in one breath. He looked at me as if I'd sprouted another head. I lost my patience. "I haven't read it yet! So, if I never see you again, that's fine, but don't take the book because I just bought it and I really want to read it!"

He had a look on his face I couldn't interpret. It was somewhere between confusion and amusement.

"I'm going to call you," he said.

"No, that's not the point..."

He held the back of my head and kissed my forehead. "I promise I will call you. I won't steal your book," he laughed.

"...I haven't read it yet."

The elevator opened and he got in, laughing, with my book. I felt a strange sort of terror—like I had officially lost my mind. I could see myself: crazy sex hair, in my bathrobe, in the hallway of my building, arguing with this stranger over a book. A stranger who ten minutes ago had been naked in my apartment. A book I had just bought and hadn't even read yet.

Menacing Becomes the Bostonian

We stood on either side of the doors, and he was still smiling as he pushed a button. The doors slid closed. In my last glimpse of him I thought, *he has a fantastic profile.* Angular. Roman. I closed my eyes and fell against the wall behind me.

I was an idiot.

I sighed and went back to my apartment to shower for work. I tried to make peace with the fact I'd just done an incredibly stupid thing. I'd have to find another annotated copy of the *Bhagavad Gita*. And I'd most certainly have to find another place to run.

* * *

That afternoon the phone rang. I didn't recognize the caller ID, and my heart sped up. I raced around the studio for two full rings before I was calm enough to answer. "Hello?"

"Hi?" He sounded unsure of himself. "This is Eliot."

"Hi. How are you?" I tried to swallow my excitement to keep from choking on it.

"Good. I'm good." He paused. "I'd like to come over and make you dinner."

"Oh? That'd be great." Yes!

"How about Saturday?"

I tried to deadpan this, "Uh, yeah okay. Sure."

"I get off work at six, so I'll come by around eight. You like pasta?"

"Yeah."

"Okay. I'll let you go then."

"Oh." *That was it?* "Okay. Bye."

By 7:45 Saturday night I had spent quality time with my loofah, my razor, and my moisturizer. I was sitting in front of the open window, craning my head out, watching for his approach as the streetcar passed below. Somehow, he eluded me, and there was a knock on the door at 8:05. My entire body shook as I ran to the peephole—he was standing there with a paper bag balanced on a big pink box.

I opened the door, "How'd you get in the gate?"

"Some guy was leaving and let me in. Take the bag?" He leaned in to kiss me.

I took the paper bag and opened it—dry pasta, a jar of sauce and a letter-sized manila envelope. I let him in.

"What's in the box?"

He took it to the table and opened it. "Seven-layer double chocolate. With ganache frosting." Inside the box was the biggest cake I had ever seen—decorated with pastel pink and yellow Easter eggs.

He looked at me, excited, with a child's eyes. "Let's have a piece now!"

"What about dinner?" I said, but it was too late. He was rummaging for a knife in my kitchenette. He removed a thin slice of cake and put a chunk in my mouth. It was, by far, the greatest chocolate cake I had ever tasted.

He shoved a piece in his mouth and rolled his eyes back in his head, "I'm dying—it's death! I've been thinking about this cake all day."

I couldn't stop laughing. "Come on, let's start the water and make dinner." I emptied the bag in the kitchenette and held up the envelope, "What's this?"

"Transcript and discharge papers." He took my only pot off the stove and filled it with water. I opened the envelope: a transcript from Berklee College of Music in Boston and honorable discharge from the United States Navy.

"Just so you know who I am," he said.

"You didn't need to do this," I laughed. "But thanks."

We were gluttonous. We gorged ourselves. We acted as if we'd been starving all our lives and had finally found food. And when morning came, we stood over that empty pink cake box in disbelief.

"How did we eat that whole cake?" I asked.

"It can't be gone," he said.

Menacing Becomes the Bostonian

He said it as if the cake had fallen somewhere, mysteriously, like under the table. For years to come, that cake would be legend between us. It was the litmus test by which we judged all future cakes, and not one ever measured up.

That morning—Easter—we got dressed together and walked through the French Quarter. We avoided the parades and the crowds that wound through the narrow streets. We saw a movie at the Aquarium of the Americas.

He took me on my first ferry trip across the river. On the other side, in his old neighborhood of Algiers, we sat on a park bench facing the skyline of downtown New Orleans. The Crescent City Connection towered above us to our left. It felt strange to see everything from this angle.

Tendrils of my hair flapped in the breeze and glints of white light flashed off the choppy waves of the Mississippi River below. Across the water, the glass façade of the Aquarium gleamed a golden yellow as the sun began to set. I linked my arm around his and leaned into him. He kissed the space between my temple and my ear, and I could see my entire life with this man stretched out before us.

It was naïve, and irrational, but it felt as real as anything I'd ever felt.

The next morning, I woke up early to run. I got dressed and sat on the futon to put on my shoes.

"Hey," I touched Eliot's uncovered back, "you want to go for a run?"

He opened one eye sleepily to look at me and then turned his head away. He said something muffled that sounded like, "no, too beat."

"Lazy," I teased. I rubbed my hand over his shoulders and kissed the back of his neck. I left him sleeping and ran my usual route, crisscrossing through the Garden District. I came home drenched and aching and gasping for breath. It was getting hotter, even early in the morning. The apartment was empty, and there was a note on the table in big, scrawled letters: be right back. I unbolted the door so he could get back in and jumped in the shower.

By the time I got out, I could smell coffee. I went in the studio, and he was unloading take-out boxes from a bag on the table.

"What's all this?"

"Breakfast. I have to go; I'm late for work."

"For me?"

"Here," he pulled me to a chair and sat me down, "I got you some potatoes and a muffin and some coffee. You should have a bowl of cereal, too."

"This is too much, why don't you have some?"

"I have to go." He was already fumbling in his pockets for streetcar fare. "Don't get up." He kissed the top of my head, "See you this weekend."

* * *

After a few weekends of hanging out in the Quarter, I started asking when he would invite me to his apartment. He was cagey and avoided the question every time.

"Okay, this is getting ridiculous. You have to let me see where you live," I said.

"I'm a bachelor; it's too embarrassing. I moved all my furniture back to Boston when I thought I was moving back last year. There's nothing for you to see—it's empty," he said. "Besides, it's just a small place. No air conditioning. I only pay $250 a month."

Comparing rent was a sport in New Orleans. It's something I noticed right away—everybody was always competing to see who had the cheapest rent. It was humblebragging before we had a word for it. Everyone I talked with, from coworkers to random people I'd meet around town, wanted to talk about rent and what neighborhood you lived in.

Menacing Becomes the Bostonian

At $575 a month, I was paying an astronomical amount for the time. It blew people's minds. Everyone at work was constantly trying to find me a cheaper place.

"How are you only paying $250 a month?" I demanded. "Now you really have to show me!"

"Fine, but I'm serious, it's embarrassing. There's nothing inside. You can come over next weekend if you really want."

He lived in the Black Pearl, a section of Uptown next to the river, within a larger neighborhood called the Riverbend (named for an obvious reason—it's where the Mississippi River bends), and it was also known as Carrollton. Neighborhoods in New Orleans were like Russian nesting dolls—'hoods within 'hoods and everything had multiple names.

You didn't simply live on Adams Street. No. You lived Uptown, in the university district, in the Black Pearl, on Adams Street, near the Riverbend. And that's where the streetcar dropped me to meet him one night.

We walked along a quiet residential street. So quiet I could hear insects chirp and maybe the faint sound of water from the river a block away.

"This is my neighborhood," he said. "What do you think?"

"It's quiet." I hadn't had a quiet night in New Orleans since moving there over a year earlier. There was the occasional familiar sound of a passing streetcar, but that was about it—as if we were in a different city entirely.

The trees smelled different here, more like sweet olive. I couldn't detect any jasmine nearby. The gardens were small, if they even existed. We walked past an eclectic row of modest shotgun homes and old larger houses that had been divided into apartments over the years. It was a little run down, but I could spot gentrification projects here and there—a fresh coat of paint, a newly installed fence.

"I used to come out here all the time when I lived in Algiers. I used to love this neighborhood, I dreamed of living here."

"And now?"

"I'm sick of it. I was planning to move back to Boston—that's where I went, when I was gone. But there was a blizzard, and I got depressed and came back."

He led me to a small double shotgun house with a broken-down front porch and a moss-covered brick courtyard. There were no porch lights, but I could see two tall doors next to each other on the porch—each door leading to a separate rental.

He swung open the rusted, waist-high gate and walked into the courtyard. It was an old wooden house, cracked paint, probably had never been renovated since it was built. Some kind of flowering vine was growing out from the rotting fascia boards near the roof, its sharp green leaves and thin white flowers overflowed from the rain gutter and spread out around the corner of the house like thin, green arms.

I followed him up the loose porch steps to the pair of doors. A TV blared through the door on the right.

"That's Mr. Watkins," he said. "Deaf. His daughter lives around the corner."

He opened the door on the left and let me through. It was too dark to make out many details, but it was much bigger than it appeared from outside. The ceiling was extraordinarily high and there was an old fireplace and mantle at the far end of the room. Next to it was a small card table and what appeared to be a drum set in a dark corner. A military duffle bag filled with what I assumed were clothes was propped against the fireplace. Adjacent to the card table, a doorway led to the bedroom. I knew beyond that would be the kitchen. There seemed to be some kind of medallion on the ceiling. With a little work, it could be a beautiful space.

"Sorry, there's no light in here," he said. "There's a light in the kitchen if you'd rather go in there."

"No, this is fine."

"I told you it was empty."

"And you weren't kidding," I laughed. "It's nice, though. I like it." The only light was coming in from the door and a tall window—moonlight mixed with a distant streetlight's glow. As my eyes adjusted, everything took on an eerie blue glow.

"I'm going to leave the door open to get some air through," he said. "It gets really hot in here." He propped the door open with the duffel bag.

It was hot. Almost immediately I felt beads of sweat collect and run down my face, one rolled into my ear, and I could feel my t-shirt already sticking to me. I found him near the window, put my arms around his shoulders and kissed him.

"Here?" he asked.

"Why not? I'm glad you brought me."

"On the floor?" He sounded disgusted.

"Sit down." I took his hand and pulled him to the floor with me. I pushed him onto his back and straddled him. His hands gripped my waist, but only to push me off.

"I'm sorry, it's too hot for this."

I wasn't sure what to say. It wasn't the reaction I expected.

He stayed on his back and stared at the ceiling. I couldn't tell if he was uncomfortable or just feeling quiet. I lay down next to him, on my stomach, propped my head in my hand. "What are you thinking about?"

"I don't know. Nothing." He closed his eyes.

I felt antsy, anxious. Something heavy beyond the heat was settling between us. "Tell me about your family, they're all in Boston?"

"I have three brothers, only one lives there."

"What do your parents do?"

"My mother was a homemaker; my father was a plumber." He sighed as if he were reading statistics from a book. "She has Alzheimer's now. My oldest brother lives with her, but he wants to put her in a home. My father's been dead for twenty years."

"Oh."

The matter-of-fact way he said everything left me confused. I didn't know what to say. "I'm sorry."

"Don't be."

I waited for him to continue, but he didn't. His silence, and the sweat that was now pouring freely down my shirt, was making me feel anxious—like I should say something, anything, to ease the tension. "Your father must've died young?"

"He hung himself."

The temperature seemed to drop twenty degrees. He didn't say anything else. "I'm sorry," I repeated dumbly.

"It was a long time ago." His voice was flat; I couldn't read it.

I couldn't think what to say next, but I felt words fall out of my mouth, "Did you—did your family talk to anyone about it? When it happened?"

"My mother didn't want to talk about it, so we never did. We just went on like it never happened."

I sat up now, trying to make out his face in the dark. This was serious. His eyes were closed, as if he were trying to sleep. His fingers were laced just below his chest. His ankles were crossed. I couldn't let it go. "Can I ask you what happened? We don't have to talk about it."

"There's nothing to talk about. He was depressed. He wanted to see someone about it, but my mother wouldn't let him. He kept saying he was depressed, he was depressed, and she told him to man up, man it out. One day my oldest brother came over for dinner and he opened the garage and found him there."

"While you were in the house?" I whispered.

"I was on my way home from class. I was 19 and got there later. My brother cut him down. He said there wasn't a note."

"And you never talked to anyone about it?"

"It was twenty years ago. There's nothing to say."

I couldn't decide what shocked me more: the story or his delivery. I told myself he had twenty years to process the experience. Whatever feelings he may or may not have had, it was obvious he wasn't going to share them that night.

As if reading my mind, he opened his eyes to look at me and said, "I should walk you to the streetcar."

"You don't want me to stay?"

"You want to stay in this heat?"

"No," I laughed. "But I'm not ready to leave yet." I reached out to put my hand on his chest.

"You should go before it gets any later." He stood up and pulled me to my feet.

"Are you throwing me out?" I joked.

"Of course not." But he was. He had me halfway out the door and was ready to lock it behind us before I'd even gotten my bearings.

We walked to St. Charles in silence. I didn't know what to say; he looked his age for the first time since we met. We didn't wait long for a streetcar. He kissed me as the doors folded open. "I'll call you tomorrow," he said.

I climbed the stairs and dropped my quarters into the fare slot. I slid onto the first wooden bench and watched him through the open window as he crossed the street toward his apartment. When the streetcar rumble-popped back to life, I turned to watch him until he disappeared down the street.

*　*　*

The phone rang one afternoon—it was the front gate number on caller ID. I wasn't expecting anyone. "Hello?"

"Hey, let me up. I have something for you." It was Eliot.

I buzzed him in, and a few minutes later there was a knock on the door. I opened it to find Eliot standing there with a red racing bike.

"What's this?"

He rolled the bike in. "You need a bike. It's so much better than walking around on foot."

"I mostly take the streetcar," I ran my hand along the frame. It was an expensive, lightweight bike. I loved it.

"I know, but this is easier—and it's free."

"Thank you! It's really nice," I took the handles from him. It was practically new. "You didn't have to do this."

"It's no big deal. I got it from a friend. Will you use it?"

"Of course!" I had been talking about getting a bike for months but didn't have the cash.

"Maybe you should think about moving Uptown? It's so busy here for riding a bike. And there's so many panhandlers around—it's not very safe."

"Eh, it's not that bad. The view makes it worth it." The view did make it worth it, but he was right. He said "panhandlers" but every week we got notices from building security about muggings around our gate.

As it turned out, I wasn't going to have a choice about moving. A few weeks after the bike, the management company announced my building was being converted into condos. I had the option to buy my unit or move. I had no cash and only made a few hundred dollars a month, so I was moving whether I wanted to or not.

Eliot and I walked to the Quarter that Sunday and I told him about the condo conversion.

"If I could come up with a down payment, I could buy the apartment. Do you want to go in on it?" I joked.

"That building is so run down. You know how much work it's going to need?" He paused. "Why don't you just move Uptown? It's so much quieter there."

"Where would I live?" I wasn't expecting him to offer his place, but I halfway hoped he would. At the very least I hoped he'd offer to help me find a place. He seemed to think things over for a minute.

"You could move in with me if you want," he suddenly got excited, "think of how much money we'd save! Only $125 each!"

Menacing Becomes the Bostonian

His excitement over the money made me laugh. It was a practical idea. It was only a few blocks from work and the park. And we were already spending every weekend together.

"Yeah. Okay, let's do it."

Five months after we met, Eliot and I moved my furniture, and me, into the empty house on Adams Street. We were so excited about this new era we adopted a puppy from one of the ladies I worked with. Everything finally seemed to be lining up—and it was better than I could have dreamed.

The 'hood

Our time on Adams Street was short. As lovely as I thought that space could be, the decay went too deep. There was a hole in the floor, covered with carpet, that was big enough to fall through. The hot water heater never actually heated much water. Wild vines constantly broke through the frame around the kitchen window. Our puppy was a mixed-breed shepherd and growing fast. We needed a bigger yard and more space.

When I noticed mold creeping up around the corners of the bathroom floor, that was my breaking point. I started looking for another rental.

"I don't see why we should move. We've already got a yard and we're not going to beat $250 rent," Eliot insisted.

"We've got a tiny yard covered in vines—and they're coming in through the windows! It's hot as hell in this place," I argued. "We both have jobs—it's not like we can't afford more rent."

"We have day jobs. We're not made of money—and why should we spend it on rent, even if we could afford it?"

Eliot wasn't having it unless we found a place under $400. He worked 32 hours a week selling cologne in a little boutique, but his main job was playing gigs with a couple of bands. I made about $650 a month working at the library. So, I understood where he was coming from. We were the definition of broke artists. He was obsessive about saving money, but I wasn't going to live in that shack for the six months remaining on his lease.

Since I worked at a university, I decided to start taking classes and finish the bachelor's degree I'd abandoned years before. I had two years left, and part-time work was great, but I had to bring in more money if we were going to move. I decided to take classes at night and work during the day.

"Do you think there's anything full-time I could apply for?" I asked Miss Viv.

"You need more work, baby?" She sounded concerned.

"Kind of. I want to move, and it would be better if I was working full time."

"Let me see what I can hear, leave it with me."

A few days later Miss Viv told me about Jaquelle—a lady in another department who needed an assistant. I put in an application with HR.

Jaquelle agreed to interview me, but she seemed skeptical the minute she saw me. She had infamously fired her last assistant very publicly and loudly in front of half the staff. She had a reputation for churning through assistants. A lot of them. Very quickly. But I wanted that job. I stepped into her office, and she motioned for me to sit next to her desk. She was stone faced as I sat down.

"You're Spanish?" she asked. It took me off guard, but I'd learned in New Orleans that race was everywhere and at the root of everything.

"Hispanic, yes," I wasn't going to get into a whole Chicano vs. Hispanic vs. Latino discussion with her, but I knew what she was asking—was I white?

"You know, everyone thinks Spanish people are white, but I worked with a Spanish guy once, and he got so mad when people called him white. I know you all are your own thing," she said.

"That's true," I had no idea where this was going, but I wanted to be agreeable.

"Miss Viv says you're a good worker."

"That's nice of her to say. I like working for her," I was touched Miss Viv put in a good word for me.

The 'hood

"Mmhmm." She eyed me over her reading glasses, and I squirmed a little. She was tough. It radiated off her.

We went through standard interview questions—could I follow directions? How would I solve problems? Would I show up to work and learn the skills for the job? I didn't get the sense that I impressed her, but she wasn't kicking me out, either. I heard from some of the girls at the front desk that she'd yelled at them in front of students—so at least she wasn't yelling at me.

"I've got a few more people to interview," she said. "You'll hear back if we decide to hire you." She shuffled through papers on her desk as if to dismiss me.

I got up to leave, "Okay, thank you."

I didn't have a sense either way whether I'd be a finalist, but I went to Ginny to ask if she knew any inside secrets. Since they were both librarians, I thought she might have some clues about how to get in—and not get fired.

"Don't worry about Jacquelle," she said. "She just likes things her way. The only reason she acts that way is because no one does their job. Do the job, and you'll be fine. Her family is connected—they run half the city."

"Okay. So, she probably wouldn't fire me for no reason?"

Ginny laughed, "Just do your job, you'll be fine. She went to school in Chicago, so she knows her stuff. I hope you get it!"

A few days later I got a call from human resources—I was offered the job. Eliot and I did a happy dance with our dog, Pixie, and he finally seemed excited about moving.

I could not wait to leave that carpet-covered hole and moldy bathroom floor behind.

From day one, I bent over backward to say yes to anything Jaquelle said. I did not want to get chewed out in front of students or be fired in front of the staff. There were a few tense moments at the start, but it felt manageable. I just kissed all the ass I could manage.

It paid off when I found out Jaquelle's family had a slate of rental properties in another part of town. She knew the rental market inside and out.

"Ms. Jaquelle, do you think you could give me advice on finding a rental?"

She perked up. The only thing Jaquelle loved more than her job and her kids was giving advice.

"Where do you wanna live? How much you wanna pay?"

"I don't know. I don't have a car, so I need to stay near work."

She leaned back in her chair and thought for a minute.

"And I have a dog," I added.

"Yeah, you need a guard dog on your salary!" she laughed.

There was no political correctness in this mission—Jaquelle was black, and she was native New Orleanian—she was the only person I trusted to point me toward a safe rental. I couldn't afford anything nice. I made about $16,000 a year at that job, which was good money for ghetto New Orleans but well below the poverty line.

"I think I know a place," she said. "It's not ours, but I know the people."

The next day we drove to a little row of Creole cottages a few blocks away from the house on Adams Street. It was only a few blocks, but this street was like a different universe. The houses on this block were all run-down shotgun houses and tiny Creole cottages—small four-room houses that had been divided into two rentals. Each side of the cottage had two small rooms: a kitchen and a bedroom.

There weren't any trees on this street. The gentrification around St. Charles hadn't spread this far toward the river yet.

This block made the Adams Street house look like luxury accommodations, but Jaquelle assured me the cottage had just been renovated. And it was only $375.

The house was one street away from the Mississippi River and the tall earthen levee that kept the river at bay. Jaquelle

The 'hood

pulled up to the house—a bright yellow cottage next to a burned-out shell that used to be a house.

A couple of teenage boys on the corner eyed us.

"I don't know about this," she said, eyeing the boys back. "But we'll take a look, since we're here."

We got out and surveyed the treeless block. There was a ragged white shotgun with a sagging roof directly across the street. The door was covered with a stark black iron security door. A small pink shotgun stood next to it, completely overgrown with vines but a full trash bin was sitting out front—it was inhabited.

All the other properties were either run down or abandoned with broken windows. A little ranch-style house at the end of the block had a construction truck parked in its driveway. It looked as if it was being renovated.

Jaquelle pulled out the keys and leaned into me, whispering, "You see that kid there on the corner?" She glanced to where the teenagers stood, and I followed her gaze. One boy was walking away, and the other, a chunky kid, maybe 15 or 16 years old, turned away from us. He had short dreadlocks and wore an oversized white t-shirt and baggy jeans cut off below the knees.

He took a quick look at us over his shoulder, saw we were looking at him, and quickly turned back around. We'd caught the end of a deal.

"Do you think the police get called around here all the time?" I asked her.

Jaquelle ushered me into the house as the boy glanced over his shoulder again. Once inside the kitchen, she closed and locked the door. We inspected the small room.

"You think the police waste their time on a kid like that? They wouldn't even show up. Even if they did, he'd be out again before anyone takes his name. And guess who he'll be pissed off at for fucking up his day? Whoever called the cops. Don't ever get involved in that shit."

I walked around the kitchen—it had been renovated. It was small but nice. The cottage had two rooms. This front kitchen area and a second room with a bathroom tacked onto the back. I walked to the back door. There was a freestanding laundry room out back with a coin-based washer and a clothesline.

This place had a washing machine! I had been using a public laundromat the entire time I lived in NOLA. A coin-wash and a clothesline would be an improvement.

"That's the kid you want on your side, hear?" Jaquelle called out to me. "He's the one that'll make sure no one steals your shit when you're out of town."

I laughed as I came back inside and inspected the tiny closet-sized bathroom.

"Yeah, you laugh," she said seriously, "but you watch. If you moved in here, this place would be hit up all the time, hear? This the 'hood. Hood folks see a white girl, they're going to think you've got money."

I was looking around the bedroom and said sarcastically, "I'm not white, remember?"

"Girl, if you ain't black, you *white*. So, get that straight in your head right now, because that's how they think. And it doesn't matter if you don't have shit, they think all white people are born with money."

I stopped and looked at her. I was joking around, but she was dead serious.

"I'm not saying it's right," she said. "I'm saying that's how it is. And you watch, if you moved in here, first thing, everybody's gonna hustle you, hear?"

"Oh, come on," I said and continued looking around the room. "I dated a guy in East L.A. I think I can handle Uptown New Orleans."

"Hmph." Her tone was clear: *you don't know shit, girl.*

"Let me tell you what's going to happen if you moved in here," she said. "First week you're here, someone's going to

The 'hood

knock on your door. Or they'll stop you in the street, hear? They'll ask you for a donation—a school drive or a church thing—they're going to feel you out. See how much you'll give. They'll say, 'Hey, can you give a little to this? Give a little to that?' They're going to see how easy they can roll you."

I went back to the kitchen and looked out the window—the boy was still not facing us. "So, what should I do?"

"Don't give anyone *shit*. You tell them you're a student and you don't have a job. Whatever they ask, you say you've got no money, hear? And don't carry anything nice. After a few weeks they'll leave you alone."

"You think so?"

Jaquelle was inspecting the cheap white cabinets installed above the stainless-steel sink.

"Girl, you mark my words, hear? You give these ghetto folks one red cent, and you'll never be able to shake them. And be nice to the old ladies, hear? Say hello, good morning. Smile like the sun shines out your ass no matter what. They're not going to like you, but it doesn't matter. The old ladies run those kids. If they see you have respect, they'll make sure no one messes with you."

I leaned against the windowsill opposite the sink and faced her. "So, I should make friends with the drug dealer?" I joked.

"You don't make friends, no." She closed a cabinet hard and turned to face me. "I'm saying you show respect. You make eye contact, hear? You let him know you're not afraid to look in his face. But don't be nice. Don't be all up in his face with that 'friendly' shit, that's bullshit. He knows it."

I was smirking at her. It's not that I didn't believe her—I did. But she was talking to me like I'd never seen a neighborhood in poverty before. I had.

She sighed. "Girl, you do what you want, hear? But I wouldn't live here if I was you. You'll get rolled. First thing."

She wasn't wrong. I knew the possibility was there.

"I'm sorry," I looked at her sincerely.

"I appreciate what you're saying—I really do. Thank you for doing this and looking out for me."

She softened a little. I did appreciate her advice. I just didn't think it would be as bad as she made it sound. I had been dealing with panhandlers and hustlers since I got to New Orleans; it was nothing I hadn't already seen.

In fact, one woman was notorious. She stopped me, sobbing, four separate times in the first year I lived in my old apartment. Every time, she approached me at the security gate, crying uncontrollably, saying her boyfriend had stranded her at the bus station, and she needed money to get home to Mississippi. Could I please give her $30? Or $20?

The first time I honestly didn't have any money, or I would have helped her. The second time she seemed familiar, so I said sorry, no. By the third and fourth times I called her out and said, "hey, you already tried this with me." Both those times she dropped the tears immediately and moved on. I saw her pulling that trick all the time, but she never bothered me again once I called her out.

I didn't hate the players, but I understood the game.

As we went back out to the car, I could see the Mississippi River levee rising behind the house. It was maybe 12-feet tall, covered with grass like a park. A big green hill where people let their dogs run free. A train track ran alongside the base of the hill. The train noise wouldn't be a problem.

That levee was the main selling point for the cottage. It was basically a built-in dog park across the street. Plus, there was a 13-mile paved road on top. We could ride our bikes or jog from the house all the way to the Audubon Zoo, and even beyond that. In the other direction, the levee road went into Jefferson Parish out toward Baton Rouge. It would be the perfect place to run when I was too lazy to go the five or six blocks to Audubon Park.

There was also a medical center on the next block. Every Tuesday I knew a local farmer's market set up in their parking

The 'hood

lot. And shuttle vans ran from the medical center to the nearby campuses every morning and afternoon. The walk to work was only eight or nine blocks, but the shuttle would be useful for rainy days.

Other than the blighted houses on the block and the burnt-out crack house next door, it was a good location and a perfect little house. I signed a year lease even though Eliot still had a few months left on his Adams Street lease. He stayed at his place while I moved into the yellow cottage, and I took our shepherd for protection.

* * *

My first night in the cottage, a steady stream of college kids blasted their BMW stereos up and down the street, pausing just long enough on the corner to pick up their party drugs. I couldn't understand the arrogance of blasting your stereo at 3 o'clock in the morning through a residential neighborhood when you're buying your drugs, but there it was. That chunky dreadlocked kid had a thriving overnight business.

My first mission was to make eye contact with that kid. I knew Jaquelle was exactly right in her advice. Morning to night, he was out there, but he never looked in my direction when I was out with the dog. I figured out he lived a few doors down across the street with his grandma. I passed the house on my way to and from work and had seen him coming and going. Grandma sat on that front porch from sunrise to maybe 8 or 9 o'clock at night every day.

I started my charm offensive by saying good morning and good evening to her every time I walked by. Every time I called out, she spat over the railing in my direction and looked away as if I didn't exist. I kept right on saying it. I kind of hoped she would eventually stop spitting at me, but nope, it happened every time. She never looked directly at me. That was fine. The sun shone out my ass regardless. I didn't need her to like me. I needed her to make sure no one would steal my shit.

Displaced

Any time I walked past the dreadlocked kid on the corner, I tried to make eye contact. No luck. Finally, after days, he looked over and I did the slightest nod and looked away. The next time I looked he nodded back, and I knew we had an understanding. I continued paying respect to grandma and ignored the spitting.

After the head nodding he moved his business two blocks over, in front of a corner store owned by a guy named Vi. The traffic would probably be better for both their businesses.

The rich-kid party crowd went with him, and they were now far enough away that I could get a decent night of sleep. The next time I saw him by his grandma's house, I gave a hint of a smile with my nod. I hoped he understood my appreciation.

A couple of weeks after I moved in, I heard a soft knock on the door around 10:00 p.m. Pixie, our 40-pound, knee-high shepherd mix, barked and I followed her to the door. There were two tall, thin windows on either side of the door. Each covered with a white paper shade—I peeked out one of the shades.

There was a lady, maybe in her 50s, standing at the bottom of the steps. She had a tight salt-and-pepper bun and wore dark polyester pants and a button-down blouse. She carried a clipboard clutched to her chest.

I shushed Pixie and opened the door a crack to see if she'd try to get out. She stopped barking and stayed beside me, so I opened the door enough to stick my head out.

"Can I help you?"

"Yes, ma'am." The woman smiled briefly and hugged the clipboard tighter. "I live just down the block there, and I don't know if you heard but there was a boy killed around the corner last week?"

"Oh my God, no!" I was genuinely surprised.

"Oh, yes. Mm-hm. Just playing outside his house—hit and run. Mm-hm. Just right there." She vaguely pointed to the area behind my house. "And his family has no money, no. It's just so sad." The woman sniffled, "Now, you just moved in here…"

The 'hood

"I did."

"Well, we sure do welcome you, and it's such a shame this had to happen right when you're getting settled. You know, I've lived here all my life, right there around the block there."

She motioned to the next block, a block with a couple of rundown rental units, a vacant lot, and a church where Mahalia Jackson once sang.

"It's a quiet neighborhood, mm-hm. And this little boy was killed just right here. I still can't believe it." She blinked hard, as if about to cry, but no tears came. "The family has no money, no. The city won't release his body until they pay a fee to get him out. It's hundreds of dollars."

"What?" She lost me with that last detail. My brain kicked in. "The city kept his body?"

"Oh yes, indeed. Mm-hm. The city's got the body. They won't let it go. It's hundreds of dollars. So, we've got a collection to help his family out, you know what I'm saying? We got to get his body out and give him a proper burial."

She stared at me expectantly. I stared back at her blankly.

A hundred questions went through my mind: Why would the city have the body? My mom was a hospice nurse. That's not how morgues work. Why would they be charging hundreds of dollars in fees? It didn't make sense.

On top of that, I couldn't believe a woman her age was standing on my doorstep at 10 o'clock at night trying to hustle me. She had to be 50 if she was a day. I got a little pissed off that she was taking me for a fool this late at night.

"You say it happened last week?" I asked.

She furrowed her brow. "Yes, ma'am."

I feigned shock. "Well, my goodness. When? I can't believe I was here all week, and I never heard a thing. Not even a siren or an ambulance."

I caught the flash of a glare before her face went placid. "I'm not too sure about the time, Miss. I know you're new to the neighborhood, so you might not know how these things go. But what can you give to help the family?"

"Sorry, I don't have any money."

She was visibly taken aback. "Everybody's chipping in, Miss. *It's for the family.*"

"Oh, I understand that. I don't have any money."

She stared at me, confused. "I live right around the corner there. You can trust me, Miss. We just need a few dollars to get this boy out to his family…"

"Oh, I hear you. I come from Adams Street, so we've probably seen each other before," I knew I had never seen this woman before, but I wanted her to know I wasn't "new" here.

"I don't have any money. I'm not working right now." I put on my most sincere, concerned expression. "But I am *sure* you'll collect what you need. God is good—He'll come through for you. I'm very sorry for the family."

"Mm-hm." She glared at me and turned up a corner of her pursed mouth. "You have a good night, then."

"You, too." I closed the door.

I felt a twinge of guilt and hoped there wasn't really a boy's body trapped in red tape. But even if I had believed her story, I wasn't going to hand out cash to a stranger at 10:00 on my doorstep. Even without Jaquelle's prediction, I knew that was asking for trouble in any neighborhood.

I never saw that woman again. She most definitely did not live around the corner. A few weeks later a young woman stopped me on the street on my way home from a night class. She told me the exact same story. A boy had just been hit by a car, and the city was holding his body hostage. It was weeks later. I said no and kept walking.

My instinct to doubt her had been correct. Either that, or the kid must've been trapped in that morgue a mighty long time. No one else bothered me after that. I blended in and went about my business in peace. Jaquelle had been right.

The 'hood

A few months after moving in, my coworker was volunteering with an animal shelter and asked if I wanted to go to an adoption event. Eliot and I were talking about getting a sibling for Pixie, even though having two dogs in that tiny cottage seemed like a recipe for disaster. If we got another dog, we agreed it had to be a small senior rescue.

Of course, once my coworker brought me and Pixie to the event, she made a beeline for the puppy pen. There was a little puppy strutting around the pen that was the exact same shade as Pixie. They could've been littermates, if not for the six-month age difference. This little pup looked like a baby fox, and Pixie wagged her tail and jumped when she saw him—they sniffed each other, both tails wagging, and that was the end of that.

We had a second dog.

When we got home, Eliot was standing in the cottage's open front door. We each had keys to both houses, so we roamed between the two, although we spent most of our time at the yellow cottage. I got out of the car, and we watched the dogs chase each other around the front steps. Pixie led her new brother into the house.

"What are we going to name him?" Eliot asked.

My coworker said goodbye and Eliot and I went in the house. "What's a good dog name?"

"Nunziato," he said.

"Nunziato? What kind of dog name is that?"

"It's my grandfather's name. Let's name him after his great-grandfather."

I watched the dogs wrestle around the futon in the tiny bedroom. "Does he look like a Nunziato? Is there a nickname for that? Nunzie? Eh, I don't know...."

"How about Cesare then?" He pronounced it Cha-zah-ray. "That's his first name. We called him Cha-zah."

"Cesar." I pronounced it Cha-zah. "Like Caesar?"

"Cesare Nunziato!" Eliot declared and rubbed Cesare's head.

Pixie jumped up and bounded off Eliot's leg and he chased her into the kitchen. I heard him call after her in a falsetto voice, "Pixie's my girl!" followed by the sound of her nails scraping the floor as she frantically ran in circles around the kitchen.

I picked up the puppy and squeezed him and kissed his furry head, "Cha-zah! My little Chazzie boy!"

Cesare—Chaz—seemed to like his new name. I put him down and he strutted in a circle and sat tall with his chest stuck out proudly. "What a little show dog!" I said to him. He looked at me sidelong with his black button eyes and I broke into laughter.

With Chaz our family was complete, and the potty training began again. I'd be outside with the dogs at one or two o'clock in the morning as Eliot was coming home from gigs, so we got to know the nighttime neighbors well.

There were only three kinds of people outside at that hour: people buying drugs, people selling drugs, and people like me who had no business being outside but somehow found themselves there.

Since the chunky kid had moved his business there were two people I saw regularly at that hour: Jacob and Marty.

Jacob was the first to approach me, and the first person I met who never asked me for money. He'd stop and talk with me at the corner where the drug dealer used to work. Sometimes he'd ask me for a job cutting grass or hauling trash, but I never had any work to give him. I had concrete front steps, and the "backyard" was just an empty lot behind the cottage. But I always promised to send him any work if I found any.

Jacob was an old-school gentleman, in his 50s at least, and he looked every bit his age and then some. His dark skin was heavily lined; his shoulders hunched from years of hauling and raking and maintenance work. But his eyes were warm and kind. He was rail thin and always wore the same faded blue jeans and work shirt. He usually wore an old blue baseball cap. I could never figure out where he stayed.

The 'hood

I never got a straight answer from him when I asked about his life. I only knew he'd been a fixture on this street for as long as anyone could remember. I think he stayed with different people around the neighborhood.

At almost any hour of the day or night you'd find Jacob walking here or there, up and down the same few streets asking for odd jobs. Whenever he saw me, he'd call my name and wave. If I had the dogs, he'd stand out on the corner with us for a few minutes to advise me on how to train them. He said he knew everything about dogs.

"When you feed them, make sure you put their bowls up on a brick or something, so they don't eat straight off the floor."

"Oh yeah? Why's that?"

"Oh!" He exclaimed, like it was unbelievable I didn't know this, "You don't want them eating off the floor! If you do, they'll put any old trash in their mouth when they walk—old chicken bones, anything. You don't want them eating that nasty stuff. Bad for their digestion. Train them not to eat off the ground. I always did that with my dogs. Never had a problem."

"Thanks, Jacob. I'll try that."

No matter what he said, I agreed. It seemed to make him feel useful to give advice, and he seemed like a person who needed to feel useful. Marty eventually filled me in on Jacob's story, or at least what she knew of it. They had known each other over 20 years by that point. They were neighbors on this block back when he still had a house. She thought he may have had a family, but she couldn't remember for sure.

Marty was so much a part of the neighborhood, especially at night, that I don't even remember meeting her. She was just there—as if she'd been built there with the houses. She lived in the dilapidated shotgun across from our cottage and worked as a bartender at some shady dive bar downtown. She never gave me the name, but she'd always be coming home as I was taking the dogs out for our midnight walk.

Marty and Jacob were our resident addicts. They were two peas in a pod, always together. Jacob, a clean-shaven black gentleman, and Marty, a petite, ruddy-faced, stringy-haired blonde in her 60s who walked around with a water bottle filled with vodka.

Jacob may have had a drug problem, but he never took a handout. He never hustled; he never stole.

Everyone respected him—the entire neighborhood conspired to keep him housed and working odd jobs, so he always earned enough to support his addiction. He always had a place to stay. I was sure he stayed with Marty sometimes, and I assumed they were more than friends.

Some nights Marty would walk with me and the dogs for a few blocks and tell me about her pet dingo. She never explained how she came to have this dingo, but she loved to talk about him like he was her child.

"Dingoes are wild. You can't get too close to them," she explained one day. "He can't be near other dogs, or he goes crazy. Don't ever come outside if you see us out front. If he charges, I can't stop him."

I had never seen a dingo before, so I couldn't say for sure if it was one, but one night I looked out the window and saw her walking it. It didn't look like any dog I'd ever seen. It was sort of dog-like, but with sharper features and looked much stronger. Marty would wait until my dogs were safely inside before bringing him out on a big leather leash.

The sight of tiny, frail Marty trying to control that dingo made me laugh, but it seemed to listen to her. It looked at her like its mama and never seemed out of control.

Most mornings I'd see Marty again when I left for work. In the mornings she looked after Miss Rebecca—the lady living in the broken-down pink shotgun next to hers. Miss Rebecca never stepped out beyond her front door. She was an elderly lady, looked as old as the sun. Never said much but was always

The 'hood

smiling. She always wore a flowered robe and waved from the doorway if anyone passed by.

Twice a week, Marty hauled Miss Rebecca's trash bin from the back of the house on trash day and dragged it back when it was emptied.

Even after the potty-training phase with my dogs ended, I would still go outside at night to check on Jacob and Marty. They became like surrogate parents, looking after me and asking Eliot how gigs went when they saw him coming home after a show.

When the Adams Street lease ran out, Eliot moved into the little cottage with the dogs and me. The four of us squeezed into that 300-square-foot house, and we settled into a cozy routine punctuated by heated arguments from living in such close quarters. Eliot kept his drum set at the church where he attended service every Sunday. He would sometimes do handyman work for them, oiling the pews and doing yard work on Fridays. Then he'd stay and practice drums in the empty chapel.

He had been playing in an upbeat Italian jazz group, and work was picking up. The church let them rehearse in the fellowship hall, which had a stage and piano, and they started getting steady weekly gigs. Eliot was a tireless promoter, hounding club and restaurant owners with their newly minted CD and press kit. They managed to pick up shows at a few bars on Bourbon Street and some corporate parties and events.

My work was picking up, too. Because I got reduced tuition at the university, I enrolled in a documentary production class that would change the course of my career. We had to write a documentary film proposal for class, and something inside me opened. I didn't want to write screenplays anymore. I wanted to tell real-life stories.

I needed a subject for this project, so I asked everyone at work if they had any interesting leads.

Jaquelle came through again. Her best friend was a gospel singer who had been murdered in the '90s. She asked if I'd be interested in using his story for the class. I was so grateful she trusted me with her memories.

She graciously shared photos and let me interview her about their friendship. I was able to interview people who knew him and put together a film proposal. One of the archives on campus had his original recordings—I spent hours listening to raw recordings of his albums. He was a singular talent, a once-in-a-lifetime singer. I was enthralled.

Unfortunately, his life had taken a dark turn. He had been robbed and murdered by a prostitute in the Quarter. In the end, the family wasn't comfortable sharing the story. It was okay for a school project, but not a feature film.

When the semester was over, I presented Jaquelle with the proposal and all the research. If she ever wanted to make the film, she had everything she needed. She started to cry when she skimmed through the outline of his story.

"Thank you for doing him justice."

It was the first time I understood the true power of storytelling. It could be a force for healing; a way to honor the fallen. That proposal was more meaningful to me than anything I'd written before.

It meant something to her, and that was more than I could've hoped. I felt a tremendous responsibility to him, and I hoped his family would one day tell his story.

The instructors of that class put me in touch with a local producer who needed a summer intern. I couldn't afford to quit my day job, so Jaquelle arranged my schedule so I could come in early and work half days twice a week.

For two afternoons a week, I got to walk over to producer Dave's house down the street and sit at his editing bay—a professional editing system—and he showed me how to log footage of his latest documentary. It was the most exciting job I'd ever had. I felt like I'd hit the lottery every time I sat down at that editing bay.

The 'hood

His film was about an eccentric Mississippi artist who lived on an island in the 1960s. Dave and his business partner decided they needed to get interviews in Mississippi. They invited me to join the crew so I could lug equipment through the backwoods and learn how to work. I wholeheartedly accepted, and Jaquelle worked her magic so I could take a week off and join the crew.

* * *

August in the South cannot be described; it can only be experienced. I would argue that Mississippi in the summer is the hottest place on earth. In fact, I'd say it's the closest you can get to hell without dying.

We filmed in the overgrown backcountry wilderness of the artist's family compound. It was unlike anything I'd ever seen. We trudged through wild green brush, ducking around man-sized cobwebs spun by unseen spiders and filled with colorful long-legged insects as large as my fist.

Although we stayed at a nearby motel, for three days we had no air conditioning and no shelter in the field. For three days, each day felt more exciting than the last because I was finally doing something I loved. I was trekking through the wilderness with a team of talented guys on a creative mission. We were creating a story from raw, wild terrain.

When it was all said and done, I felt like one of the boys. I could go out and make my own film if I ever had an idea for one.

By the time I got home, I'd decided to return to school full time to finish the degree faster and focus on documentary work. I had managed to save enough money to get through my last year of studies. It was fall 2004, I had one year left, and I figured that was enough time to establish myself in production work.

I quit my job with Jaquelle, but the library kept me on as a part-time student worker. Ginny was about to go on maternity leave, so they put me in charge of opening her archive while she was gone. That wasn't normally a "student worker" kind of job, but I'd been there long enough that they trusted me.

Displaced

Everything was bustling in our lives by the end of 2004. Eliot's band was taking off. I was doing double time to finish my degree, and the blighted houses on our block were starting to be snapped up by investors and house flippers. Gentrification was coming to the Black Pearl.

Instead of BMWs blasting their stereos at 3 a.m., we now had demolition teams and heavy machinery rolling through at the crack of dawn.

One afternoon Eliot and I walked home from the grocery store through the medical center parking lot. We saw two teenaged boys leading young, muscular pit bulls by thick stainless-steel chains. They glared at us, but I looked right back at them and slowed down a little to watch.

Eliot walked faster, "Come on."

The other side of our cottage was rented by a tatted up goth girl with jet black hair and face piercings. Kimee worked in a veterinary office and had two little yappy dogs. She was standing on her front step smoking a cigarette when we got home.

"Hey, you see those boys with dogs around back?" I asked.

"Oh, yeah. I've seen them," she scowled. "I'm pretty sure they're using that blue house for fighting."

Eliot went in the house, giving me a "don't get involved" look.

"You think we should do something?" I asked.

"I already called animal control. It's a fucking voicemail box. I left my information but who knows if they'll do anything. Stupid motherfuckers."

She never heard back. Well, she didn't hear back from animal control. But we both heard from the kids.

A few days after she reported the dog fights, Kimee woke up to find her car completely keyed from front to back. Her car was no prize to begin with, but she was furious. She got on the phone with the cops. They never came, but she kept calling.

I also got a surprise that day: my bike was missing from our locked side yard.

The 'hood

Oh, no, they did not. Not my bike from Eliot. I loved that bike! I was *pissed*.

A few mornings later my bike frame turned up, mangled and tireless. It was dumped two doors down, blocking the sidewalk where I walked the dogs every morning. I took it as a childish attempt at retribution.

I was beyond angry. It was left across the street from the chunky drug dealer's house, in clear view of grandma's front porch. I walked my dogs to the bent frame and let them pee on it, then faced the chunky kid's house and glared. I thought, *You think this intimidates me? Try something else. See what I do.*

For the next two days, every time I passed it, I didn't acknowledge it was there. I looked directly at the dealer kid's front porch and yelled greetings to grandma as she spat over the railing. But now I glared at her.

That kid had to know who did it. The bike frame disappeared after a couple of days, and no one bothered me again.

Some investor bought the last blighted house on the block and the dog fighting house, too. By the end of the year the streets were lined with construction trucks.

Gentrification had arrived.

The Last Good Year

Something in the zeitgeist shifted the year before the flood. Seemingly out of nowhere, throughout 2004, people we knew who had lived there for years started to move away. There was more grumbling than usual. Our friends were fed up with the potholes and the poverty. Some of them couldn't afford the rising rents. The places we frequented in the Quarter were getting more expensive or closing completely.

Eliot and I had a tradition of spending Christmas and Easter with Pete and Andrew, a flamboyant couple who always hosted an eclectic group of friends on these two holidays.

Pete, Andrew, and Eliot had known each other about 15 years before I came along. They were fellow runners at Audubon Park and somehow—probably Andrew and his outgoing nature—they had adopted Eliot many years earlier. When I came into the picture, they adopted me as well.

On Christmas of 2004, we met them for their annual brunch at one of the Quarter's high-end hotel restaurants. As we entered the lobby, Pete, Andrew and three of their friends were entering from the parking entrance. Andrew, a tall bald man in his 60s, towered over them.

His voice bellowed through the lobby, "I just don't see why they have to charge so much for parking our car!"

My heels clacked on the marble floor as we rushed to meet them. Pete, a petite muscular man a little younger than Andrew, reminded me of Jack LaLanne. He put a hand on Andrew's arm to calm him down.

"Now, I really don't think it's a big deal. Should we see if our table's ready?"

He waved to us as he went to ask about our table.

We reached Andrew and he kissed each of us. "There you are! Do you know how much they charged us for valet parking? It's just incredible what they get away with over here. We are never coming back; I'll tell you that right now."

He said this every year, and every year we came back. No one in the lobby was paying attention.

He introduced us to their friends—a couple visiting from Argentina and an old friend of theirs from Treme. Pete came back with a young blonde hostess and kissed us, and she led us inside to be seated.

The front dining room of the restaurant was appointed in dark wood, rich upholstery, and fine linen. A lush courtyard with a fountain stood at its center. Because Pete and Andrew had been eating at this restaurant for at least 30 years, they were accustomed to having the best courtyard table. However, another party occupied their space. We were being escorted toward the center of the room, near the aging piano player.

"Peter, don't you let them put us in steerage!" Andrew said a little too loudly.

"They're not putting us in steerage," Pete said. He looked at me and motioned to a back room, "That's steerage."

I had walked through "steerage" on my way to the bathroom on previous visits. Unlike the front dining room with its private buffet and courtyard, the diners in "steerage" were packed tightly into a hotel ballroom with folding banquet tables and cheaper tablecloths. Their buffet was separate—and located by the bathrooms.

People in the front room had dedicated waitstaff who had been serving the same customers for decades. In steerage, the most you could hope for was the occasional bus person that made the rounds. I'm not sure why they called it "steerage" though. I was pretty sure the price of admission was the same for all of us.

The hostess seated us at a table near the pianist, who raised his eyebrows and smiled at us. Pete went to drop money in his glass and spoke to him for a minute. Eliot waved at him and leaned into me, "He's an old timer. Had this gig for years."

Our server was an older lady who caught up with Andrew for a few minutes after pouring our champagne. He kissed her cheek, and I noticed he discretely pressed some folded bills into her hand as she left.

We served ourselves from the courtyard buffet and fell into our usual conversation. Eliot and Pete, the Catholics, discussed the latest church controversies with the Argentinians. Andrew and I discussed his childhood growing up in New Orleans and the antique store he used to own.

"This place just breaks my heart," he told the table. "Things were so much better in the '80s. You wouldn't even recognize this place."

"Times were different then," Pete agreed.

Our conversation rolled along with whatever tidbits people offered for discussion. I drank mimosas by the pitcher and ate a few bites of smoked salmon. Eliot and I split every desert on the buffet line, leaning into each other and sniping bites from each other's plates.

That Christmas we all lamented the economy. Gigs were down. Eliot's band was reduced to corporate gigs and a few festivals. Venues were paying less, and fewer people were tipping. When we ran out of things to complain about, we discussed the weather, because it was unusually cold that year and the forecast called for snow.

We weren't disappointed by the forecast. By the time we dragged our drunk, stuffed bellies out of the restaurant it was already snowing. A thin layer of white covered the street. We all stood outside looking at the sky like it was falling.

"Well, we were going to walk the Quarter, but I guess not," Pete said.

"You're darn right we're not!" Andrew said sassily. "I'm not walking in this!"

We began exchanging hugs and stomping our feet in the cold.

"Give us some sugar," he said to me. I kissed him goodbye, and we left them waiting for their car. I looped my arm around Eliot's, and we walked quickly to catch the streetcar home.

People were standing at the streetcar stop saying it hadn't rolled by in over an hour.

Much later, in the newspaper, I saw a picturesque photo of the streetcar decorated with red velvet ribbon and evergreen garlands, traveling through the snow that day. I'd love to know when those photos were taken, because we waited half an hour for that streetcar before the rumor mill confirmed service was suspended due to the weather.

"What do you think, should we walk?" Eliot asked.

"Yeah, it'll be nice—something different!" I said, clearly drunk.

It was a long walk Uptown, but it was a romantic scene, and it was a walk we'd taken hundreds of times. We got about half a mile—as far as the Pontchartrain Hotel—before our feet were frozen solid.

"Forget this," he said when we saw cabs parked at the hotel.

"Yeah, get a cab," I laughed.

We laughed the entire ride home, where we found our dogs sprawled out on the bed napping. He turned the on the space heater as I put two frozen pies in the oven.

"What movies did we get?" he called from the bedroom.

For the last two years we each rented a movie on Christmas that the other hadn't yet seen. Then we'd have a double feature. That year I picked It's a Wonderful Life.

"My movie's on the bookshelf," I called back.

He appeared in the doorway with two DVDs. He was reading the back of It's a Wonderful Life. "Nice, I've always wanted to see this."

"What'd you pick?"

"The Omen."

I laughed out loud. "What? That's not a Christmas movie!"

"I know! I don't know, it seemed funny. There's a priest—that's kind of Christmas-y. You haven't seen it, have you?"

"No," I laughed. "Okay, that's quite a double feature."

We cuddled into bed with our dogs and ate two entire pies—blueberry and pumpkin—watching the snowfall along with our movies.

* * *

As remarkable as that snowstorm was, it was mostly forgotten by New Year's Day. As 2005 rolled in, we found out our rent was going up to $425 in the spring. For both of us, that was an outlandish amount for a glorified closet in this neighborhood. I went on the hunt for a new rental.

A shotgun house around the corner had just been renovated. The owner wanted $650 a month—more than either of us had ever paid, and more than other places in the neighborhood. But it was completely insulated with new storm windows and a new roof with hurricane clips. The owner said it was renovated to Florida hurricane codes. Being a woman who loved building codes, I was impressed. It also had central heat and air conditioning. Central A/C! That was unheard of in this neighborhood. We'd been living with a broken-down window AC and space heater for two years.

As soon as I found it, I took Eliot to see it.

"Look at the hardwood floors! There's a fireplace in the living room! We'd have a full bedroom and living room and kitchen!" I wanted him to love it as much as I did.

He was not impressed.

"Wait, I haven't shown you the best part," I took him to the most important room: a newly renovated bathroom in the back of the house with a claw foot tub and stacked washer and dryer.

I was ecstatic. He looked miserable. We stood together on the bathroom's gray slate floor.

"A brand-new washer and dryer," I said tantalizingly. "No more coin-op laundry."

He looked at it. "Uh-huh."

"And a claw foot tub..." I tried my best suggestive voice.

"Uh-huh." He stared blankly at the tub, completely oblivious to my attempts at a bathroom seduction.

"It's $650 a month, J."

"That really isn't a lot when you think about it."

"We pay $400 now. That's an extra $125 each we're going to have to come up with every month."

"This has more than twice the space. And look at it—look," I waved my arms. "Eliot, there's a dishwasher! Everything's brand new. Look at this place! Come on! $650 is nothing compared to L.A. or Boston. It's a steal. You know that."

He went back to the fully appointed brand-new kitchen, and then he looked back in the bathroom. "Uh-huh."

"You know it's worth it."

He looked at the tub again. "The tub is really nice."

"See! Let's get the lease signed before someone else rents it. Come on."

We had to go to through a leasing agent. She dropped off the paperwork and told us we could drop off a check to her office. I filled out the leasing agreement in both our names and we each cut a check for $650: first and last month's rent.

The next morning, we walked to the leasing office and Eliot started to sweat. He started to literally sweat. He was sweating profusely, and we had to stop several times so he could put his hands on his knees and lean over to catch his breath.

"What is the matter with you?" I more than a little irritated.

"I don't think I can do this."

"Can't do what?"

"This is a lot of money. What if you stick me with the lease?"

I stood next to him while he was bent over trying not to hyperventilate. "Are you kidding me with this?"

"Where am I going to get $650 dollars a month?"

"You have a job! And you have gigs! What the hell are you talking about?" I was yelling now. "We both make more than this. And why do you think I'd leave you with a lease? You don't trust me?"

"No, no," he stood up and took a breath. "You're right. You're right. I can do this. You're not going to stick me with a lease."

"For God's sake, pull it together." I slapped him on the back. "It's just a lease."

He walked into that leasing office like a man facing an executioner. But we handed over the checks. We each signed the lease—Eliot with his face clammy and hands shaking—then we took our keys and left.

"That wasn't so bad, was it?" I asked as we walked home.

"I guess not." His pace picked up a little, "It'll be fine, right?"

"Of course it will."

We moved into that house the following month, and all anxiety was gone.

We basked in the glory of central air conditioning and did our laundry in our own washer and dryer. We cooked meals in a brand-new kitchen. Eliot loved to cook, and I'd come home from class at night to find elaborate pasta dishes and salads waiting for me. Even the dogs were happier with a bigger yard, and we were directly across the street from the levee. Every morning we'd take the dogs out along the river, and life had never felt so on-track. Everything about that home was perfect for us.

Two: Forget About Today Until Tomorrow

A Flood in Three Parts

I. The Preparation

Every Katrina story starts on Saturday. Even though the storm made landfall early Monday morning, Saturday was the day it became undeniable that the storm was heading toward us. That's the day the "cone of uncertainty" had narrowed enough to make it clear New Orleans was in the landfall trajectory. The cone of uncertainty was a National Hurricane Center phrase for the many computer models that predict where a storm will hit. When mapped out, they create a spaghetti-like mangle of lines across the gulf. I liked to call it the "cone of confusion" because there was no telling where a storm would land until 72 hours before landfall.

Computer models varied hundreds of miles—it could hit Alabama, it could hit Texas, it could hit New Orleans—you wouldn't know until the models started to line up a few days out. And even then, a storm could take a jaunt, and you'd end up with nothing.

After four hurricane seasons in New Orleans, I knew it was anyone's guess where that storm would land until a day or two before it hit.

Hurricane Ivan, one year earlier, was absolutely, positively going to be the storm of the century for New Orleans. No question! The news had everyone worked into a frenzy. The contraflow evacuation system—where all the freeway lanes were directed outbound to help people get out—had completely failed during Ivan. There were massive traffic jams. People ran out of gas on freeways. And then, at the last minute, the storm turned east. We didn't see a drop of rain in our neighborhood that day.

We went through this drill every summer, and every summer it was a lot of drama for nothing.

On Saturday, August 27, 2005, I woke up, brushed my teeth, made some tea, and turned on the television. It was around noon. That's when I first heard the word "Katrina" in relation to New Orleans. The storm had already hit the Bahamas and south Florida, but until that morning the Cone of Confusion projected that she'd travel up Florida and stall out over Georgia.

I half-listened to the warnings, as I did every year. Each summer there was a catastrophe on the way. And each summer nothing happened.

Something about the messaging seemed more intense that day. The newscasters kept saying: If you don't have a second floor and a hatchet, you have no business staying in town. I couldn't remember them saying that in previous years.

Second floor. Hatchet. For the first time, I was concerned. How long does it realistically take to hack through a roof in rising water? The longer I watched the coverage, the more I was freaking out. Eliot had already gone to work that morning. Most of our friends were staying and riding out the storm. What if this was really the big one?

"Hey, should we leave tonight?" I called him at work.

"No, it'll be fine. No one here is leaving."

Eliot's boss claimed she had no intention of evacuating and said evacuation was for weak-willed people (of course, she flew out that night in a private plane).

"Can you see if someone will lend us a car? I tried finding a rental but there aren't any." Even if it turned out to be nothing, I was still scared.

"I'm telling you the storm will move east like Ivan. It's going to blow over just like it always does," he said.

A Flood in Three Parts

"I still think we should leave."

"We'll go to the church—it's brick and there's two stories. Even if the city blows down, the church isn't moving."

"Can't we borrow someone's car? Ask around."

"Everyone I know is staying. I'm telling you we're going to be fine. I've been through 15 hurricanes. This isn't even going to last a week."

Not being able to convince Eliot, I took the Tchopitoulas bus to Walmart, where I fought for the last four gallons of water. I knew there was nothing I could say to get him to leave. He's what they called a diehard. He took great pride in retelling how he rode out Hurricane Georges in 1998 in a shack with broken windows. The man had never evacuated. Ever.

I was a mess, though. I spent the rest of the day filling Ziploc bags with ice until our freezer was packed full. Filled the bathtub with water. Thankfully, we had an ice maker, so I stacked bags of ice in the fridge. Yes, it would melt, but it would be clean water.

For some reason I felt compelled to cook everything in the pantry, even though it made no sense. The last thing anyone wants when it's 100 degrees in Louisiana, with no electricity, is lentil loaf and bean casserole. But I had to do something with my hands. Had to feel busy. I put all our photos and important papers in plastic bags in a storage bin and put it in the attic crawlspace, just in case the house flooded.

Despite the fear, I was cautiously optimistic. The Army Corps of Engineers building was built on the levee across the street. Engineers don't build their own offices in flood zones.

My faith in engineering was unshakable.

At some point I went to the bank for cash. I banked with a local credit union, and if I had known how difficult banking was about to become, I would've taken out a lot more cash.

When Eliot got home, he said the church manager, John, would be riding out the storm with us and our dogs in the church. His wife and kids had flown out to Missouri, but he was

Displaced

staying to watch their properties. I couldn't stand John, but at least we would have company.

* * *

Sunday was preternatural.

We got up early and started packing. If the house flooded, or we couldn't get back to it for a few days, we needed enough essentials at the church to survive. Bob Breck, a local weatherman, called out from the TV while we packed: *Do you have a hatchet?*

They wouldn't give it a rest with that dang hatchet.

"Does the church have a hatchet?" I asked.

"We don't need one. The church has two stories and an attic. Worst case scenario we go upstairs. There's a pastor apartment and storage rooms up there and everything. We could live there if we needed to."

Bob Breck stood in front of an overhead satellite image of the storm—a storm nearly as big as the Gulf of Mexico, a storm bigger than Bob Breck himself.

The size of that image terrified me, the hole in the center looked large enough to stick your fist through.

We each packed a bag of clothes in silence. I packed my laptop and camera equipment into an overnight case. Eliot packed his military duffle bag with percussion equipment and music books, sticks and brushes and a metronome. When he put the bag on his back, one of the drumsticks fell out through a hole in the bottom. He picked it up and stuck it in the waistband of his shorts.

I got a spool of thread from my sewing box and slid a needle into the spool. I stuck this in my bag. I could fix the hole while we were gone. As an afterthought, I put a pair of knitting needles and skein of yarn in, too. As if I'd have time for needlework.

We loaded a bag of dog food and four gallons of water into the rolling metal cart that we used to carry groceries. We stacked two overnight bags on top of that: one with my equipment, one with his clothes. He had his military bag on, and I pulled a messenger bag over my shoulder. It contained two changes of clothes, a towel and two washcloths.

Our life was reduced to six pounds of dog food and four carry-on bags.

"You ready?" Eliot handed me one of the dog leashes.

We leashed the dogs, locked the house, and walked in silence to the church a few blocks away. It was completely silent on the street, already a ghost town. By the time we got to the church, there was a strong breeze bordering on wind.

"The storm doesn't hit until morning and it's already windy," I said. He didn't respond. He was unlocking the church's side door like a man on a mission—focused.

Inside, Eliot flipped on the lights and a radio. We unloaded everything in the fellowship hall. A newscaster was reporting the contraflow evacuation system had worked perfectly for the first time in its history. No traffic jams. No people stuck on the freeway. It had been smooth sailing. The city was mostly emptied, they said.

"It's like a sign something is coming," I said.

"Maybe. Let's take the dogs for a walk."

The church was adjacent to Audubon Park, so we took the dogs for a lap around the track. Pixie wanted to run, so Eliot jogged ahead with her. Chaz wanted to lie in the grass and roll around, so I sat with him while he stretched out on his back for belly rubs. In the grass, a perfectly preserved butterfly carcass was lying nearby. I delicately picked it up with my thumb and forefinger and held onto it like a talisman.

We're going to be okay.

Eliot and Pixie jogged back to us and the four of us started a lap around the two-mile track together.

"It's so quiet," I said.

"It's always quiet before a storm."

"Yeah, but last year there were more people out before the storm. It's dead today."

We didn't see another soul until we got back to the church. John was unloading a sleeping bag and case of Diet Dr. Pepper from his trunk.

"You been here long?" he called to us.

"Just got here," Eliot replied. "We're going to set up in the fellowship hall, if that's okay?"

"Yeah, I'll be in my office. I'm only planning to sleep here tonight. I'll be back at the house tomorrow."

I went into the church lobby and pulled out my mobile phone to call my mother. There were no smartphones then, just the old candy bar cell phones. My stomach churned and my hands shook as I paced the tiled front entrance of the church. I hadn't seen my mom in about a year, maybe a little longer. She was living with her soon-to-be third husband in Denver.

"You guys ready?" she asked.

"Yeah, I think so. So far so good."

I covered my eyes with my hand and told her we weren't nervous at all.

"Okay, be careful. Let us know how it goes."

"Watch the news for us," I laughed. "We'll tie a red flag to Chazzie's tail so you can see us on the church roof."

"Don't even joke."

"It'll be fine." I hung up and hoped I was right.

Eliot and I set up camp in the fellowship hall, a cavernous room in the back of the church. The floor was tiled with cold white asbestos tile and there was a small stage at the far end of the room. On one side of the stage was a door to the kitchen and stacks of banquet tables and chairs that were folded and stacked neatly. Next to that was an empty vending machine that was easily 40 years old.

A row of frosted windows spanned the length of the room and let in a moderate amount of daylight. The ceiling was two stories high, and the rest of the large room was empty. It was an open space for banquets and church performances.

On the other side of the stage was a second door and an upright piano. I didn't ask where the second door went, but I assumed to the upstairs apartment Eliot talked about.

We took cushions from a couch in the lobby and made a makeshift bed on the floor. Set out water bowls for the dogs and stacked our gear in a corner.

John set up his own little camp in his office, a small room off the fellowship hall.

Then we settled in to wait. I took out my yarn and cast on some stitches. There was nothing I wanted to make, but it was something to do with my hands.

As night fell, John brought out a tiny black-and-white battery-operated TV, and we watched about 20 minutes of news together. The storm was set to pass over us around 8 or 9 in the morning. The local news stations were broadcasting from 70 miles away in Jackson, Mississippi. My stomach was in knots. When the newscasters leave, you know trouble is coming.

John retired to his office. Eliot fell asleep with the dogs on the couch cushions. Around 10:30, I turned out the lights and fell asleep on the cushions next to them.

*　*　*

There's a sound, like a wooden heart beating, it's beating perfectly in time—ba-bommm (pause) ba-bommm (pause) ba-bommm (pause)—at first I think I'm dreaming, but my eyes open slowly and I look up toward the stage and the piano and I see the two wooden doors creak open maybe an inch and ba-bommm shut again. I realize every door in the old church is opening and closing in unison.

A thought, like a whisper: We're inside God's beating heart.

I turn over to face the frosted windows where gray overcast light is coming in and I can hear the wind howling against the panes. Eliot is sitting like a Buddha facing the windows, his back to me. He is perfectly still.

"What's with the doors?" I ask.

"Air pressure," he says. "The upstairs windows blew in around 3:00, we put boards up. Don't go up there, there's a lot of glass."

He doesn't turn, doesn't move a muscle. I notice there's a blue plastic bucket to his right and I hear a steady drop-drop-drop into it. I look up to the ceiling and see a large tan wet spot in the acoustic tile.

"How long has it been going?" I ask.

"A little while. Everything's fine, go back to sleep."

So I did.

* * *

Somewhere there's a video I shot that day.

It opens with the water I woke up to—about a foot of water outside in the street. It had receded by noon, and the streets were dry.

The footage cuts to Eliot clearing branches from around the church. The pile he built was nearly as tall as he was; he moves through the yard picking up each branch and tossing it onto the pile with smooth, even strokes of his arms. He sweats profusely in his Navy muscle shirt—he tore a hole in the front where one of the branches poked through. When he took it off at the end of the day, it looked like a bullet hole went through the stomach.

In the video, I call out and say something that makes me laugh, but you can't make out what I'm saying. The audio cuts out. He pauses long enough to roll his eyes at the camera and continues plowing his way through the yard.

In the background, a bulldozer travels down St. Charles, followed by a tanker truck. That was Monday. I joined the crew of neighbors in the street, moving branches from the streetcar tracks. We cleared the nearby yards by hand.

A Flood in Three Parts

An older woman with bleach-blonde hair led the effort, saying, "The sooner we get the tracks clear, the sooner the streetcar can come back."

* * *

Early Tuesday morning, we went to check on our house—no damage. We stopped at Vi's corner market down the street to see if he had any juice or Gatorade. A handful of people were hanging out around the doorway trying to catch a breeze off the fans running off his generator. We went in and looked around but the shelves were pretty bare.

"This all that's left?" Eliot asked Vi's wife, who was standing behind the register.

"Everything in the refrigerated case is a dollar," Vi said. "Generator's probably going to give out by end of day."

We got a dozen miscellaneous drinks and paid him cash.

If we'd waited two more days, we could've had it all for free. But we didn't know that at the time. And even if we did, we couldn't wait. It was over a hundred degrees outside, and we were saving our water for the dogs.

We stood out front with about a half dozen people from the neighborhood. A woman and her husband had just driven up to Baton Rouge and back.

"Doesn't seem to be much damage," she said. "Roads are pretty clear through Jefferson Parish. Couple days, max, for power to come back."

Vi came out to join us and sucked his teeth. "City's gonna find a way to turn it into a month."

We all laughed.

A guy I recognized from around the block pulled up in his sun-bleached burgundy Cadillac.

"Hey, the city is flooding!"

I could swear I heard a twinge of excitement come through that guy's voice.

His wife was in the passenger's seat and leaned over him to yell out, "Y'all need to watch yourselves!"

We all leaned down to look into their car window, and I imagined how we must look—this collection of mismatched neighbors—me and Eliot with our plastic bags of drinks, Marty and Jacob with cigarettes hanging between their fingers, the elderly black gentleman from across the street leaning on his wooden cane, Vi and his wife who had come outside, and his cousin from around the corner, all Vietnamese, the rotund blonde woman and her husband from Baton Rouge, and a few kids playing tag in the street.

None of us said anything. We just looked into the sun-bleached Cadillac.

"Industrial Canal breeched, so did 17th Street," the wife continued. "It's all over the news—we tried to drive up to 17th, but the water's almost up to Tulane on the Claiborne side."

Claiborne Street was on the other side of Tulane's campus; the water didn't have far to travel before it reached us.

Vi said, "What do you mean? When did this happen?"

The husband spoke, "Last night? This morning? I'm not sure, but that shit's still rising. I'd get the fuck out if I were you. River Road's open to Causeway all the way to I-10, we just checked. It's a clear shot out. Good luck, y'all."

"Yeah, thanks," Vi said. The couple drove off with a wave.

"I'll check the news," Vi's wife went up to their apartment above the store to turn on the TV. A minute later she called down to us through a window, "Yeah, it's flooding. Those jackasses want to drop giant sandbags on the levees! By helicopter!"

"Dumbasses!" Someone called out. It might have been me.

"What's going on?" Vi called up.

"I can't tell. It's pretty flooded, though. I don't know, I can't tell what's going on. There's just water everywhere."

Marty was the last to speak before our congregation split up.

A Flood in Three Parts

She put her hand on my arm and squeezed it, "Don't worry about it, honey. We're on the highest point in the city." To the group she said, "Hell, worse comes to worse, we see two, three feet tops. But that's not gonna happen. We're above sea level."

"Yeah," I said. I didn't say this out loud, but I remembered we lived across the street from an Army Corps of Engineers building. I was confident a group of engineers wouldn't build their office below sea level. They might put other things down there, but not their own building.

If there was panic brewing, it wasn't on the surface. We were murmuring our disbelief, but none of us seemed panicked.

Eliot and I walked back to the church with our bags of drinks.

"How much water do you think there could be?" he asked.

"I have no idea. If it's up by Claiborne, how much more could there be?"

He paused for a minute. "How long do you think it'll be before the power's back on and everyone comes back?"

"I don't know. Depends on how much water?"

We got to the church and pulled John's little battery-operated TV from the office. It only had a small screen about as big as my palm, but that was all we needed. We put it on a banquet table and pulled up two chairs. Our legs and shoulders pressed together as we huddled in front of the tiny gray screen. It took a minute for the picture to form clearly. When it did, all we saw was dark gray water punctuated with the tips of rooftops.

"Where are they? Where is that?" Eliot asked quickly. That was the first moment of panic I felt.

The video was a helicopter shot, and the camera panned out. There was nothing but water, gray-black water and the tops of a few trees and slivers of triangular rooftops as far as we could see.

A broadcaster may have said "Lakeview" or maybe "Lower Ninth Ward," I didn't hear where we were looking, and it didn't matter because it was all the same: *underwater*.

Water upon water—on and on with nothing left.

Displaced

I heard my voice whisper, "Dear God Jesus."

I looked at Eliot, and he looked at me, and I realized we were both crying.

"Turn it off," I whispered. He did.

We sat there and cried together for I don't know how long. Then we put the TV back in the office, locked the door, and left it there.

II. The Chaos

Once the city flooded, there was no concept of time. There was light punctuated by dark, or dark punctuated by light—it was gradations of light that came and went but nothing eased the late summer heat that continuously beat down on us. It only took one cycle of light for chaos to rein—less than 24 hours.

My first clue something was wrong came the morning after we saw the flood on the little black-and-white TV. We decided to check our house and ask what everyone else was planning to do. We headed down St. Charles rather than our usual path through the park.

About two blocks from our street, Eliot grabbed my arm and pulled me across the streetcar median to the other side of the street. I was about to get mad, until I saw what he was looking at: a large man with greasy shoulder-length hair was barreling toward us.

Not toward us, directly, but he had come around a corner, walking fast, and he was speed-walking straight down the middle of the street. He had a crazed determination on his face and a full-length machete—at least half the length of his arm—was raised in his right hand. He was poised to cut through anything in his path.

A Flood in Three Parts

We didn't dare look in his direction, but I watched him pass in my periphery.

"What the fuck was that?" I said, when the man was safely out of earshot.

"Who knows?"

We crossed back to that side of the street and turned down our street.

On the next block I saw the chunky dreadlocked drug dealer kid turn the corner toward us with four other teenage boys in a tight pack.

"Maybe we should turn back," Eliot said.

"No, keep walking."

We kept to one side of the street, they kept to the other, and I glanced at the chunky kid. He glanced at me with a nearly imperceptible nod. I saw the black metal handle of a gun protruding from the front of his pants; it stood out against his white t-shirt. One of the boys had a rifle slung over his shoulder with a black strap. I didn't look for more than a split second, and I couldn't say what kind of gun it was, but it was one I'd see frequently in the days to come.

Getting closer to our house, we saw Marty dragging Miss Rebecca's trash bin into her yard. "I keep telling her the trash isn't coming, but she doesn't listen."

I couldn't tell if she was talking to herself, or to us, but we stopped. "You need help, Marty?"

She looked at us, her thin face was red and sweaty. She looked to be beside herself.

"I keep telling her! I keep telling her, Miss Rebecca, don't be putting your trash out. There was a hurricane. No one's coming by to pick it up. But she doesn't understand!"

"She didn't notice the storm?" I asked.

"Oh, honey, you know how she is. She don't remember a thing from one minute to the next. It's all I can do to keep an eye on her."

We continued to our house—everything was still fine.

"Aren't you glad we rented this place?" I asked.

"We lucked out."

Our neighbor had evacuated, and it looked like part of her roof collapsed. We debated whether to find a tarp and cover it or let it wait until she returned. We decided it would be fine until she got back. The heat was blazing and there were no signs of rain.

We got back to the church as John was carrying in a fresh case of diet soda.

"I'm going to be spending more time at my house to keep an eye on things," he announced. "You know, my neighbors would appreciate if someone would sit out on their porch during the day. Just to maintain a presence, you know? They've got food in their pantry, and I'm sure they'd be willing to compensate you for watching their property until they get back."

"I was thinking maybe we should leave," I said.

"Oh, you don't want to do that," John said. "This'll be over in no time."

I was still thinking about the guy with the machete and the kids with guns patrolling the streets.

"You think so?"

"Most definitely," John said.

"I think so, too," Eliot agreed.

"Plus," John said, "think about all that flooded property. In a few months you'll be able to buy blocks of houses for nothing. Just wait, six months from now this is going to be a different city. This is the best thing that could've happened to this place; it washed out the trash."

I had never liked John, but now he made me want to vomit. I didn't like his excitement. I knew what he meant by "watching their property"—acting as armed guards. I wasn't going to get in a gun battle with a bunch of kids if they decided to rob some rich guy's house.

A Flood in Three Parts

"Think about my neighbor's offer, they'll be grateful for your help." John said.

Fuck off, I thought.

* * *

There are two little boys riding bikes, fast, racing toward us on Benjamin Street. They're shirtless, wearing khaki Dickies that have been cut off at the knees. They wear white tube socks pulled up to their knees and pristine white kicks and they're racing toward us as fast as they can. We're walking the dogs, and we stop to watch them pass.

They are eight, maybe nine years old. I can almost see the sweat flick off their skin as they race past us, each of them weighed down with two semi-automatic rifles each, crisscrossed across their shoulders, the guns clattering against their pumping legs, barrels pointed backward. The straps make thick black X's across their chests.

One boy also clutches three small handguns against his bare belly to keep from dropping them. He swerves a little to keep his balance. They have shaved heads and serious, determined looks on their faces.

They're riding so fast, so hard, I'm scared they'll fall. I worry especially for the smaller one, because he's gripping the handguns and only holds one handlebar. They turn the corner, out of sight.

We resume walking as if this was nothing out of the ordinary.

* * *

One day we walked down St. Charles and realized all the stores in the neighborhood had been broken open. We peeked into the shattered glass door of the Rite Aid on Broadway and saw the liquor shelves had been wiped clean. A can of Dinty Moore chili sat in the open doorway.

I picked it up and threw it back into the store.

A guy named Gary—and old friend of Eliot's—rode by on his bike and waved. He had a large, heavy looking, blue duffle bag strapped across his shoulders.

Gary pulled up next to us. "Hey, how y'all doin'?"

"Just came from our house," Eliot said.

"How'd y'all make out?"

"No damage. You?"

"Naw, we're all good. I'm just taking my guns up to my mama's house in River Ridge. All these fucking kids breaking into houses, don't want them getting their hands on 'em, you know? Things bad enough as it is."

We agreed. I tried to imagine how many guns he had in that big blue bag. It was as large as Eliot's Navy duffel bag. He noticed me eyeing it.

"Hey, you all need something? You got protection?" He started to unzip the bag.

"Oh no, that's okay," I said.

"You sure, baby? It's no big thing."

I laughed because I'd never even held a gun, "No, really. It's all good."

He smiled, "Suit yourself. You all leaving?"

"We're going to see what happens," Eliot said.

"Yeah. I'll probably head up to my mama's house. Things getting a little too crazy down here with these kids—you know what I'm saying?"

We did.

"Hey, watch yourself up on Oak Street, hear?" he said. "There's a kid with his head blown off in the gutter. Don't head over there if you don't want to see it."

"Ugh," Eliot made a face of disgust.

"Right. I don't want some fucking crackhead breaking into my house while I'm gone, you know what I'm saying? This shit is crazy."

We didn't respond.

"Y'all come by the house if you want anything."

He rode off and Eliot and I stared at each other a second. There was a kid with his head blown off on Oak Street? We kept walking back to the church.

As we crossed the park, we saw Pete running toward us in his American flag Speedo. I felt awed and inspired how Pete had kept up his running routine in all this. He really was a regular old Jack LaLanne.

He waved as he passed and shouted, "Andrew is behind me with the dogs!"

A minute later, sure enough, Andrew and five of their seven golden retrievers came speed walking around the corner toward us. We smiled and waved as they approached.

He stopped and the five dogs mingled around him. "Listen, you all know Whole Foods is open? You need to go down there and get yourselves some food before everything's gone."

"Whole Foods is open?" I was incredulous.

"Oh, baby, yes. Pete and I pulled the car right up to the back and loaded up! Honey, we got all our vitamins for a year!"

I realized what he meant by "open" and laughed.

"Don't laugh, baby! You know all that stuff is going bad in this heat! Someone may as well use it! And don't you think they're going to mind, either. They're insured. It's just a crime for all that perfectly good food to go to waste. You all should come over. We're stocked up on wine and good cheese. The whole freezer is stocked."

"Thanks for telling us," I laughed.

He gathered his pack and speed walked on. "Get yourselves down there, sugar!"

When he was gone Eliot looked at me with excited eyes, "We should go."

"I am not looting Whole Foods."

He looked disappointed.

We weren't criminals. That felt like a bridge too far.

Displaced

* * *

It was morning, early, and the air was still a hazy grey. It couldn't have been long after dawn. We were in the habit of sleeping at the church because it felt safe and cool inside. But every time the sun came up, we walked the dogs from the church to our house—we'd open our door, look around inside, walk around restlessly for five or ten minutes, lock up, then cut back through Audubon Park on our way back to the church. We repeated the process in late afternoon.

On that morning, our neighbor around the corner was packing a suitcase into his car trunk. He came over to stop us before we went down his street. As he approached, I thought his eyes were too large, the pupils too dilated. His face was too red.

He said, "Watch your dogs around the corner, there's a body over there."

I didn't understand what was saying, but we stopped to listen. He took my arm, his eyes welled up, his face turned more red. "I was just talking to him last night, and I found him there this morning. I don't know what happened."

He was crying now, heavily, and I put my hand on his arm, but my sense of touch was malfunctioning. *Who was dead around the corner?*

"I covered him with a sheet of Tyvek, there was Tyvek there from the house next door...you know?" His eyes were large and crying, looking into mine, like wells.

I feel like I'm falling in.

Yes, I remembered, there was a house on this street that was being renovated before everything happened. He's talking about the white paper they wrap houses in—Tyvek—before they put on the siding.

There was a roll of this white paper with the word TYVEK printed all over it—I remembered—in front of a house. Tyvek is waterproof and keeps the elements out. The post office makes envelopes out of it. I know what Tyvek is, I've sent packages in it, and I finally understand what he's saying—this man has covered his friend's dead body with it, here, down the street.

My chest feels like it's filled with electric eels. *Who died on this street?*

"We're going to Baton Rouge," he said. "I don't think we're ever coming back."

We nod at him.

"Watch yourself going down the street." He hugged me and said, "God Bless."

It was surreal. We continued walking and there was a downed power line in the middle of the street. There hadn't been any power, or water, in days. We stepped over it like it wasn't there.

Out of the corner of my eye I saw a man-sized cloud of white Tyvek lying on a porch. The eels squirmed in my chest. I averted my eyes, looked at the ground, held my breath. I looked at the dogs walking before us. Irrationally, I continued to hold my breath until we were half a block down the street.

I knew that house. I knew who died.

* * *

Two or three times a day, depending on our degree of restlessness, we walked to a nearby gas station where a payphone sporadically worked. Our cell phones were useless, except for an odd occasional text message that would go through. Calling collect from this half-assed payphone was our only link to the outside world.

I would call my mom in Denver, and she would tell me what CNN said.

CNN said they were going to float a giant barge down the Mississippi River to deliver water and collect all the people and deposit them in Baton Rouge. (Oh, that's a good one, I said. Complete bullshit.)

CNN said the Red Cross would set up shop any minute now (I wasn't holding my breath). CNN said stand around and wait because "the officials" are going to come up with a plan any minute now. (Meanwhile I'd sell my soul for a piece of ice.)

I finally told her CNN was full of shit. I was on the ground, on perfectly dry land, talking to people who said the back roads were clear and dry, and the only police car I'd seen was loaded down with junk and headed out toward Jefferson Parish.

I told her we were thinking about walking to La Place, or Baton Rouge if we could make it. We were going to follow the levee road out toward Baton Rouge, because the unknown was probably safer than the known. She told me to wait because the geniuses in charge would have a plan any minute.

It was all an exercise in futility. There was no plan from any government agency. It was hotter than hell. We were almost out of water.

And we were all losing our damn minds.

On these daily payphone treks we'd stop in front of a small apartment building where a few of our friends used to live. Everyone in the building had evacuated except one kid: Pharez. He hung a white blanket from the third-floor balcony that said "S.O.S." in giant black letters.

Pharez couldn't have been older than 20, if that, and he sat up in that balcony all day drinking and watching the street. I suspected he had barricaded the front entrance since he hadn't left the building since the storm. There were only six units, and everyone else had left.

"Hey, Pharez!" Eliot would call up and wave.

We barely knew Pharez before the storm. He had only moved in a few months earlier. He was a little guy, thin and dark-skinned with a short fade. He'd been a hairdresser in Opelousas before coming to the big city.

Any time we passed his building, he'd lean over the balcony and toast us.

"You get through to your mama?" he'd ask me.

"Yes," I'd call up.

"What she say? They coming for us?"

"Not today. Sorry."

"I found a really good wine in my neighbor's refrigerator," he held up a bottle. "She won't mind. I finished it off."

Pharez lived by the new law of the land: if you left it, it's fair game. He'd gone through all the apartments collecting whatever food and water were available.

*　*　*

Somewhere there's a video of Eliot and I talking in the fellowship hall. I was filming him as he wrote out sheets of drum music by candlelight. He was working on a new rhythm. I asked him, "What'd you think about the kid on Oak Street?"

He says, "It's fucked up."

He doesn't look up; he's tapping out beats with his fingers and jotting them down in pencil. Jot. Erase. Tap. Jot again.

Just after I put the camera away, we took stock of our fluids. We saved the water for the dogs. We'd already gone through all the melted ice in our freezer. We'd finished off the case from Vi's market. We didn't eat much, but the liquids went fast. It was so bloody hot, the minute you drank anything it came right out your pores.

"It's time to hit Whole Foods," I said.

Eliot couldn't hide his excitement. I didn't know whether he was excited to get free stuff from Whole Paycheck or excited to get more supplies—probably both.

When the sun came up, we walked through the haze toward Magazine Street. We didn't have a plan. We didn't even talk about it. We just knew we were low on supplies and didn't know where else to go.

Pickup trucks barricaded the street we usually took to get to Whole Foods. A large piece of plywood was propped against the trucks. Spray painted across it was: PRIVATE STREET. YOU WILL BE SHOT.

"That seems unnecessary, don't you think?" I asked.

Eliot didn't respond. We took a different street. The world was silent and empty. I decided not to speak again.

I heard Whole Foods about a block before we arrived. A siren alarm was blaring out, as it had been for God knows how long. I was grateful we didn't live closer. It was incessant and especially loud in the silence of the morning.

The glass front door was shattered. We stepped carefully over the shards and entered the heart of the siren sound. The decibel level inside made my shoulders hunch up and I wanted to cover my ears, but I needed them to carry supplies. Why hadn't we thought to bring earplugs?

We split up. I went to the water aisle but there wasn't much left. A few bottles of cranberry juice and half a dozen bottles of mint-flavored water. I took what I could carry. If I had been thinking clearly, I would've taken bags from the registers to carry more, but my stomach was flipping, and I was afraid we weren't alone.

I was afraid people were living in the refrigerated areas—they might be the only places in the city that were still somewhat cool inside. I was afraid of territorial insanity. Everything felt like a zombie film. And that blaring siren made it impossible to think about anything but getting out. I ended up with two bottles of juice and an armful of designer mint water.

I was petrified.

Eliot met me at the front aisle, taking his time to get there, and we climbed back out through the shattered glass. He was eating chocolate covered peanuts from a plastic bulk foods bag. A brown paper bag was looped over his wrist. Of course, he had the foresight to pick up a bag when he walked in. I kicked myself for not having a plan before we went in.

We started down Magazine toward the church.

"What'd you get?" I asked.

He opened the bag.

A Flood in Three Parts

"Tea cakes. Lemon and pumpkin bread." There were four loaves of sweet bread in the bag.

"And a bag of chocolate candy?" I fought the urge to hit him. I couldn't with my arms full.

"So?" He sounded defensive.

"So, how are you going to drink tea cake and chocolates? Those fucking chocolates will be melted by the time we get back to the church. How are they not already melted?"

"They will not! What do you want me to do? Go back? I'll go back! What the hell difference is it what I got?"

"The difference is I got water and you got useless shit!"

"Get off my ass, will you? You got water and I got food, that's what matters. We split the difference—divide and conquer!"

"That is not what matters! What matters is this is serious! You're walking around with your head up your ass—as usual!" I didn't know why I was losing my shit. I really didn't. We didn't go in with any plan, but I was losing it. Maybe because I knew that water wasn't going to get us very far.

He stopped and let out a primal yell. "Christ! What the fuck difference does it make? Look around! You want me to put it back? Will that make you happy?"

We were standing on the corner of Nashville and Magazine streets. I looked up Nashville. Downed tree branches blocked the street. Power lines leaned at 45-degree angles. The world looked so fucking desolate I wanted to cry, but I couldn't summon the energy. Or the tears. I gave up.

"Take these bottles. I need a drink," I said.

We put the bottles in with the bread. I was tired. Parched. We weren't sleeping in this heat, and it was catching up with me. We shared a bottle of overpriced designer mint water, the kind of water we wouldn't be caught dead drinking in our previous life, and we didn't speak the rest of the walk back.

I was silently ecstatic when he discovered the chocolate had melted into a wet glob by the time we got back to the church.

***

Helicopters fly overhead all day. They refuel behind the park, so there's constant movement in our skies. The constant whak-whak-whak of their blades is our daytime soundtrack. On the radio, we hear crying voices: *people trapped here, people trapped there, someone please come save us.* We listen to the radio for five or ten minutes at a time then shut it off because there's nothing we can do. It's too depressing.

John rides his bike to the Convention Center and brings back word: the place is overflowing with the dead and dying. He tells us we should walk down and check it out for ourselves. We try to go once, but I hyperventilate a few blocks away from the church. We turn back home and stay there.

One day we cut through downed trees in Audubon Park, and I notice one of the helicopters has been circling us for a few minutes. We're knee-deep in branches, but we stop to watch it circle. It's small and white. I can't find any insignia.

"What kind of helicopter is that?" I ask.

Eliot shields his eyes from the sun; we watch this little two-man helicopter circle back toward us. "I can't tell," he says.

"Why is it circling us like that? You think it's media?"

We're both squinting up at it now and it's low enough I think I can see someone leaning out the side to look at us.

"Vultures," I hiss. I cup my hands around my mouth and shout at them, "Hey! Make yourselves useful! Drop some fucking ice!"

Eliot gets a kick out of this and laughs, "I don't think they can hear you."

"I don't care."

The helicopter makes another circle, a little closer this time—they're definitely watching us. It looks like the leaning guy might have a camera. I raise my middle fingers, "Hey!" I yell, "I've got a shot for you, motherfuckers!"

Eliot laughs and raises his middle fingers, too.

A Flood in Three Parts

"How's this for news?!"

The helicopter rises quickly and flies away. It's the best laugh we've had in days.

***

John and Eliot liked to sit out on the front steps of the church at night to catch the slight evening breeze and listen to the radio. There were six, maybe seven, concrete steps leading up to the front entrance of the church. They'd sit up on the top steps, sip diet soda for an hour or two, and listen to the only signal broadcasting in NOLA: the United Broadcasters of New Orleans.

There was only one radio tower in operation, so all the stations joined together to broadcast from a small room on the west bank of the river.

It seemed like every time we turned on the radio, the broadcaster Garland Robinette was interviewing a city official or taking calls from listeners who gave reports from the ground: *there are people stuck on this bridge, there are people trapped in that neighborhood, the Red Cross isn't coming.*

People called in to give eyewitness reports. A mall had reportedly burned down. Parents searched for children, and children were found without parents.

Eliot and I would say to each other: surely, they must have found all the people by now.

How many people were still out there? How many bodies had they recovered?

Normally I would stay inside with the dogs at night, barricaded in the fellowship hall, but one night I sat with them on the steps just after the sun went down. It was maybe ten degrees cooler at night, which was still in the 90s, but at least the sun wasn't beating down on us and there was a hint of a breeze.

The first couple of days after the storm there were emergency floodlights shining on Tulane's campus, close enough that they illuminated the church steps. But by that night there was no light left.

It was pitch black. Like a nightmare of falling down a black well, only without the vertigo. Sitting out there, I marveled at how I couldn't see my own body, but I could make out the faint flicker of fireflies in the streetcar median.

From the front steps of the synagogue across the street, I heard a sound—several low voices talking over each other and a woman laughed loudly; then it went silent. I heard the rustle of someone walking in the median, and the scrape of someone's shoes against the asphalt on the far side of the street. The only steady sound in the dark was the quiet, low hum of our radio broadcasting a recap of the day's searches. I wished they'd turn off the radio. The sound was like a beacon to our doorstep.

I strained to listen for voices from the makeshift villages in the park. I knew they were out there. I knew men had gathered in the park and in the broke-open buildings of Tulane and Loyola universities. I'd heard a rumor there was a nightly bonfire somewhere on Tulane's campus and people made gumbo ya-ya in a big pot. That was the rumor. Half the campus was flooded; I'm not sure how true it could've been.

It was difficult to judge distance in the dark, but somewhere down the street, maybe a block or two down, a flashlight flicked on and sent a thin beam of white from waist-level to the ground. I think all three of us, and probably everyone hidden in the nooks of the street, turned to watch it move.

The blade of light was moving toward us. My stomach started to churn. I debated crawling down the stairs and making my way to the side entrance of the church. But I needed air. I needed air to keep from vomiting up whatever fluids I had left inside me. We'd saved all our water for the dogs, and they preferred the cold asbestos floor at night, which somehow managed to stay cool even in this heat.

The light was maybe half a block away when I heard someone, probably John, snap off the radio. The night went deathly silent, but I knew the light was close enough now to locate us in the dark. It moved slowly, swerving back and forth a bit as it crossed the median toward us. The light lifted and pointed toward us. I suspected it was a Mag-Light because the bright blue-white beam washed over us. It burnt my eyes, and an electric tremor flashed through my chest. My heart sped exponentially. It was a clear act of aggression—shining this light in our dark.

Not one of us moved. Not an inch. I'm not sure any of us were still breathing. As the light came closer to the steps I could make out the shape of a man behind it. My heart jumped when he called out, "Hey!" too loudly given how close we were.

He moved up the steps and scanned each of us with the light. "Hey!" He said again, too jovially, too forced.

We didn't speak. We didn't breathe. I felt terror, true terror, crack through my chest.

"What are you guys doing?" He asked loudly. I assumed he was drunk from the aggressive pleasantness in his voice. "You all stay here?"

John broke our silence, calmly, "What's your name, man?"

He focused the flashlight on John's face, making him cringe and recoil.

The man laughed, "Finally! Was starting to think you all were mutes!" His laugh was more of a cackle. The way the light skimmed his body I couldn't make out his features, but I could tell he was white, maybe in his 30s and stocky.

"What can we do for you?" John asked, again very calmly.

"I need a place to stay, man. I've been staying out in that school there, but it's not really working out for me, you know what I'm saying?" He cackled again.

"We don't have any room," John said plainly.

"No room?" He yelled. "You got this big old place, here!"

"We don't stay here," John lied. "We're just out here enjoying the breeze."

"Enjoying the breeze. Yeah." The guy spat on the steps.

He turned the flashlight to me and came up a few steps, so his face was level with mine. He was within grabbing distance. The light was inches from my face, I was momentarily blinded, but I could smell him now. Crown Royal if I had to guess.

That was the first and only time I was aware of my vagina and the danger it put me in—and something in me snapped.

It happened so quickly, so unconsciously, that I would be tempted to question if it happened at all, except it happened with perfect clarity: The man said something to me, I didn't hear what, but the light dropped to just below my face. I could see violence in his eyes. I saw his mouth move aggressively and his body leaned so far into my space that I could clearly smell the alcohol on his breath. And out of the corner of my eye, I saw the two men next to me, in unison, subtly lean back and turn their heads away from us.

I was on my own with this man, and a funnel of rage moved through me so completely I was re-blinded. If he was speaking, I couldn't hear him. I leaned forward and stared into where his eyes would be if I could see them, and in my mind, in my head, I screamed so loudly, with all my power: *I dare you to touch me, motherfucker. I will rip your fucking chest open with my bare hands and piss inside your fucking corpse. Just give me a reason to do it.*

I channeled 28 years of tightly coiled atomic fury at a father who smelled the same way, at the men who had subtly turned away, and in that second, I was more than ready to take this fucker out. All he had to do was step closer.

He must've seen it in my eyes because the flashlight wavered. I felt him step back. He stepped all the way down the stairs and lowered the light back to the ground.

I was in my body, but it was completely numb.

I must have been sweating. I knew I was shaking, but I couldn't feel my body. I had been re-engulfed in pitch black darkness and I couldn't see, but I knew my heart was racing and my body shook.

A Flood in Three Parts

I was vaguely aware that the man said a few more words and took his flashlight and left.

My knees gave way when I tried to stand up and go inside. Eliot tried to take my hand to guide me back in and I pulled my arm back forcefully. I felt my own way around the church. That was the last time I sat outside with them.

I would have killed that man, and I knew I would've killed him. I let that knowledge empower me. I felt stronger in its presence.

* * *

I am standing in the street alone. I don't know why I'm in the street alone. I'm standing in the middle of Hurst Street, or maybe it's Garfield, or it could have been Benjamin, I don't know, and it doesn't matter. I'm standing in the street in front of a faded yellow house with cracked white trim. Four houses down and around the corner from my house.

The sun is so white, so bloody bright, that if this were a film there would be a stunning solar flare across the lens. It would bleach out the sky and cast purple-red orbs into the frame.

But this isn't a film, though for a moment I think it is.

The sun is just so bloody bright I'm nearly blind and think I'm hallucinating, but I know I'm not.

I'm standing in the middle of the street, next to the downed power line that's been down so long I forget it was ever up, and I am looking at my neighbor's body decomposing on his porch.

A body decomposing in the heat is nothing like it is on film. It isn't flat and limp like a living actor hired to portray it. It's rolling up on itself like a piece of parchment, contorting, with knees bent up and back arched. It has one hand pointing toward the sky, the other suspended above the torso.

The contorting body had dislodged the white Tyvek wrapper that once covered it. The Tyvek would flap away if there were a breeze, but there isn't, so it still slightly covers the rotting ankle and denim shorts and brown-stained white cotton shirt.

I stand there in the street because I want to remember. I want to remember this man when he was sitting on his top step with a 40 in one hand, raising the other in a wave. I want to remember our laughs as I raised my hand in return, with the full knowledge he's going to watch my ass as I jog by.

I want to remember how we'd laugh. But nothing came.

I stand in the street and I'm no longer sweating because I don't drink enough fluids to sweat. I feel every granule of salt stuck to my body. Each one clings to my skin individually when I move, millions of them like parasites covering me.

As I breathe, the dried salt marsh of my back cracks apart and re-forms. My hands hang at my sides, and I feel every speck of dirt lodged under each fingernail; each nail is black from clearing branches, and I have no place to wash them.

I have no desire to wash the dirt from my hands.

I know then: someone has taken a sharp rock, a Paleolithic rock, and skinned me from within. The dried salt caked on my skin holds me together; the dirt beneath my nails is the only thing I feel.

I have solar flares in my eyes.

And nothing comes.

III. The Exodus

Eliot and I had one radio that still had battery power—a little cheap plastic thing with no speakers, so we had to sit close together and share the earbuds, each of us having one ear bud tucked in an ear.

We flipped on the radio and heard the Jefferson Parish President say he was seceding from the Union and declared himself the dictator of a new nation called "Jeffertonia." He was

A Flood in Three Parts

making a point about how much faster the federal government responded to foreign emergencies than what they were doing for us. It was a valid point we all agreed with, but Eliot and I rolled our eyes.

"What do you think?" I asked.

"FUBAR," he replied. *Fucked up beyond all recognition.*

The Jefferson Parish Sheriff declared he'd lock down all roads out of the city starting tomorrow. No one could leave New Orleans. We would be trapped between the Jefferson Parish Sheriff and the United States military, which was currently sweeping through neighborhoods and rounding up residents. They were placing people on busses to destinations unknown.

It was too hot to cry, but I wanted to. An irrational thought went through my mind: *I have to conserve water. Fluids are precious. Tears are wasteful.* I realized I was starting to come apart. *Did I really just think that?* I did. No tears. I already had heat exhaustion.

I took out my ear bud and stood up.

"I'm leaving in the morning." It was no longer a discussion. No longer up for debate. I was done. "Are you going with me, or am I going alone?"

"I'm going with you," he looked up at me, surprised.

"Then let's get ready."

I turned on my cell phone, which had a measly bar of power. No service. I sent a text message to my mom in Denver, hoping it would go through: *leaving for La Place in the morning please start driving will call when out of city.*

I had no idea if it would send. I left the phone on for a few minutes. No response. I turned it off to conserve the remaining tiny bit of battery power.

We walked to the pay phone. Dead line.

On the way back we stopped at Pharez's building. He wasn't on the balcony, so Eliot yelled his name. A minute later his head popped out an upstairs window.

"Yeah?"

"We're leaving tomorrow. Walking. You wanna go?"

"Thank God! I was too afraid to leave by myself. Yeah, where we going?"

"La Place? That's probably closest."

"Yeah, sure. Hey, if we get to Opelousas, I'll be home!" He sounded excited.

"We're leaving first thing in the morning," Eliot said.

"Honey, we could leave right now!"

We all laughed.

Spirits were suddenly high. We told him we'd be back around 8:00 to pick him up, then went back to our house for a final look around. Marty and Jacob were hanging out on the corner with a couple of guys from down the block. Eliot went to check the house while I stopped to tell them we were leaving.

"When are you going?" Marty sounded concerned.

"I'm not sure, maybe tomorrow?" I don't know why I felt evasive, but I didn't want to say too much.

"You have to come to my house, then. Come on, I have something I've been meaning to give you."

I followed her around the corner to her house, the whole time feeling anxious. I couldn't put my finger on why—it was a dark feeling. I didn't want to follow her.

We got to her little shotgun. The roof had collapsed and flattened the entire back of the house, but the front door and part of the living room were still standing. She unlocked the front door.

Oh, lord, please don't let her be staying in a collapsed house.

"Marty, you aren't staying here, are you?"

"Oh, hell no, honey. I'm staying at a place Vi's got down the block. No, I just wanted to give you something I left in here's all."

I held my breath while she entered the precarious house.

She came out a minute later with an old, bundled up sock. Please God, I thought, don't let her risk her life for an old sock.

A Flood in Three Parts

She unwrapped it and took out a gold necklace and cross and two pair of small gold hoop earrings. She stuffed the sock in her pocket and closed the jewelry in her right hand while taking my wrist with her left.

I instinctively made a fist. "What's that?"

"They were my mother's. I want you to take them." She rubbed her fist against mine to make me take the jewelry.

"I can't take those, Marty." I twisted my wrist out of her grasp and stepped back.

She took my wrist again, but I didn't open my hand. I tried to twist again, but she gripped tighter this time. Her bony fingers were remarkably strong.

"I don't have any family, who am I going to give this to?" She tried to pry my hand open with her knuckle, "Please take them. You can trade them if you want. It's real gold. You might need the money."

"I can't. They're your mother's. They're yours." The air had been sucked from the atmosphere. I couldn't inhale.

The harder she tried to push them into my hand, the tighter I made my fist. They were the only valuables she had. She had herself and Miss Rebecca to look after. Her house collapsed. I knew she needed that money more than I did.

"It's not much," she said, "but you don't know what will happen out there, please take it." She looked like she was going to cry.

I started to feel panicked. I had to leave. I had to run. I had to get the hell out of there, because I was about to cry, too.

I pulled away from her, and she let go. She carefully folded the jewelry back into the sock. "You don't want them."

She didn't look at me.

"It's not that. What if you need them? Look at this place. You might need to trade them yourself."

She laughed. "Me? Honey, I've been living in this neighborhood 64 years. You think I'm going anywhere? Hell no."

"I'm sorry, Marty. I'd feel too guilty if something happened to you and you needed the money." I tried to show her with my eyes that I loved her, that I was scared for her. She rolled the sock into a tight ball.

"Take them when you get back, then. I'll keep them for you." She stuffed the sock in her pocket.

"When I get back. I promise I will." I put my arms around her frail little frame, and she hugged me tight.

As we pulled apart, she said, "You take care of yourself. And don't you worry about a thing. It'll all work out fine."

"Yes, ma'am. Thank you."

I went around the corner to our house and tried to put Marty far from my mind. It was too painful to think of what could happen to her. But she was a tough lady. Everything would have to be okay.

Eliot was in the kitchen, throwing everything from our refrigerator into a black garbage bag.

"What are we taking?" I asked.

"I'm just taking my Navy bag. Everything will be here when we get back."

I went through the cabinets to throw out open boxes of cereal and anything else the rats and mice might enjoy while we were gone. We bagged up all the perishables and closed them in our plastic trashcan outside, then returned to the church to pack.

We planned to follow the river—eventually it had to lead to Baton Rouge, and we hoped there'd be somewhere along the way to call for help. We had to pack light. I decided not to bother with clothes. We hadn't showered in days, so it didn't matter if I changed my clothes at this point.

I packed a messenger bag with my computer, a couple of cameras, and my journal. We threw a few granola bars and the last of the designer mint water into a smaller Army surplus bag and I tied a plastic bag of dog food to it. We had half a gallon of water left for the dogs.

As we were packing, John came in for the night. He stopped on his way to the office to watch us. Eliot said, "We're leaving in the morning."

"I think you're making a big mistake," he said coolly. "You don't know what's out there." He jangled his keys in his hands. "I'm telling you, if you give it another week everything's going to be fine. Go up to my neighbor's and get whatever you need, stay at their place. I think you're better off doing that."

I didn't even look up. I shuffled the contents of my bag. I felt Eliot look at me, as if waiting for me to snap.

"No, I think we're going to go. But I'll be back as soon as I can," he said.

"It's your decision." He left us and went to his office.

When he was gone, I told Eliot we weren't going to be herded onto a government bus—we'd probably wake up in Iraq. I was joking, trying to make him laugh, but we both knew that scenario wasn't too far from the truth. There was genuine fear spreading through our neighborhood that we would be forced at gunpoint to board government busses to nowhere.

The panic with Jefferson Parish shutting down the roads hadn't helped.

The morning we left was as hazy gray as any other morning. I was reminded of early morning runs through the Garden District. The smell of jasmine didn't exist here, but the fallen trees had released their very essence. The air was woody sweet and heavy with an earth-scented dew. We stopped outside the church for a final gear check and to leash the dogs.

Eliot wore his Armed Forces School of Music t-shirt, the same shirt I had admired—coveted, even—when I used to watch him run. He wore the same olive drab Aussie hat he'd been wearing since we met. I had on scruffy cargo shorts that matched his hat. I thought, *we must smell awful.*

We took off down St. Charles toward Pharez, and I felt light, lighter than I had in my entire life. We joked about what we were going to eat and how long we were going to shower when we finally reached civilization. We were damn near giddy.

About half a block ahead of us a man in a cream colored dress shirt and brown pants came limping toward us. As he got closer, I could see his shirt was wet and clung to him and contrasted starkly against his skin. He was barefoot and haggard. We met him in front of Tulane.

"Where's the registration?" he asked. His eyes looked wide and hollow.

"Sir, what are you looking for?" Eliot asked.

"My kids. I don't know where my kids went. I went out. I swam out to get help and I came back, and they were gone. Where do I go?"

"Sir, I'm not sure," Eliot said, "but I heard there's some National Guard on Napoleon, they can help you."

The man looked relieved and seemed to relax a little. "How far's Napoleon? Which street is this? I don't know my way round here. I just came up through the school." He motioned toward Tulane's campus.

"Just keep walking straight," I said. "This is St. Charles. You'll run right into it, maybe six or seven blocks? Not even that far. They can help you."

The man's face relaxed, "You going that way?" He glanced behind him.

"Yes, sir. We're on our way out."

"You better get yourself a story straight, hear? They're stopping everyone on the street. You can't get out to Jefferson."

Damn that sheriff—he'd really done it! I hoped the blockade threat had been a bluff.

"You sure?" I asked.

"I was just there, baby, they turned me back. Not letting no one go through. Get yourself a story straight."

I sighed. "Thanks for the warning."

I felt the need to reach toward him, and we hugged.

"Thanks, hear? God bless you," he said into my hair.

"And you. Good luck," I whispered as we parted.

We got to Pharez, where he was waiting on the balcony.

"Be right down," he waved.

A few minutes later he appeared at the front door wearing a baseball cap and a blue schoolboy's backpack and carrying a medium sized cat carrier. He looked like a teenage boy going on a field trip, and I felt the urge to protect him.

"This is Miss Baby," he said. I peeked in to see a fat gray tabby cat hunched in the back corner. She hissed at me. "Don't mind her, she doesn't like to travel. Which way we going?"

"I think we'll have to go up the levee," I said. "We heard River Road's already blocked off."

"Those fools. It figures," Pharez spat.

We climbed up the grassy levee hill to the path that ran along the top. The sky was still hazy, but the sun was so golden it felt like the first morning I'd ever been alive.

We started walking away from the city, toward the Jefferson Parish Sheriff officers that we knew would be blocking the road below us a few blocks away. Eliot took up the lead with our dog Pixie, I was a few feet behind him with Chaz, and Pharez brought up the rear with Miss Baby.

Up ahead, below us, I could see two sheriff patrol cars in the distance. They were parked sideways to block the road into Jefferson Parish. An old blue pickup truck was pulling up and stopped on the Orleans Parish side.

Two officers walked to either side of the truck, each holding a black semi-automatic rifle pointed toward the sky. We picked up our speed as we approached the blockade below us.

I could see now, they were talking to a white woman in the driver's seat. She leaned out the window. She had to be an older woman; I could tell by her yellowed peroxide hair pinned up in soft bouffant curls. She looked like the kind of woman who did her hair and makeup every morning, even on a morning like this.

She started screaming, crying, her voice carried up to us and ripped through my ears: *Why are you doing this to us? Why are you doing this? My family is in Metairie, can't you understand? I have to get to them! Let me though!*

An officer barked loudly: *Ma'am! Turn the car around NOW. Turn back! You will not be warned a second time!* One lowered his gun to 45 degrees. They looked like the same guns carried by the kids on bicycles a few days before.

One thought is pounding through my mind: *walk faster, walk faster, before they see us...walk faster, faster, run, run,* run.

Without speaking a word, all three of us broke into a jog and didn't stop until we were well past the scene unfolding below us.

As we ran past, the woman let out an animal scream, a wounded scream, and I heard tires burning rubber. I assumed she had backed up her truck up and turned around, but I wasn't going to turn around to find out. We slowed back to a walk, none of us saying a word.

I realized my face was wet with tears. I wiped it with a dirty palm and gave a prayer of thanks that this woman provided the distraction that let us through. I prayed she would get through somehow herself.

* * *

As the morning haze lifted, the river shone to our left. We kept to ourselves, walked in our line. I passed the time by singing into the river breeze. Miss Baby's carrier had wheels, so Pharez tied a belt to the handle and dragged her along behind him. I listened to its steady scraping sound a few feet behind me.

Rows of suburban brick houses stretched out to our right. A few fences were down, a few roofs had damage, some trees were down, but overall things looked about the same as I imagined they had before.

We walked for about an hour before we came to a concrete picnic table and stopped for a rest.

A Flood in Three Parts

Pharez unzipped his backpack and pulled out three bottles of apple juice, the kind in small glass bottles shaped like apples. "From my neighbor," he said as he handed us each a bottle.

I handed out granola bars and Eliot poured water into plastic bowls for the dogs and Miss Baby. We sat on the table, watching the river. A few minutes later a man called out to us from down the hill. He was a large man, trudging up toward us.

"Hey! You all come out from the city?" he called as he approached.

"Yes, sir," Eliot answered.

"How is it?" He started to cry. We didn't respond, so he continued, "I just can't believe this is happening, I just can't believe it. You all lose everything?"

"No, sir. We were Uptown," Eliot said. He'd become our spokesperson.

"Even still. I just can't believe it. Where you all headed?"

"We're not sure. Maybe La Place? Wherever we can get."

"Well, God bless you. God bless you. We're going up to Baton Rouge ourselves. I wish we could take you, but I got too many people to take already."

The man was really crying now. Red-faced sobbing, "I'm so sorry." We tried to comfort him, told him not to worry about us. "I just can't believe this is happening," he said when he'd composed himself.

Then he went back down the hill.

"That was weird," I said.

A few minutes later another man rode by on a racing bike. He was in brightly colored red and yellow race gear, as if he were training for the Tour de France. He didn't stop, but he slowed down to take a look at us. As we were getting up to leave, he came back in the other direction and stopped. He was middle aged and ruddy skinned.

"You in the military, son?" He asked Eliot. I assumed the Armed Forces School of Music shirt had caught his eye.

"Sir, yes sir. Ten years United States Navy."
"What are you all doing out here?"
"Sir, we're going to La Place."
"La Place! What the hell they got in La Place for you? Ain't nothing in La Place," he was disgusted. "Where you from?"
"Sir, I'm from Boston and she's from California and he's from Opelousas."
"Oh, you all are fools. You really are. How are you planning to get to La Place?"
"Follow the river. Maybe all the way to Baton Rouge, sir."
The man scoffed. "You know what you're going to find if you follow the river? Swampland. Alligators. You all are really something foolish coming out here like this. You have no idea what you're walking into."
"Well, sir, we had to leave the city."
He seemed to consider this for a minute. "Let me give you some advice then. You walk to Kenner, and you go to the airport. You can probably get some transport there. But don't you dare go following the river, that's just straight foolish."
"Yes, sir. Thank you, sir."
The man rode off and we continued walking. We briefly discussed it amongst ourselves: he was right. The new plan was to get to the airport. We had no idea how to get there, or what we would find, but an airport sounded a whole lot better than wading through swampland.
Then we returned to our marching line.
Somewhere near the Huey P. Long Bridge, the first man who had approached us panted his way behind us on an old rusty mountain bike. He called out, and we stopped and turned around. He had a plastic grocery bag looped over one of the bicycle handles.
"I feel just awful we can't take you with us," he said as he stopped and handed me the bag. I opened it and found a gallon of water and three red apples.

I started to cry, and so did he—again.

"That's for you all, hear? I'm sorry we don't have more to give you. Our car's just packed full, we can't take you. But God bless you. I just can't believe this is happening," he cried.

He maneuvered the bike around and peddled back toward his house. We each took an apple and fell back in line. It was the greatest apple I had ever tasted. I held it in my mouth and tied the plastic bag with the water to my messenger bag.

It wasn't long before the racing man raced toward us again. He stopped ahead of us and waited for us to approach. He seemed to be deep in contemplation. "You all know how to get to the airport?"

"No, sir, but that's okay, sir. We'll find it." Eliot took the lead for us again.

"Well, damn it, how are you all going to get to the airport if you don't even know where it is? What are you all thinking? How can I be a good Christian and let you wander all over creation like this?" He seemed genuinely angry with us, which made me want to laugh. It was the definition of absurd.

"Sir, you've been very helpful. We thank you, sir." Eliot was really laying on those "sirs." I secretly hoped it would make this guy give us a ride.

"Alright, listen. I can't just leave you all out here like a bunch of fools. I'm going to talk to my friend—he's patrolling up the road here. I'll see if he'll give you a ride up to St. Rose. I've got a truck parked there. I can take you to La Place. You'll have to ride in the back with my bike, though."

"Oh, thank you, sir! That'd be great!"

Suddenly we were all pulling out our "sirs" and thanking him profusely. We were like kids at Christmas meeting Santa.

"Now wait a minute," he said, "I don't know if he'll do it. And I want you to know I'm only doing this because you all are a mess of fools who'll probably get yourselves killed out here. I can't in good conscience let that happen."

Displaced

He rode off and our pace picked up considerably. We were practically dancing along that road.

We walked for maybe 20 minutes before a shiny white Expedition SUV came rolling up the hill about a hundred feet ahead. I could see Jefferson Parish Sheriff emblazoned across the side. It rolled slowly toward us on the asphalt path, then stopped and did a 3-point turn so the back faced us. The break lights went out and the engine died as we approached.

A stout man in a sweaty navy t-shirt stepped out and walked toward us. He had a short military haircut and wore iridescent wrap-around sunglasses. There seemed to be a permanent crease in the center of his forehead. I noticed he had a fresh dark red sunburn across his forehead, nose and cheeks. He pulled open the back of the Expedition and Eliot spoke, "Thank you for coming, sir."

"I wouldn't have done it. We got enough to do out here without playing taxi to a bunch of fools," this man was clearly not in the mood for our sirs. "Jerry's a good friend of mine, so you be sure to thank him."

He took Miss Baby's carrier from Pharez and placed it in the back, then helped our dogs jump up and closed them in. I assumed Jerry was the racer on the bike.

Without speaking, Pharez and I climbed into the back seat with our bags and Eliot climbed in shotgun. When the engine kicked back up the air conditioning felt so glorious I had to close my eyes tight and press my head against the window to keep from crying.

Pharez leaned against the other window; I imagined he felt the same thing.

"Sir, I bet you've seen a lot this week," Eliot said.

"Haven't slept in six days. We got strict orders to turn you all back," he glanced over his shoulder at us in the back seat. "We got enough problems without having to babysit you all."

He looked out his window at the river, still glistening and bright in the midday sun. "It's a damn shame," he said to no one in particular.

The air conditioning lulled me into the first real sleep I'd had in recent memory, but it was only a few minutes until we reached St. Rose. A small blue pickup truck was parked on a dirt access road leading up the hill.

"This is it," the officer said. He helped us unload the dogs and Miss Baby and shook our hands, "Good luck to y'all."

We thanked him and watched as he drove down the dirt access road and went back on patrol.

Jerry climbed out of the truck and called to us. He'd changed into jeans and a white t-shirt and helped Pharez lift Miss Baby over the side of the truck. I got into the passenger seat while the guys climbed in the truck bed with the animals. Eliot lodged himself in a corner and had a death grip around each of the dogs' necks. He looked comically terrified.

I laughed and called through the back window, "Don't forget to let them breathe!"

"I don't want them to jump out!" he called back. Poor Pharez looked dazed and gripped Miss Baby's carrier.

I turned my cell phone on. No service. Jerry pulled a phone from a belt holster. "You're not going to get a cell signal out here. I got satellite." He handed me the phone, "You have the numbers to call your people?"

"My mom, yeah. To see if she's coming." I looked up my mom's number from my phone and dialed it into his.

He started the engine. "She meeting you in La Place?"

"I'm not sure yet," The phone rang. My mom answered.

"Hey, we're on our way to La Place," I said. "Did you get my text message?"

"We're outside Dallas, we've been driving all night. Where are you?"

I was too relieved to cry. "I don't know, somewhere on the other side of Jefferson Parish."

"It's going to take us until tonight, maybe tomorrow morning, to get there. Can you get closer to us?"

"We can try to get to Baton Rouge."

"Okay, we'll keep heading that way. Try to get further north if you can."

"We'll try. I'll let you go. I'm so glad you got my message."

I didn't know if she was crying, but I didn't want to start. I wanted to get further down the road. I gave Jerry his phone and thanked him.

"Your mama's coming?" he asked.

"And my stepdad. They're driving from Denver."

We got to La Place and Jerry was right: there was nothing there but a gas station. Pharez bought all of us a cold drink. Jerry fueled up his truck and we stood around looking at the wide expanse of overgrown trees and brush and nothingness. There were a few cars gassing up, though.

This was La Place.

"Listen, y'all," Jerry said. "I can get you as far as Baton Rouge, okay? City limits. Your mama and dad will have more luck getting you from there. They're not going to find this place."

We thanked him again and loaded ourselves back in the truck. He drove us to the first exit in Baton Rouge: Siegen Drive.

At that time, there was nothing on Siegen Drive but a McDonald's and a strip mall with a big parking lot. And that parking lot was packed full of people. It was like a refugee camp where people from the city had been dumped—it looked like at least a hundred.

He dropped us at the McDonald's and gave me his card. "I don't care if it's two years from now, you let me know what became of you all, hear?"

I put the card in my pocket. We all shook his hand and thanked him, and he left us among the mass of newly homeless people who sat huddled in groups in this parking lot with stunned looks on their faces.

Pharez saw a payphone at the strip mall, so we walked over with him to call his mom. He'd used the satellite phone in the truck to let her know we were on the way, but he needed to tell her where we landed. She was driving down from Opelousas.

As he dialed the phone, he turned his back to us so we couldn't see his face. We stepped back a few feet to give him privacy. He had been incredibly brave in that apartment building by himself, but he was still just a kid. He'd never been anywhere as big as New Orleans and had only just arrived a couple of months before this happened.

If that sweet kid wanted to cry to his mama, he had the right to do it with privacy.

A few minutes later he came over and said his mom and her sister would pick us up.

"You all can stay with my cousin in Opelousas, and your mama can get you from there. I'm going home—my mama's place is a way out from there," he said.

"That'd be great. Thank you so much, Pharez," I said.

"When we're all back in New Orleans we'll have a big laugh about this," Eliot said.

"I never want to see New Orleans again," he deadpanned.

I used the payphone to call my mom—she said they were nearly in Shreveport in northern Louisiana.

"We got a ride to Opelousas," I said.

"Oh, thank God," she sounded relieved. "We didn't know how to tell you this, but there are barricades up on all the roads going in. We wouldn't have been able to get into Baton Rouge. We didn't want you to worry, so we didn't say anything...but we can get to Opelousas. It'll be about six more hours."

Of course the roads were blocked. Nothing could be easy.

I asked Eliot if he wanted to call his family.

"I'll wait until we get to Denver."

Displaced

I sat on the curb with the animals while the boys went to McDonald's to eat and use the bathroom. A woman was sitting next to me on a red and white Coleman cooler. She had her head in her hands, elbows on her knees. An oversized white t-shirt hung around her body like a tent, and she wore too-large denim cutoffs. She had no shoes.

After a few minutes she looked over at me with barren eyes. "You come out the city?"

"Yeah."

"Yeah," she repeated. "We got nothing left."

She put her head back in her hands. Darkly, I wondered if she floated out with the cooler. I wondered if she had been asleep when the water came. Was this her nightshirt, were these too-large shorts from a stranger? I didn't want to ask.

I looked around the parking lot: there had to be about a hundred people sitting in small groups and huddled in the shade of the strip mall overhang.

How did they get here? Where would they go?

Pharez's mother and aunt arrived in a black Ford Explorer just as the sun was starting to set. He immediately climbed in the backseat, curled up against the window, and closed his eyes. His aunt was a little older than his mother and she stayed seated in the passenger's seat. His mother helped us load our bags in the back. She was red-eyed, and we embraced as Eliot helped the dogs jump into the back.

He closed the door and put out his hand to shake hers.

She laughed. "Honey, you're not from around here, are you?"

"No, ma'am. Boston."

"Yeah, you're from the north alright. Give us a hug, baby. Now's not the time for pretense."

He hugged her as I climbed in the backseat next to Pharez. The news was on the radio—an evacuation bus had just flipped off the road and caught fire somewhere nearby.

A Flood in Three Parts

"Lord! These people have enough sorrows!" Pharez's aunt called out.

We set out on the back roads. "It'll take a little longer, but there's too much trouble on the interstate," his mom said.

"What's been going on? Where are people going?" I asked.

"Lord have mercy, you haven't been watching the news?" The aunt asked.

"Of course they haven't!" His mom snapped. "Child, it's just awful. Terrible what's been happening to these people. They got people all over, under bridges, all over everywhere. Putting them on busses to God knows where. Lord have mercy, it's a crime."

"And that morgue," the aunt clucked her tongue.

"What morgue?" I asked.

"Child, they're putting up a big, refrigerated morgue in Gonzales. For thousands of people."

That was all any of us wanted to say about that.

We listened to the news coverage of the bus that overturned on a freeway on-ramp. Several people were killed. I couldn't imagine how things had gone so horribly wrong. I thought Contraflow had been a success and the city had been emptied? We didn't even have a flood until the day after the storm. What the hell was happening?

I watched the sun sink toward the horizon; pure gold light skimmed the fields on either side of the road. Pharez had fallen asleep. Eliot reached over and took my hand, but his face never left the window.

We got to Opelousas not long after dark. The aunt's daughter, Nica, was waiting for us at the door of her townhouse. She was about my age, built a little larger than me, with a soft dark face and stern eyes. She helped us bring our bags into her living room. Pharez hugged us briefly, sleepily, and stretched out to sleep in the backseat of the Explorer. His mom and aunt took him home.

Displaced

Inside, we tried to contain the dogs in the tiled entry of Nica's townhouse but they were running wild.

"You can let them in the living room," she said. "It's okay, we don't mind dogs. I put clothes and towels out for you in the upstairs bathroom, so you all can take a shower."

Eliot took the dogs through a short hall into the living room. I looked at the photos in the hall: photos of her in Army fatigues, hugging buddies in the desert. Eliot called over to say I should shower first.

I tried to keep it short, even though I wanted to stand under that hot water for a thousand years. Days of salt and dirt and debris rolled off my body and swirled down the drain. I watched thick suds do the same from my hair, and I was suddenly starving. I pressed my hands against my eyes, starving and weak. I turned off the water and put on the clothes Nica laid out for us: a too-large white t-shirt and too-large denim shorts.

I balled up my dirty clothes and cleared the way for Eliot to have his shower.

Nica was in the kitchen. "I ordered some pizza, is that okay?" she asked.

"It's perfect. Thank you." I saw she had more Army pictures on the refrigerator. "Where'd you serve?"

"Afghanistan. Two tours. I'm in the Reserves now. Just got back last week, actually. You want some water?" She took a glass from a cabinet.

"Please."

"I know what it's like to not shower for a week." She poured water from a filter pitcher and handed it to me, "I wanted to make sure you guys could shower as soon as you came in. On patrols we'd be out for weeks at a time. The sand would get so thick in my nose I couldn't breathe."

I pulled a face and took a drink of water.

She smiled, "I know. It's disgusting. That sand gets up in everything. The first shower is the best, isn't it?"

A Flood in Three Parts

"Yes."

She took a plastic grocery bag from a drawer and handed it to me. "For your dirty clothes." I thanked her again and went to the living room to put the clothes in my bag.

Nica's brother and his friend burst into the townhouse with paper bags of soda. They looked to be in their late teens.

"Hey, Pharez here?" They asked me.

"He went home with his mom," I said.

Nica came in the living room to greet her brother, "We got pizza coming, you guys going to stay?"

Eliot came out of the shower in an oversized white t-shirt and cutoff denim shorts as the pizza arrived. We all sat on cream leather couches and talked about that bus that crashed and caught fire and whether any government leadership knew what the hell they were doing.

"Okay, I don't understand," I said. "Where are they taking all these people?"

"Oh, shit! You haven't seen the news, right?" Nica's brother asked. Eliot and I shook our heads, and the kid dramatically fell back on the couch and threw up his hands. "Oh sheeet, your head's going to explode! Yo, Nic, where's the remote?"

She turned on CNN for us.

It was all a blur to me—endless panning shots: crowds in the street in front of the Convention Center; limp babies in crying mother's arms; crowds of people under overpasses. It was beyond anything I'd imagined.

Eliot slid off the couch onto his knees. I leaned forward and put my hand on his shoulder. Troops on Canal Street and bodies covered in sheets on the red carpet of the Convention Center. So many bodies. Nowhere to put them. A morgue in Gonzales. A woman who died in a wheelchair and was left covered in a corner.

People were there to film this, of course. Someone's always there to replay that footage, ad infinitum.

In my periphery, I saw Nica's brother pull a plastic bag from his pocket and roll a joint on the coffee table. He lit it and said, "hey" and motioned it to me. I shook my head and went back to the TV.

I don't know how long we sat there. I don't know if we cried. I only know I felt the warm cotton of Eliot's shirt beneath my hand. I know I rested my eyes on the back of his neck when I couldn't look at the city anymore. I know at some point I walked away to call my mother, and Nica talked my stepdad through the directions to her house. I know they arrived for us that night in a Lexus SUV full of food and pillows and a gun tucked in the pocket of the driver's side door.

I knew I was grateful on an indescribable level. Grateful we got out.

We packed our bags in the trunk and put the dogs in a large kennel my stepdad had brought. We all hugged and thanked Nica and my mother whispered to me, "Should I give her money? Would that insult her?" I shrugged. I had no idea the etiquette in this situation. My mother kept her wallet in her purse, and I felt embarrassed that we were whisked away in such comfort when so many people had nothing.

That feeling lasted exactly as long as it took for me to lean on Eliot's shoulder in the backseat and fall asleep. I slept most of the 20-hour drive to Denver.

The Katrina Tour

Neither of us had ever been to Denver, but when we arrived my mom helped us get settled with fresh clothes and Eliot called his brothers to let them know he'd be going to Boston until we sorted things out. There was no word on when electricity or water would be restored in New Orleans. It could be a month; it could be six months. No one had any answers. The city wasn't even drained yet, and people worried the soil and water were so contaminated it wouldn't be safe to return for months.

That first night, we got into bed in the guest room but didn't speak for a long time. I knew we were both awake, but what was there to say?

Finally, I heard his voice in the dark.

"Do you remember that time you went running and I stayed behind in your apartment?" he whispered.

I did. There was only one time that happened. We always ran together. "You brought me breakfast while I was gone. Coffee and potatoes and a muffin. It was so much food."

We both stared at the ceiling. I felt the heat from his body a few inches away.

"I watched you run," he continued. "I got up when you left. I watched you run down Thalia Street. I never told you that."

Something sad in his voice pulled at my chest. I wanted desperately for him to stop talking, but he didn't.

"You had that red bandana on your head, do you remember? I lost you when you turned the corner, you ran behind a building."

"What about it?" I whispered.

"I wish I'd run with you that day." His voice was constricted, I thought maybe he started to cry.

"It was a good breakfast." I reached over and took his hand. "The best I ever had."

"I'll always remember watching you that day. It's my biggest memory of you."

He was crying. I felt a surge of irritation, but I squeezed his hand.

I closed my eyes. I didn't want to sleep, but I wanted to shut him out. I couldn't deal with any emotions yet. I couldn't deal with my own, and I certainly didn't want to deal with his.

In the silence between us I heard his breathing become calm and slow. I kept my eyes closed. I hoped he would fall asleep.

Instead, he spoke again, this time his voice was flat and tearless, "I haven't been home in three years."

"I know."

"My mother's in a nursing home."

"You'll be fine once you get there. It'll feel good to be home."

I let go of his hand and rolled away from him. Even if I didn't want to sleep, I didn't feel like talking about anything. Maybe I should have, maybe in years to come I would regret turning away, but that night I was too tired to do anything but roll over and close my eyes. I refused to be strong.

I felt him turn his back to mine. I must have fallen asleep, because the next thing I knew I was jolted awake in a cold sweat.

I dreamed I was drowning. People were drowning all around me—we were thrashing in dark water that never ended. I couldn't make it to the surface. I was kicking furiously, desperately, but drowning. We were all drowning. We were dying together, and it terrified me.

I grabbed my journal on the nightstand and scribbled it down. I didn't want to remember, but it would be worse to forget.

I looked over at Eliot. He seemed to be sleeping.

I wrapped my arm around him and pressed my face into his back. His hand closed over mine and squeezed, and I went back to sleep.

The next day we took the long road out to the Denver airport, and I walked Eliot into the terminal. It was the first time we'd been separated in almost three years. He was going to Boston, and I'd follow in a few days. I hugged him, and he kissed me briefly on the corner of my mouth.

"I'll call you when I get to my brother's."

"Okay."

"You'll come out soon?"

"Yes, call me. Be careful."

He kissed me again, a second longer, and walked away.

There was no goodbye. I felt an irrational fear that we'd never see each other again. Maybe he wouldn't call. Or there'd be a terrible accident. One of us might die before I got to Boston. I watched him walk through the terminal with his canvas Navy-issued duffle bag slung over his shoulder. And I felt very lost.

Back at the house, I filled out my FEMA registration form online. It was an extremely long and detailed form that took half an hour to fill out. I wouldn't have bothered, but no one could say how long the city would be "closed."

Some news reports said it could be three months, others said six. Either way, there was a general agreement it could be months before the city was fully drained and utilities were restored. We had no idea if we should find jobs in Denver or Boston, or if we should go back and live without services.

Some of our friends from Baton Rouge had already gone back and they told us there were checkpoints to get back into the city. Only people from certain non-flooded zip codes were allowed in the area, so there was a lot of creative maneuvering to get in and assess the damage to their property.

Our zip code was on the early re-entry list, so technically we could have gone home any time. But there was no water, no electricity, no trash pickup or grocery stores. I found an old 1992 4 x4 Pathfinder and bought it just in case we went home.

Eliot and I weighed our options and compared notes nightly on the phone. His brother tried to get him to stay in Boston.

My mother's coworker stopped by and said, "I just don't see how you could go back. I mean, all that stuff on TV, I had to change the channel. I'm sorry, but it's like some third world African nation down there."

In the middle of all this "when will we go back?" confusion, my mom suggested I go to the FEMA aid center that was set up in an abandoned Air Force facility just outside Denver. It was housing about 1,200 people in barracks and all the disaster assistance programs had set up shop there. The local news advised any evacuees to go there and register for temporary jobs and housing. So, despite my better judgment, having already seen what the government was capable of, I went down to register for a job.

The first thing I noticed when I parked was how orderly everything was. There were official-looking volunteers with clipboards directing traffic and guarding the gated entrance. There was a bright orange fence around the barracks to separate it from the parking area. There was only one way in or out: the check station where a big sign said ID Required.

A table had been set up at the check-in station, and two volunteers in official-looking orange vests stopped me as I approached.

"Can we help you?"

"Uh, yes. I'm here to register for FEMA assistance. Am I in the right place?"

"Yes, fill out this sign-in sheet." A woman handed me a clipboard. "Do you have an ID?" I pulled out my driver's license. She looked it over, "Will you be staying here or just visiting?"

"You mean like living here?"

"Yes, do you need to register for housing in the facility?"

The Katrina Tour

"No."

"Where are you currently staying?"

"Do you mean who do I live with or in what city?"

"Both."

"With my family in Aurora."

"Okay." She handed me back my ID and held out a square white Visitor sticker. "Here's a visitor pass. You'll be issued an evacuee card inside. Once you get that, you can get in or out by showing it here at the gate."

"Okay." I took the sticker. "Am I supposed to wear this?"

She looked at me and scrunched her eyebrows. "Of course."

I put the sticker on my chest and walked along a dirt path that led to the barracks. It looked like a sad brick apartment building. A Salvation Army food truck was stationed in front of the barracks entrance. Next to it was a mobile sheriff trailer. There were large tents in the distance. Event tents. I could see some had clothing inside; some had books and shoes. There was a white trailer marked "Toiletries."

People loitered by the food truck and walked from one tent to another. Other people sat on folding chairs in front of the barracks. There were people everywhere. It was more crowded than I expected. How the hell did all these people get to Denver? I felt completely overwhelmed.

"Do you need some help?" A little woman in an orange vest put her arm around me and I involuntarily shuddered. "Is this your first time here, sweetheart?"

She spoke to me the way I spoke to my dogs, with exaggerated sweetness.

"Yeah, I—I guess I'm a little overwhelmed."

"Well, of course you are!" She squeezed me and I backed out of her arm.

"I just need to see about temporary jobs?"

"Oh, well you're going to need your evacuee card, have you gotten that yet?"

Displaced

"No."

"Okay, well come with me." She put her arm through mine and led me to the sheriff's trailer. "Do you have a photo ID, sweetheart? You know, something like a driver's license?"

Did she think Katrina had washed away my knowledge of what a photo ID was? How did she think I got in the gate? I could feel my irritation rising.

"Yes, I do."

"Okay, well I'm going to hand you off to this lady here," she motioned to a woman behind a table in front of the sheriff's trailer. "She's going to walk you through the process, okay? And I'll be right here when you're done to get you to the next place, so don't you worry."

I started to feel like I was missing something. I thought this would be no big deal. I'd go in, ask for information, receive information, and leave. But this woman was acting like I was going into surgery. Like I had a terminal disease.

Since I was in unfamiliar territory, I assumed this woman must know something I didn't, because she was acting like I wouldn't be able to navigate this process without her. I started to get a little nervous.

At the table, the seated woman handed me a clipboard with a form. "You need to fill this out and take it with your photo ID up that ramp into the trailer. You'll get instructions inside."

No problem. I filled out the form: Name, Date of Birth, Social Security Number, Former Address, Current Address. Do you plan to return? Check yes or no. If yes, when? Fill in the blank.

I walked up the ramp and was told to sit on a bench behind two other people. I'd never been booked for a crime, but I imagined the process was very similar. Once in the trailer we were photographed, fingerprinted, and issued a color-coded photo ID card.

The colors signified whether we were housed "internally" (within the facility) or "externally" (with friends or family). I quickly gathered the people housed externally could come and go freely, but those housed internally could only be off campus at designated times. Although I didn't know where they would go. They had no cars.

Was this better or worse than whatever folks left behind in New Orleans? I felt extremely grateful that I didn't end up on a bus ride from one hell to another.

I came out the other end of the trailer, wiping ink from my fingertips, with a freshly printed external evacuee card in hand. Sure enough, that little lady in the vest was standing there waiting for me. I put the card in my jacket pocket.

"Oh, no," she said. "You can't do that. You have to wear it where we can see it. They put a clip on it for you."

I looked at the card. Sure enough, it had a clip on the top. I clipped it to the edge of my denim jacket.

"You can take off your Visitor pass now." She held out her hand, as if to take it.

I peeled the sticker off my shirt and folded it up. She put her hand closer to me, so I gave it to her. "Now you need to take the bus to the processing center and get your paperwork filled out."

"I just want to see about temporary jobs..."

"Oh, I know sweetheart, but you have to fill out all your papers first."

"Oh! I did all that online. I have a FEMA number already..." I started to reach for the folded paper in my pocket where I'd written my FEMA processing number, but she looped her arm around me again.

"That doesn't matter, sweetheart. You need to go to the processing center," she led me to a line of people standing on the sidewalk next to a yellow loading zone.

"The next bus should be here in a few minutes. You just ride it to the stop and fill out your Red Cross papers and you'll get everything you need taken care of, okay? I'll still be here when you get back, so don't worry about a thing."

I was no longer worried about anything. I was pissed off. I was shuffled onto a bus to God-knows-where to fill out God-knows-what while people in vests with clipboards made sure I had the correct color-coded badge attached to my jacket.

After a twenty-minute ride I ended up on a hill somewhere in another line of people snaking through a beige building.

I was told to go into a basement to fill out my FEMA form on one of the 20 computers set up there. I said no, I already had a number. I showed the printout proving I had already done it online. So, I was shuffled into a second line where I ended up facing a woman behind a Plexiglas window like a bank teller.

Without saying anything, she slid a plastic EBT card and brochure through the slit at the bottom. I scanned the brochure.

"Is this food stamps?" I asked.

She looked at me with the bored, irritated, expression seen in all motor vehicle offices across the country. "It works like a debit card. You get $125 per month for three months. If you require an extension, you'll need to meet with your case worker and show proof of need."

"I didn't apply for food stamps. Did I?"

Her eyes were dangerously close to rolling as she glared at me. She pushed a clipboard through the slit. "Sign the form, please. There's a line behind you."

There was indeed a line behind me—a long line. I signed the form and took my EBT card and was shuffled outside to a cluster of banquet tables set up under white event canopies.

I made my way around this circle of table-hell in confusion: a signature here, a form filled out there. Did I have my birth certificate? Did I need a new driver's license? Would I like to register for something or the other?

Someone from the Red Cross counted out three hundred dollars in $20 bills from a gray cash box and put it in my hand. Another person from somewhere else handed me a brown sack lunch: an apple and two pieces of white bread with a slice of ham

The Katrina Tour

in between. I was so hungry I ate the ham, and I'd been a vegetarian for 15 years.

By the time I got back on the bus and rode the twenty minutes back to the Air Force barracks I was exhausted on every level. When I got off the bus, I stumbled around trying to get my bearings and find my way out. That little lady somehow found me again, this time she was joined by an older woman in orthopedic shoes. They each took hold of my arms and led me to tent filled with clothing.

"Do you have a winter coat?" Orthopedic lady asked.

"You'll need a winter coat. It's supposed to snow next week." Little lady agreed.

"I'm sure my mom has a spare coat," I said.

"Oh, no! We have lots of coats here!"

Yes, it was true, there was an entire tent full of thrift store clothing to choose from. Piles and piles of old coats and these two ladies were trying to find one that fit me. Orthopedic lady started to cry and put her arms around me. "I just couldn't believe what I was seeing. What you poor people have been through! I just can't imagine. I'm so ashamed of how you've been treated."

"I didn't lose anything," I said. "I just came to find a job."

She looked at me, confused, "You people have suffered so much. I feel so terrible."

I felt repulsed by her touch. I didn't want her touching me or crying on me. I pulled out from her arms.

Let her go cry on that other lady.

I wasn't trying to be a bitch. I felt humbled and grateful toward the people who genuinely tried to help. But women like this were treating me like a token. I was a symbol of poverty to them. A symbol of loss. My reality had no bearing on them. I was *The Katrina Survivor*.

It was as if I was only there to be pitied and cried upon to make themselves feel better. They had the nerve to make this situation about their feelings, as if I should be wiping *their* tears. As if I owed them absolution for whatever they might be feeling.

Women like that made me feel like I was a performer in their grief porn. It was grotesque, and I wasn't having it.

I wanted to get out of that place as fast as possible. I didn't want to be touched by these women. I was already tired of catching their tears. I called Eliot to say I was coming to Boston, and then we were going home.

Boston

If it was possible, I felt emptier on the plane to Boston than I did when we left the city. I missed our life. I wanted to go home. But the city was still flooded—even all these days later—and there was no telling what would be left when we returned.

In my darker moments, I wished everything we owned had been washed away. A clean start. As much as I wanted to go home, I was afraid of going back. If we went home, what was left? How would I walk those streets again? Nothing had ever terrified me more.

On the plane, I sat in a window seat and looked out at the black night around us. The world seemed upside down in the dark, and I strained to make out something familiar. We passed Manhattan—an orange island in a black sea. And then it was gone. Onward to Massachusetts.

As we circled Logan Airport, I felt inexplicably lighter. I was finally landing in something familiar. A piece of home: *Eliot*. I stepped off the plane into the cold confusion of the airport terminal. There were only a few people walking around. I scanned the entrance for Eliot and finally saw him walking toward me.

The Katrina Tour

I expected to feel excited, expected him to embrace me, maybe even to cry after all we'd been through. But I felt hollow. I'd missed him. I needed him. I expected a movie scene where lovers reunite after a long, terrible absence. I expected us to be jolted into a deeper togetherness.

I expected too much.

He came toward me with a vacant stare. He still looked shellshocked, pecked me on the cheek, and put his hand on my arm. I felt a distance between us was greater than the country I'd just flown over.

I went rigid and silent, but I wasn't surprised. There was a comforting familiarity in our inability to say what we felt. Our ability to inflict cold indifference on each other, even when we didn't mean to. He took my bag and hurried me along, making small talk about the flight, shepherding me onto the shuttle bus that took us to the train.

I was in a daze as he bought our train tickets, and we passed through a futuristic turnstile. I knew then that we had entered a terrible dream. A nightmare. I looked at the train map on the wall: one direction went to a place called Wonderland; the other direction went to downtown Boston.

"Are we going to Wonderland?" I asked.

"What?" He stood at the edge of the platform and watched for the train.

"Wonderland?" I pointed at the map.

"No, we're going downtown."

"Oh." I stood next to him, but we didn't touch.

The train pulled in and slid to a stop. We piled in with a few other people, but the car was mostly empty. We rumbled along, side by side, listening to the train's clacking. It was after midnight when we got to the stop near his cousin's house.

The air was warmer than Denver, but colder than New Orleans. I breathed deeply—the air was so crisp, it felt colder and sharper than any air I'd breathed before.

I followed him up a hill to a silent old colonial. We walked through an open door into a low-lit hallway where a petite Italian woman in a silk dressing gown was waiting for us. The house was elegantly decorated in warm whites and beiges.

Eliot bent to kiss her, "We made it."

She came over to kiss me. "How was your flight? Do you want something to eat? I'm Abby."

"Nice to meet you." I kissed her cheek.

"You're probably starving. Eat. There's food in the fridge."

"I'm good, thank you," I had never met Eliot's cousin, but she radiated warmth.

"You're tired. Of course. Your room is upstairs on the right; the light is on." She squeezed my hand. "Eat if you're hungry."

She kissed Eliot again. "I've got to be up early. I'm glad you made it. We'll catch up tomorrow."

"'Night," he said.

"Thank you." I called as she went upstairs.

He opened the fridge. "You want to eat?"

"No, I want to go to bed. But I see where you get it from."

"What?"

"Always eating. Never mind."

The guest room was entirely white. White antiques, white goose down comforter and linens. I looked out the window onto mature trees that surrounded the house and a pool in the yard. I was so tired I barely undressed before passing out on the bed.

A bright white sun woke us. Eliot opened the windows, and the air was crisp and perfect for early September. That morning felt like the sharpest, most important day of my life. I woke up with a longing for the stability of a family like this. Almost all of Eliot's family still lived in this suburban neighborhood; everyone except him and two of his three brothers.

Ever since their grandparents came from Italy, the family had all lived in this area. Eliot's family had *roots*. His grandparents had lived a few streets from his parents, who lived down the

The Katrina Tour

street from his aunts and uncles, and all his cousins. I longed for those kinds of roots. I went down to the kitchen.

"You want breakfast?" Eliot asked, pulling a box of cereal from a cabinet.

"No. Maybe some toast." I shuffled through the refrigerator.

"I want to stop by my brother's before we go downtown. Get some water and fruit." He reached around me for the milk.

"Okay," I said, making the toast.

"You can see the house I grew up in." He shoved a spoon of cereal into his mouth.

We set out after breakfast, past a colonial graveyard and a monument to Quincy Adams, grandfather to John Quincy Adams. Eliot gave me a history lesson on the Adams family. I hardly heard him. As we made our way down the hill toward his parents' house, the houses got smaller, and the streets got more winding. Walking next to him, listening to the history I'd always slept through in school, I felt a tremendous love for him wash over me. It overwhelmed my senses.

"I want to get married," I broke in.

"What?"

"I think we should get married."

"What?" He stopped and looked confused.

It wasn't the reaction I expected, not that I'd consciously thought about it. "I think we should get married." His look of confusion didn't change. "I want to be with you."

"Where is this coming from?"

Now I was confused. We stood in the white New England morning and stared at each other.

As strangers.

"Everything that just happened and you're asking me where this is coming from?"

"You never—I never thought you were the kind of person who wanted to get married." He sounded unsure of his words. "That's the great thing about us."

"What?" The air suddenly felt too thin. It burned cold on my face. "I never said I didn't want to get married."

"You and me, we're not that kind of people."

"What are you talking about?" I was honestly confused. The world had hollowed out beneath me, and I felt like I was falling underground. His expression matched my feelings.

"We're *artists*." He emphasized the word as if that would make its meaning clear. "That stuff...it's not for us. We're not like other people."

I wanted to believe he was joking. I wanted him to laugh and put his arm around me and say of course we would get married. We would find a way to put our lives back together. We would be a team. But he stared at me with as much confusion as I felt.

When my voice returned, it was sharp and venomous, "You are so full of shit. You know I said I want a family."

"No," he sounded panicked now. "We—our life has never been about that. We're going to travel around the world and live in different countries—" I could tell he had fallen into this hole with me, confused and stumbling over his words.

"Why are you acting like you just met me?" I snapped.

"Why are you doing this to me? *Right now?*"

"Because we're standing in the street and I want to spend my life with you!" I yelled. "I want us to figure out what we're going to do with this fucking mess we're in, and I want to know we're doing it together!"

"Well, I don't know what I want anymore!" He yelled back.

The vacuum that opened between us in that moment was physical. We both stepped back, away from it.

He should have taken a knife and stabbed me. It would have been a less painful death. I looked for his eyes, but he wouldn't look at me.

"Please, let's drop it," he said quietly.

I saw him for the first time. He would never want more than what we had.

The Katrina Tour

"Two years together? Everything we just went through?"

I wanted him to take it back. I wanted him to apologize, to reassure me, to make me feel secure. I wanted him to feel what I felt—that we should make a grand gesture and create the illusion of stability. I needed that illusion of stability.

He wouldn't look at me. He was looking at the sky.

"After all this," I continued, "you can't look me in the face. You say you don't know what you want anymore?"

A breeze whipped by and I realized my face was wet. I was so cold I couldn't feel anything.

"Whatever you want, it obviously isn't me."

"Why can't we just go back to what we had?"

"We don't exist anymore."

He looked at me now. "Don't be that way."

I tried to read his eyes, but I couldn't. He looked as hollow as I felt. Exhausted. As if our life together had fully unraveled in a span of minutes.

"I should go back to Denver," I said.

He sighed deeply and stepped toward me. "If you want to go, I'm not going to stop you. I'm too old to play games with you." His voice sounded a hundred miles away, but I could feel the heat from his body as he put his arms around me.

"I would rather you stay. I'm glad you came."

His arms closed tightly around me, and I didn't fight him. I returned his embrace and dug my face into his neck. He tightened his hold on me.

There was nothing else to say.

I knew I was crying, but I couldn't feel it. I was disconnected from my body. I let him hold me because I needed him to. If he hadn't held me there, I was sure I would have dissolved into ether.

He squeezed me tighter, and I heard him whisper into my hair, "Try to think of this like a vacation. Let's go to New York. Everything will be there when we get back. We'll figure it out."

It felt like a lie, but I was too tired to argue. I was too tired to carry any feelings.

Ultimately, it didn't matter whether I stayed or went, or whether I laughed or cried, because we would still be trapped at this impasse. The circumstance would be the same no matter what I chose to do. More than anything, I wanted to go home.

I took a deep breath and chose to make the best of the trip. I pulled back, wiped my face, and we kept walking in silence. I followed him to his family home.

We got to a white Dutch colonial with a detached garage and he stopped. "This is it. I'll show you the trees around back."

The back of the house was filled with beautiful old trees with branches that spread out like the oaks in our neighborhood. It was a modest house set in a cluster of trees. His brother who lived there was a landscaper, so the flower beds were colorful, and the lawn was thick and deep green even in September.

"Do you want to sit outside while I go in?" He motioned to a picnic table under a tree.

"It's kind of cold out, don't you think?"

I could tell he was trying to keep me from going into the house, but I wasn't going to sit outside by the trees. He just stood there, looking out toward the houses behind their lot. He looked lost in a memory.

I put a hand on his arm, "Should we go inside?"

"We don't use the back door anymore, so we'll have to go around to the front. We used to use it, but we don't anymore." He looked like he was in a daze, but he walked me toward the path between the house and the garage.

The back door faced the detached garage, and for the first time it really hit me why he never came back here. Selfishly, I hadn't been thinking about his father. The weight of what happened here filled the air as we walked past the garage.

The garage windows were thick with dust and spider webs. A rusted brown chain and padlock hung from the door. I wanted to

The Katrina Tour

ask, but it looked like it hadn't been touched in many years. Probably not since his father went in there that day.

"Come inside," Eliot called from the front door. I had been lingering at the garage window without meaning to.

Their home was one of those old houses that looked large from the outside but felt suffocatingly small once we were inside. I imagined four teenage boys growing up here, rumbling up and down the old narrow staircase, crashing into the kitchen. It must have been noisy.

The house was filled with mismatched antique furniture, and everything had a layer of dust on it. His brother was divorced and not much of a housekeeper, by the looks of it. Eliot gave me a quick tour.

His mother's room upstairs looked as if she would return to it at any moment, despite the fact they'd placed her in a nursing home for people with Alzheimer's over a year ago. The decision came after she left the stove on and almost burned down the house while his brother was at work.

I was uncomfortable looking at her perfectly made bed and the dresser probably still filled with her clothes.

"Can we get going?" I asked.

"Sure." He led me down the narrow stairs into the kitchen. "Should we take some lunch downtown?"

"Whatever you want."

The kitchen was small and dark. Dark wooden cabinets, wood paneling, and only one window above the sink. I stood at the sink and imagined his mother cooking dinner in this kitchen. I looked out the window—a direct view into the garage. You would be able to see inside if its window wasn't thick with dust. I felt a chill.

Did she see her husband go into the garage that day? Did she know what he was planning to do? Did she stand here and replay that day in her mind every time she washed the dishes? I couldn't think about it.

"I'll be in the living room." I left him rummaging for snacks in the pantry.

I passed through a formal dining room and saw old photos lining the wall leading to the living room. Long-dead Italian aunts and uncles and grandparents smiled and frowned at me in sepia tones. One man looked remarkably like Eliot. Maybe he was Cesare Nunziato.

There were no recent pictures. I scanned the walls and the mantle in the living room. There were no pictures of him or his brothers as adults. No photos of his brother's kids.

On a sideboard I found a black and white photo of four children. Three little boys sat around a young girl with big, black curls and a thick ribbon bow in her hair. They were wearing clothes from the 1950s. She was laughing, and she had Eliot's eyes. I picked up the picture; they looked so happy I had to smile and laugh with them.

"Who are these kids?" I called into the kitchen.

"What kids?"

"On the sideboard, there's a picture of some kids."

He came in with apples and bottles of water and looked at the picture I was holding, "That's my brothers and sister."

"Your sister?"

"Yeah, before I was born." He set the food on the couch and came back. "I told you about her."

"I don't think so."

He took the picture from me and put it on the sideboard. "Yes, she died when she was six."

"Oh my God. What happened?"

"An accident. I told you this." He went back to the couch and started rearranging my bag to pack the water bottles inside.

"I would've remembered, don't you think?"

He sighed as he fumbled with the contents of the bag.

"She had to have an appendectomy, I think, and something happened with the anesthesia. It was an accident, but my father almost killed the doctor when they told him. My grandmother was screaming in the hallway, pulling her hair out. They had to get security to make them leave. It was a scene."

He closed the bag and stood to leave. He faced me, and I just stared at him.

"You ready to go?" he asked.

"I'm totally shocked."

"It happened before I was born. I never knew her."

"But Jesus. I can't believe it."

"I know, it's crazy. Are you ready?" He slung my bag over his shoulder.

"Yeah, I guess." He was so nonplussed I didn't know how to react. He led me out the door and locked it behind me.

As we walked down the driveway he continued, " What's really strange is my grandmother had a sister who died in a fire when she was six, too."

"What?"

"Yeah. There was a fire in their house, back in Italy. Her sister was inside, and my grandmother managed to save her. But she was burnt so badly she died at the hospital."

"Oh my God."

"It was the same grandmother, can you imagine? She lost her sister and her granddaughter, both when they were six. It was my father's mother. It's why she acted that way in the hospital. My father, too. They never got over it."

"Oh my God."

"I know."

He was walking fast, and I struggled to keep pace. I looked over at him, but his expression was blank.

"I don't know what to say! I'm so sorry about your sister."

"I never knew her."

"But still."

He seemed to mull things over as we speed-walked to the train station.

After a block he spoke again, "They think that's why he did it. He never got over losing her."

"I'm so sorry that happened." I wrapped my hand around the inside of his elbow, and he bent his arm to hold it there.

"It was a long time ago."

A few days into my visit, we arrived at the nursing home where Eliot's mother lived. At one time the building had been a mid-sized hospital, and now it offered Alzheimer's care. We rode the elevator up to her floor. He was wringing his hands in the compulsive way he did when he was worried about something. I put my hand over his to quiet them.

"My brothers picked this place," he said.

"It's really nice."

We rode the next few seconds in silence. The elevator doors opened on a sterile nurse's station and a hall full of hospital doors. A friendly-looking nurse was manning the desk, looking through some files.

"I'm looking for my mother, Aurora."

"Oh, yes," she smiled. "You're taking her out today, right? It's the fourth door on the left. Her name is on the door."

He paused. "Do we have to sign her out or anything?"

"No, it's fine. We know she's with your family."

His handwringing returned and I didn't try to stop him this time. We walked to her door—it was open, and we stood looking in for a second.

It was a small hospital room with a view of blue skies. There were pictures of her children and grandchildren posted above her bed. Small bottles of lotions and creams and a box of tissues dotted the top of a small dresser.

Aurora sat in an oversized waiting room chair looking out the window. She was a small woman, even smaller than I imagined, with her thinning gray hair up in a bun.

"Hi, Ma—"

Eliot went in quickly and she turned and smiled broadly.

The Katrina Tour

"Oh, hello! How are you?" She moved as if to get up, but he leaned over to hug her, and she settled back and embraced him.

He held her briefly and stepped back. She saw me and looked puzzled. I was still standing in the doorway.

"This is my friend, Jocelyn," he told her.

"Nice to meet you," she said.

"Nice to meet you," I repeated.

"Did you come for a visit?" She asked me.

"Yes, she's here for the week." He answered for me. "Ma, we came to take you to Abby's for dinner. Do you still want to go?"

"Oh, that's nice." She made no movement to leave but just smiled at him. It seemed to me that she was trying to take in as much of him as she could.

He was her baby. Her love for him was so clear and deep it radiated through the room and hit me like a wave—I leaned against the door, my eyes filling with water. I was not going to lose it in this doorway.

I had to pull myself together.

"We're going to go, Ma. Are you ready?"

"Oh, are we going right now?"

"Yes, are you ready to go?"

They talked in circles as Eliot helped her out of the chair. I watched him fumble around for her things, and I knew he'd been avoiding exactly this scene for years. His face was heavy with lines I'd never seen before. I was glued to the doorway watching them, mute and impotent. I wasn't emotionally prepared to witness their exchange.

I rode behind him in the car as we picked up a few other family members.

Abby had planned a big cookout to celebrate Eliot being home, and everyone welcomed us boisterously when we arrived. A few of his cousins asked about New Orleans, but everyone was too busy catching up and watching the kids in the pool to make a fuss about it. There were probably 30 aunties and uncles and cousins and kids filling that house, and more food than any of us could eat.

As the party wound down and the cousins drifted home, I snuck off with a drink to the sunroom. When I got there, I found Abby sitting on a chaise puffing away on a cigarette.

Abby had been an executive for much of her career. She'd been married twice and was about to retire from running a large non-profit. She was the kind of woman who wore power suits and had cocktail parties and kept a cabin in New Hampshire so her kids could go skiing. Her children were now in college, and her ex-husband still hung around her house. She was petite, and she was loud, and she always had a cigarette in one hand and a drink in the other.

"So, what do you think of Boston?"

"I like it," I took a drink. "Thank you for hosting me."

"You're family." She had a kind smile with something sad behind it. "We're all glad you're here."

I saw an opening to ask the question that'd been killing me for days, "I didn't know Aurora had a daughter?"

"Oh..." The sadness in her eyes grew. "Such a beautiful girl. It was a tragedy. Jimmy never recovered." She took a long draw on her cigarette. "You know about Jimmy? How he died?"

Jimmy was Eliot's father. "Yes."

"He never got over losing that little girl. Never."

"What happened?"

She sighed. "Oh, we were all there. All of us. It was a terrible accident. She was such a beautiful girl." She smiled as she said it. "When she died, I thought they wouldn't go on. But then Auntie got pregnant again and we thought it would be okay."

She took a long drag off her cigarette and looked into the night. "But it wasn't. I felt so bad for that little boy. He was always in her shadow. He never knew them happy. And Jimmy was never a kind man—even before that happened. Of course, then he hung himself." There was disgust in her voice.

"Auntie never came back. She wouldn't let anyone talk about it." Abby's eyes were distant, but she didn't cry. "I don't blame Eliot for not wanting to come home. They were never right after that baby died."

I felt as if every puzzle piece had been put in place. I could put Eliot in context. Everything about his emotional distance made sense to me. And there was nothing I could say.

"We're all glad you're here," she said again and smiled at me. I felt the pressure of an unspoken expectation I knew I wouldn't live up to.

Aurora wandered into the room as if looking for something.

"Auntie, what do you need?" Abby asked.

Aurora looked thoroughly confused. Abby put her hand out, "Come have a seat with us, Auntie."

She sat in a chair next to Abby and smiled at her. "Oh, yes. How are you?"

"I'm good. Did you get enough to eat? Are you still hungry?"

"Oh, no." She patted her stomach for emphasis.

"Auntie, we were just talking about you. How many kids do you have?"

Aurora's face brightened. "Oh, I have four boys. You know my mother used to take them down to Wollaston Beach in the summer. We'd have Sunday dinner at her house."

"Sure, I remember Nonna's dinners."

"She wasn't a very good cook."

"No, she wasn't," Abby laughed. "Auntie, what about your daughter? Do you remember her?"

Aurora's face went dark as she appeared to be searching her memory. "No. No, I have four sons. They're all grown up now. I never had a daughter."

Abby looked at me, her brow tight.

"Do you remember when my mother would cook dinner for everyone on Sunday?" Aurora asked.

"Yes, I remember."

Abby turned to me. "She's getting circular. Will you get one of the boys to take her back?"

I went and got Eliot. He went through the same ritual of finding and collecting her belongings and together we went to gather her from the sunroom.

"You don't have to go," he told me.

He kissed my cheek and led his mother from the room.

"He loves you," Abby said when they were gone.

I sighed a deep sigh and looked at my empty glass. I longed for another drink.

"Will you go back with him?"

"I don't know."

"It's a hard thing to decide."

"He told me he doesn't know what he wants," I confessed.

"What do you want?"

"I don't know anymore." I lit one of her cigarettes.

"My ex-husband and I have been married twice—to each other," she laughed.

I joined her laughter.

"I don't think we'll make it to once," I said.

She gathered her pack and lighter and glass and pulled herself to the edge of the chaise.

"I can't imagine what you're going through—whether you'll go back—but I know he loves you. He might not be able to articulate it, but don't be too quick to throw that away."

Abby patted my knee and left me alone in the dark sunroom.

Nothing needed to be decided tonight.

The Katrina Tour

New York

As a kid, I imagined I'd live in Manhattan one day. I thought it was the only place I could be happy—a fantasy fueled by too many viewings of Annie Hall and Manhattan Murder Mystery. That Manhattan, if it ever existed, had changed just as surely as New Orleans had in the early aughts.

We rode in a Chinatown bus from Boston, surrounded by students and grandmas and girls with funky bags. We rumbled across the Manhattan Bridge, crumpled into tiny seats as the people around us laughed, snored, and spoke in voices that boomed over the clattering air conditioner. When the bus dropped us on Canal Street, everybody scattered into the midday crowd.

It seemed to me that we were walking in a time-lapse shot. Eliot slung our bag over his shoulder, closed his hand around mine, and pulled me across Bowery toward the subway. I looked up at the buildings. They seemed to hover, oppressing me with the shadows they cast.

The crowd was too thick. I felt claustrophobic from the body heat. The noise was too loud, the people too close. With each block I felt more aggressive. The faster we walked, the angrier I felt. The anger made it easy to forget anything else I was feeling. I leaned into it.

I wanted to go home, but we couldn't go home. We had to wait for the all-clear, and still, no one could say how long it would take. Another week? Another month? We were forced into indefinite exile.

We made our way to the train to Brooklyn.

Eliot's friend Jason lived on the third floor of a walkup, about two blocks from the train. We walked there quickly, and a buzz-click sound spit out from the steel door to allow us inside. We made our way up three flights of narrow stairs.

Jason's door was open. As we approached, his smiling head poked out, "I heard you coming!"

He held up two mason jars. I had never been so happy to see a jar filled with cheap alcohol.

"I'm so glad you made it." He kissed us both and closed the door behind us. "I have a friend who wants to meet you, do you mind going back into the city?"

Eliot put down our bag and looked through CDs on a shelf near the door. He was silent, in his own world.

"Of course not!" I said, overly enthusiastically.

The apartment was so small, there was only room for a two-person table and chair and a twin bed. A small sink and mini fridge lined the wall next to the bed. An open window led to a fire escape and there was an open door to a bathroom.

"I think you're really going to like him," Jason said, his eyes were wide and dilated. "He has this great place. You're going to love it. He was one of Andy Warhol's friends, you know? The artist? He was one of the great drag queens of all time—not Andy Warhol, my friend."

He let out a high-pitched laugh that made me think he had a very good pharmacist.

Jason went on talking, catching up with Eliot, and I was grateful he filled the room with sound. It gave me an opportunity to drink in peace.

Before long Eliot was one drink ahead of me. From my seat on the bed, I watched him slowly walk in a circle around the apartment. He nodded at Jason's talk. He stopped to look at Jason's paintings. He smiled at snapshots of Jason in drag with his friends.

I had never known him to drink. In three years of New Orleans club gigs, he'd kept an alcoholic's abstinence. Had I been sober, I might have questioned him about it. But that afternoon he was besting my consumption.

Jason kept our glasses filled from cheap bottles of wine, and I watched Eliot carefully. It seemed to me he never spoke. Or maybe he was speaking, but I'd lost the ability to hear him.

The Katrina Tour

"Where are you from?" Jason asked me suddenly.

I cleared my throat. "Los Angeles mostly."

"Oh my God. Don't say that. I dated a guy from L.A. once. He was such an asshole. He never called me! No offense, but I hate people from L.A."

"None taken. We are assholes." I took a drink. "In fact, I promise never to call you."

He laughed. "Don't say that!"

I finished off my third glass and stood up. "Shall we?"

A few minutes later we were rambling back into the city. My vision was a blissful blur; it was afternoon, and the sun had bathed everything in gold.

We ended up on the Upper East Side, carried along by Jason's incessant chatter. When we crossed the street toward his friend's building, I took Eliot's arm to steady myself. My head was suddenly too light for my body, and the lines on the street seemed to shift with every step.

We walked into a beige building and packed ourselves into a tiny pre-war elevator. Jason closed an iron gate behind us and pushed a button. We jolted and rumbled up slowly, our bodies pressed together.

"Oh, I should tell you," Jason said, "He's dying of AIDS, so he doesn't look very good. Don't be concerned."

Eliot was still in his silent haze. I wasn't sure he'd even heard.

The elevator stopped and Jason opened the gate. We nearly fell out into a dark gray hallway. It was too dark after the golden sunlight outside.

At the far end of the hall a black door was cracked open. The tiniest sliver of blue-gray light slid through the crack to beckon us. Jason bound down the hallway ahead of us and burst through the door.

"We're here!" Jason shouted. We followed him in. "Go around the corner," he told us. "I'll bring the drinks in."

More drinks, please.

Jason ushered us toward a dark hallway, but I wasn't ready to see what was waiting around the corner. It was too dark. It smelled like stale air and old men and death.

This was not a Woody Allen Manhattan. It felt more like a Roman coliseum, and we were the Christians.

I looked at Eliot. His poker face was solidly in place. I wasn't sure if he was still breathing, but he was walking, so I took that as a good sign. I put my hand in the crook of his arm, and we walked around the corner into a long, dark room.

At the far end of the room, in front of a wall of bare windows, an elderly man rose from behind a mammoth oak desk. He opened his arms to greet us.

"Come in."

I had to fully take him in before I could move closer.

Thick bottle glasses weighed heavily on his nose. He had no hair on his body. He was skeletal, and his pale skin was nearly completely exposed. He wore a loose crocheted lace poncho over his shoulders and underneath was something that looked like a diaper. I didn't want to stare to confirm that.

Still, as we approached, I could see he had a regal presence. He had a magnetism. It was easy to see the shadow of his younger self still burning in his eyes.

"Sit down." He motioned to three chairs in front of his desk. "Don't be shy."

We moved forward and I caught sight of us—the three of us—in a wall-length mirror to my left. Our mirror-selves took their seats in unison with us. My mirror-self surveyed this dark, cluttered room with me.

Bookshelves lined the wall across from the mirror. They were crowded with papers and books. Above the shelves I saw a row of paintings—Warhol's? I couldn't be sure. There wasn't enough light. The bright daylight tried to stream in from the windows behind the desk, but it was strangled by tall buildings across the street. I looked back to our reflections.

The Katrina Tour

As if reading my mind, the old man switched on a lamp beside his desk. The room caught fire with orange tungsten light.

Jason came in with a tray of wine in proper wine glasses. He offered me the first, and I thanked him with my eyes.

"So, you were there?" The old man asked. He was matter of fact. I watched him pull a white plastic box from a drawer. "Tell me everything. What was it like? How did you get out?"

I looked to Eliot, but he was staring at the bookshelves. I began an abbreviated version of our story, a highlight reel. As I spoke, I watched the man pull a set of dentures from the plastic box. He methodically applied pink adhesive foam to the smooth plastic of the upper denture. I was transfixed, but I continued telling him our story.

Every few words the man would glance up and peer into my eyes and nod. Jason pulled a pipe from somewhere and I watched him prepare it out of the corner of my eye. I couldn't figure out which action fascinated me more: the dentures or the pipe. Before I could decide, Jason wordlessly passed the pipe to me, and I inhaled deeply.

"The two of you are bonded in this. Forever." The old man motioned to me and Eliot with the denture then pressed it into his mouth.

My lips were frozen shut. I watched in slow motion as he carefully pressed in his lower denture.

The world faded around me. All that remained was orange tungsten light and shadows that expanded in the mirror and the vision of this dying man with his dentures sitting before me.

I felt Jason brush past and turned to watch him disappear into a dark hallway.

"Do you know the meaning of the Mardi Gras?" The old man asked us.

"What?" *Was that my voice?*

"Do you think that could ever happen here?" He demanded.

I stared dumbly at him.

"Mardi Gras," he said sternly, "keeps the workers begging. It makes them *grateful* to beg. It celebrates the ruling class and reinforces the weakness of the masses."

There was venom in his voice, but his words got tangled my ears. I tried to tease apart their meaning, but it was all a web of sound. I was drifting in cotton.

"Do you understand what I'm telling you?" he asked.

I nodded. *I understood the world.*

"Do you think what happened there would happen here? In this neighborhood?"

"No," I laughed.

"Of course not!" He shouted. "And why is that?"

I laughed again.

"Exactly," he said with contempt. "That happens anywhere except where the ruling class lives. All the planes in the world can come here! But do you think for one minute this building could ever be touched? Never."

He jabbed his finger on the desk, "*This* is where the money lives. Everyone else can go to hell."

He spoke as if he were spitting something foul from his mouth. I had never seen that intensity in anyone else's eyes. He had the look of a raging man with nothing holding him to this world. I wanted to sink into his eyes and stare back at myself.

Jason came back with a small wooden box and placed it on the desk. I rose to meet him and whispered, "Where's the bathroom?"

He pointed back toward the hallway, "On the right."

I walked through and fumbled for a light switch in the bathroom. A bare white bulb lit four walls scribbled with decades of graffiti. Over the paint and drawings and messages, there were snapshots of laughing drag queens shouting out from where they were pinned around the room.

There was a lot of love in this room. It was possibly the most beautiful room I'd ever seen.

The Katrina Tour

It felt like sacrilege to pee sitting down.

When I went back into the living room, I saw a young man sitting on the floor behind the desk. He was wearing only a pair of shorts. His skin was creamy and soft, his eyes big and dreamy, and he stared up at me smiling as I walked by.

Had he always been there?

"I remember the smell of the bodies." Jason was speaking. He and the old man and Eliot were leaning toward each other across the desk. "I was living near Battery Park then. I helped people look for family."

I sat next to him, but he didn't notice. "The smell. That's what I remember. It was burning flesh."

"My cousin lost two friends in one of the planes." I was surprised to hear Eliot's voice.

"It's ironic," I said. All three of them looked at me as if I'd broken the spell between them, a shared memory that belonged only to them. I was afraid to go on, but I did, "I moved to New Orleans because of 9-11. And now I'm here."

They all leaned back in their chairs.

"My turn," the old man said and stood up. "Jason?"

Jason got up and helped him to the bathroom. Eliot stared out the window.

The young man behind the desk crawled over to me and sat by my feet.

"Hello," he smiled.

Am I hallucinating? I looked at Eliot and he was looking at the young man with a disgusted look on his face. I felt sure he saw him, too. It wasn't my imagination.

The young man looked clammy and space eyed. He leaned against my leg and put his chin on my knee.

Should I pet him?

He smiled dreamily, "You have a gap between your teeth."

"I do."

"It's distinctive."

I couldn't figure out where this was going. "Yes, it is."

"I always wanted a gap in the front of my teeth," he said. "I always thought I would look better that way. People would notice me."

He turned his head and rubbed his forehead on my knee like a cat. I was about to pet his hair, but Jason and the old man came back from the bathroom, and he crawled back to the desk.

"Give us a kiss then," the old man said as he shuffled toward us. It was clear he was done with us and wanted us to leave.

We got up to say goodbye. Eliot shrunk behind me and inched toward the door.

I stood in front of the old man, close enough to touch. He had seemed so frail behind the desk, but he was much taller than me. Looked much stronger than I thought.

He grabbed my face in both his hands. His eyes were huge brown rings of iris—as I stared into them, I felt like I was falling.

Time slowed down as he planted a hard, flat kiss on my mouth. I closed my eyes and felt his spittle across the closed line of my lips. It reminded me of kissing an old great uncle I'd long ago forgotten.

When he pulled back, he kept his face inches from mine. His hard, bony fingers held tight against my ears.

"You're superhuman now," he growled. "Don't forget it."

He released me with a flick of his hands and turned back toward his desk. I stared after him, but it was as if we were no longer there. He had dismissed us.

He went back to shuffling items in his wooden box, never looking back up. I felt Jason's hand pull my arm. He was dragging me back to the front door.

Jason was beaming and moist with sweat as we waited for the elevator.

"Isn't he great? Didn't I tell you? Let's see Alice before we go."

Our silence was taken as an agreement. We rode down the elevator as packed together as we had been on the way up.

The Katrina Tour

I was dizzy and parched and suddenly heavy with the weight of the thousands of miles I'd traveled in the last couple of weeks.

We emerged from the building and walked through the fading light into Central Park. Jason took us to the Alice in Wonderland bronze—only a short walk away, past the sailboat pond I recognized from a hundred films.

A hundred films and a hundred dreams of living in this place, and here I was, too empty to care.

Alice reached out between the White Rabbit and the Mad Hatter, all frozen together in bronze. I touched the White Rabbit's well-worn ear.

"I love this place," Jason said.

The park felt deserted. I wondered how long we should stay, and if it was safe.

"In winter I come out here at night," he continued. "When it's late and quiet and she's covered in snow, it's like you're the only one alive."

He went into his thoughts, so we left him there and walked to a nearby bench.

Eliot and I sat next to each other in silence. We were close enough to touch but didn't. I could feel us crashing. I looked across to the pond and in the corner of my eye I saw him lean back and close his eyes. I heard him sigh.

My eyes moved to Jason as he climbed the toadstool. The light was still vaguely gold, but it had sunk beneath the trees. Before it got completely dark, we left the park.

For the next three days, I avoided any thoughts of home. I didn't know any more if we could go back together. I didn't know where I'd go on my own.

Alice made it back from her trip beyond the looking glass. I would've given anything to know how she navigated the rest of her life.

Three: Watching a Sunrise From the Bottom of a Sea

The Long Road Home

We drove for sixteen hours straight, from the frigid Denver sunrise to a small humid town outside Shreveport. I drove as if my life depended on it. I couldn't bear the thought of stopping. Not even for gas or to let the dogs out. Stopping filled me with a nauseating panic. We didn't eat. To keep the panic at bay I had to feel like I was constantly in motion. I had to outrun my fears of what we would find when we got home.

Eliot sat silently in the passenger's seat of the Pathfinder I'd bought in Denver. He slept and snored or stared out the window. It had a manual transmission, and he couldn't drive stick. So, I drove every mile.

When we spoke, we argued, so we didn't speak. He had already returned to New Orleans two weeks before me, and he didn't want me driving all the way from Denver alone. Flights had restarted from the NOLA airport, so he flew out to Denver to drive back with me and our dogs.

When we hit the Louisiana border, I knew I had to sleep. I was half-dead exhausted, and my eyelids felt like sandpaper against my eyes. I exited at a cluster of cheap motels and pulled into a parking lot.

"You want to get the room?" I asked him.

He looked at me for the first time in hours. "Oh, I didn't bring any money."

"What?" I was sure I hadn't heard correctly.

"I didn't bring anything to pay with. I don't have my bank card." He stared at me blankly.

"Are you kidding?" I wasn't quite angry yet, because I honestly hoped he would say he's joking.

He looked at me, and I knew he was serious. He didn't believe in credit cards. He only used cash. And apparently, he didn't bring any.

I fought myself—I fought the urge to lash out and slap him. It was almost midnight. I'd just driven sixteen hours straight. I had the strength to control my hands but not my tongue. There was pure venom in my voice.

"You came out to Denver—to go on a two-day trip—and you didn't bring any cash with you?"

"Yeah."

"What the hell were you thinking?"

"I don't know."

"Yes, you do. You're thinking I'd just pay for everything."

"I didn't even have to come. This is all your stuff you wanted to drive back. You could've just flown."

"My stuff? So, these are my dogs going to my house that you just happen to live in? Is that it?"

"No. It's our dogs, our house."

The house was the reason we were in this predicament. After the flood, the housing shortage had turned the rental market into one of the seven circles of hell. Landlords were doing some crazy shit—and getting away with it.

Most of the people we knew had been evicted during the city's month-long shutdown, and some of them had returned home to find all their belongings dumped in the street and the locks changed. No warning.

A few people we knew were given eviction notices—but they still came home to find everything in the street (and picked over). Others refused to pay the higher rents and just left everything behind. Landlords were able to say there was "flood damage" (even if there wasn't) and throw everything in a dumpster, change the locks, and double (or triple) the rent. It seemed to be a free-for-all.

If you got evicted, good luck finding a new place. Rents had more than doubled overnight. The little two-room yellow Creole cottage we had moved out of before the storm was now renting for $650 and four construction workers were living in it.

The only reason we were able to keep our house is because Eliot was friends with our landlord and went back after three weeks—even though there was still no electricity and the water was under boil notice. We kept paying our rent the whole time the city was "shut down" because we knew it would be a clusterfuck if we lost that house.

I was only moving back now, six weeks after the storm, because the water was finally declared safe and we could bring the dogs back.

While I was gone, Eliot had talked our landlord into letting us pay $900 a month—an overnight rise of $250—even though the guy wanted to raise the rent to $1,200. We were lucky—he worked with us, and he wasn't greedy. He only wanted enough to pay his insurance increase. Houses that had been renovated like ours were easily renting for $1,500 a month and more. He let us sign a new lease at $900 to lock in that rent, but we'd have to pay market rate next year.

There were no places to live. We both had a death-grip on that lease, and it was in both of our names.

"Fuck you," I said. "You know what? If this is all 'my stuff' and you don't even want to be helping me, then why don't you get out of the house when we get back?"

"Don't start with me, alright? I'm sorry I didn't bring any cash, okay? I'll write you a check when we get home."

"And what if I don't have any money on me either?"

"Then we sleep in the car."

"You're really something, you know that? You know I won't sleep in the car, and you know I'd have money, so you know you'll get a room no matter what."

"Oh, come on." He rolled his eyes in a dismissive way that made me want to reach over and scratch them out. "You're making a big deal out of nothing."

I grabbed my purse and opened the door to get a room. "You sleep in the car then."

"Fine! I don't care," he said as I slammed the door shut behind me.

The motel was full, and so was the one next door. All the parking lots were filled with the overstuffed cars of families who lost their homes. It was like something from a nightmare—nowhere to stay and nothing but chaos.

At the third motel I finally found a room. The night manager said we were lucky—he had a few empty rooms, and they were probably the only rooms available in northern Louisiana. The whole town was packed with people who had been living in motels for almost two months. Lucky was the last thing I felt that night, but at least this place didn't care if we brought the dogs inside.

We got to the room—because of course he wasn't really going to sleep in the car—and I did my best to swallow my rage. We would get through the drive tomorrow, we would get back into the city, and I would figure it all out from there. I repeated these steps like a mantra as I brushed my teeth and got ready for bed. Eliot took off his pants and collapsed into bed without a word. The dogs went to sleep on the bed next to him.

I tried to lie down, but I felt like the walls were closing in around me. The sound of raucous people on either side of the room and the fear of what I'd see when we got home—I felt like my feet and my head were no longer connected to my body and they were spinning in opposite directions.

The Long Road Home

I got up and walked back to the bathroom. Then I walked to a table and chair. Then I fussed with the air conditioner. Then I peeked out the window. Then I walked back to the bathroom.

"Stop it," he said from the bed.

I couldn't stop. To stop moving felt like death. The dogs picked up on my anxiety and whined and barked at every little noise. Eliot put a pillow over his head to block us out. When I picked up their leashes, he sat up.

"Where are you going?" he demanded.

"Walking."

"It's after midnight."

"And?"

"You can't go out there by yourself."

"I need air." The dogs ran around me as I leashed them.

"You need to sleep. Leave them alone."

I sat on the bed to put on my shoes.

"You're not going out there alone," he said again.

"You coming?"

"I'm trying to sleep here. Christ."

"So, sleep." I stood up to leave.

He hurried out of bed and cursed me and pulled on his pants.

"I said you don't have to go."

"You think you're going outside alone?" He pulled on his shoes angrily.

We went out and walked the dogs in a field behind the motel. He fumed at me, but I felt better in the air. I couldn't breathe in there. I had a pain in my chest like I was being crushed. After a few minutes he took one of the dogs back toward the motel and I followed with the other.

We walked through the parking lot, through a crowd of people loitering, and I was reminded of what we were returning to. Hundreds—thousands—of families were living in motel rooms and tent cities. They were scattered with the wind.

I should have felt overjoyed that we were able to go home, but I wasn't. I wanted to throw up. I wanted to vomit until there was nothing left inside me, and maybe then I could face the shell of the city I once loved. Maybe then I could face the things I saw and who we had become in these few short weeks.

As soon as we got back to the motel room, the calm I had collected outside evaporated. If anything, I felt worse. I started crying as I locked the door behind us.

Eliot dropped back into bed, and I removed the dogs' leashes. I was vaguely aware that I had started to sob and hyperventilate. I went to the window and opened it and looked out at the field we had just walked in. I put my face against the screen and closed my eyes. I felt like I was suffocating, like I would never get enough air, and I couldn't stop crying, which only made things worse.

"Come to bed," his voice was distant. "Please?"

"No."

"Come to bed." He was tired of me; I could feel it.

"I can't." I was crying, but I felt removed from it. I heard the sound, but I had no power to stop.

He got up and grabbed me and half-dragged me toward the bed. I struggled, but he got me to lie on the bed.

I snapped.

I did not want him to touch me. I did not want him to tell me what to do. I did not want him near me. I couldn't contain myself—I lashed out and slapped him, hard, and we wrestled. We fought viciously on that bed for control. I was raw and primal and full of rage thrashing at him, and he was trying to catch my flailing arms to stop me from hitting him.

When he finally pinned me down, I felt an ugly animal yell come out of me. I was rabid.

"*I hate you,*" I hissed.

I tried to throw him off, but he had me pinned—straddled my waist and held my arms tightly. I wanted to claw his eyes out to keep from ever having to look in them again. I hated him, I hated myself, I hated the city and everything we'd become. My hatred was the only thing strong enough to eclipse the fear and hysterics that gripped me. I felt his fingers dig deeper, painfully, into my arms and he shook me.

He put his face in mine, his eyes hot and angry. I was sure I saw my own insanity mirrored back at me.

His voice was sharp and icy, "I don't give a *fuck* if you hate me, do you understand? Shut up and get some sleep."

The sound of his voice and the look in his eyes snapped me out of my rage.

I dissolved into quiet sobs, and as soon as I did, he slid off me and tried to go back to sleep. Every feeling I'd been suppressing rose to the surface at once. I was fetal and sobbing and my mind started to unthread. I felt lost at sea, unmoored, with no way to find my way back.

Finally, he pressed his chest into my back and locked his arm around me in a hug. The pressure and safety of him was enough to bring me back from my feelings. I felt relieved he was there. I let that relief wash over me—I needed him. I needed him to bring me back.

"Please pull it together," he whispered into my hair. "We have a long day ahead of us."

Eliot already knew what was waiting for us back home. I did not. We loaded up the car in the morning and drove the last few hours home in silence.

When we got to the bridge leading from the suburbs into New Orleans, I wasn't prepared for what we drove into. There was a layer of grey-brown muck on every surface.

I wasn't prepared to see the gaping hole at the top of the Superdome as we drove by. The tattered buildings. I was stunned by the wreckage.

Yes, I knew there was damage. Of course, I knew there would be mud, and muck, and ponds of water still blocking some of the streets. I wasn't prepared for so much damage almost two months later, though. *What had we come back to?*

We pulled up to our house and a group of teenage boys—not any I'd seen before—stood guard on the corner, their hands resting on the bulges of guns protruding from their waistbands. They eyed us defiantly. These weren't the usual kids from our neighborhood, and they looked like they had no fear of getting caught doing whatever they were doing.

"What's with the kids?" I asked when we got in the house.

"They've been here since I got back. I don't know. Vi said they came from Baton Rouge. They're staying down by his place," He let the dogs out the back door to play in the yard.

I unpacked the dog bowls and put their food under the kitchen sink. Eliot put a few gallons of water in the fridge.

"Where's the other kids?" I was referring to the chunky kid and his friends who ran drugs on our block.

"Never came back, maybe? I haven't seen any of them."

"Guess Baton Rouge won the turf war," I deadpanned.

"Right."

We unloaded the food we'd brought from Denver—boxes of canned and dried goods from Costco. There were no grocery stores open in New Orleans. The closest store was 20 minutes away, and Eliot had already told me it was packed solid 24-7 and always out of stock. People were bringing in supplies from as far out as Baton Rouge.

No garbage pickup. No grocery stores. The water was still sketchy, in my opinion. But at least we had electricity, and we were finally home.

The first months passed like a lucid dream. We flowed through this nebulous new world with no sense of who we were before. Nothing to anchor us. Eliot and I had half-hearted arguments, but we were too tired to do anything but push forward.

I'd say, "I want you to leave. Let me have the house." And he'd say, "Where am I supposed to go? This is my home, too. You leave if you want to leave."

Neither of us had the strength to fight, and neither of us would kick the other out. So, I moved into the living room, and he stayed in the bedroom. The kitchen and bathroom were our neutral grounds. More than any personal disagreements, we both wanted this city back. We wanted it rebuilt a hell of a lot better than it had been.

Eliot got a job gutting houses with a friend, and I started classes at a temporary campus the college set up in an office building about 40 minutes away. The main campus was still closed for renovation, but they offered a handful of 6-week classes at this temporary location. I was determined to graduate on time. I would give the city a year. That had to be enough time for us to right the ship.

Eliot would leave the house at sunrise and come home late in the afternoon, covered in dirt and dust and smelling of mold. I thought about the asbestos that must be in his hair. The contaminants he brought through our house. He came home silently, stripped off his clothes in the bathroom, and stepped into a hot shower. He had a cough, the "Katrina cough" everyone had. Irritation from the mold and debris he inhaled all day.

More than once, I stood next to the claw foot tub while he showered—listening to him cough and choke in the shower's steam.

"Do you have one of those ventilator masks when you work?" I'd ask.

"I can't breathe with it on."

"Do you want me to get you some gloves?"

"I can't work with them on. Can you let me shower?"

There were so many choices I could have made. I could have stripped and climbed in and helped him wash the city's dirt from his skin. I could have said nothing and waited for him to finish and held him when he was done.

We could have done any number of things—both of us. But we retreated into our corners.

Despite the half-hearted arguments and avoidance, on Friday and Saturday nights we would go out together and visit any restaurant that was open. We had to support the businesses that reopened. We had to keep everyone open, if we could. It was like an obsession—a singular focus we shared. We had to bring everyone home.

The first few weeks there was only one place open in our neighborhood: Louisiana Pizza Kitchen. The food was served with plastic utensils because there was no one to wash the dishes. We either walked there, or we drove to the Quarter and spent what we could to help the restaurants come back.

Two nights a week I took classes at the satellite campus. Most of the students were driving in from Baton Rouge. Some people managed to find a rental near the city, but they were living with eight, ten, or twelve people to a house.

The guilt set in immediately. The more I thought about how lucky we'd been, physically at least, the deeper I sank. We had a house all to ourselves. It was a luxury most couldn't imagine in post-Katrina New Orleans.

Maybe Eliot was right. Maybe we could pick up our life where we left it—maybe it was still here to reclaim.

Except it wasn't. Nothing was the same.

I got home from class one night to find our neighbor, Miss Hattie, sitting on an old rusty kitchen chair in the space between our front steps. She had a tall can of beer in her hand. Miss Hattie had to be 70, petite, a full woman with short, coarse graying hair and a sharp nose that reminded me of my grandmother. She lived with her middle-aged son. The back half of their roof was still blown open. Even though it now had a blue tarp covering it, they were still repairing water damage to the back two rooms of the house.

Her son and his friend had spent the last few weeks dragging molded sheetrock and yellowed-pink insulation out the front door. They piled it on an ever-growing impromptu garbage dump that had formed in an empty lot across the street.

That garbage pile had steadily grown to at least six feet—three refrigerators were in that pile, along with untold bags of garbage and sheetrock and moldy debris that had been stacked and piled there for months at that point. No word on when regular garbage pickup would resume. The whole region was buried in waste.

Every morning Miss Hattie would take a bottle of bleach out to the pile and splash it in high arcs over the pile—like a priest tossing holy water—high arcs of bleach that would fly higher than her 'do-wrapped head and land on top of that rotting pile.

"Gotta keep out the rats," she'd say.

It didn't work. Several rodents had moved into the walls of our house, but I appreciated her effort.

It was late for Miss Hattie to be out that night—after ten o'clock—and I'd never seen her drinking before. I got out of my truck and fiddled with my keys, trying to make eye contact with her, but she looked dazed.

"Miss Hattie?" I was tentative, but she looked up at me and I could see she was red-eyed and crying.

"They can't find my brother."

"I'm sorry?" I didn't understand.

"He's gone." She looked out into the night and sighed. "Thought he was in a hospital up north, but they can't find him. Nobody can find him." Her eyes were blank, her weathered face emotionless and flat except for two wet tracks down either side.

"I'm sorry." I sat on my step next to her. We didn't say anything. We stared out at the pile of garbage that had become our permanent landscape. She took a sip from her can, looked over at me, and put out her hand. I took it and squeezed. "You don't have to sit out here with me. Go on inside." She squeezed my hand again.

"I'm sorry, Miss Hattie." I stood and turned to my door. "I hope you find your brother."

It was silly of me to think I could sit out there and do anything. There was nothing I could say. Nothing I could do to alleviate the depth of her grief. We were all in this together, but I wouldn't have had the strength to survive losing a family member. I prayed for her brother; it's all we could do.

A couple of weeks into the shortened semester, I went to the library where I used to work. There were no student worker positions because campus was closed, so I had no job anymore. But I had to return some books I borrowed before the storm. The campus was empty except for construction workers and maintenance crews.

The library's automatic sliding glass doors silently opened as I walked toward the book sorting area. I remembered listening to the ladies discuss their family dramas and the latest Lifetime movies. The library was a ghost town now.

Miss Viv was standing next to a large metal bin filled with books. She was wearing her signature orange-red lipstick. I watched her for a moment as she counted books onto a wooden book cart and wrote a number on a clipboard. She didn't look up as I slid my books into the metal bin beside her.

"Miss Viv?"

She looked up, her eyes hollow then bright, "Hey, baby!"

"Hey!" I beamed at the sight of her. "How are you?"

"Oh, you know. We're on the West Bank. We did alright." The West Bank was Algiers and the other side of the river. They were high and dry.

"That's good."

"The West Bank is the best bank," she said. It was a saying I'd heard her say a hundred times, but this time she said it with a tinge of bitterness.

"Where's Miss Dee and Miss Gabrielle?" Those were the other ladies who worked with us.

"Oh, baby. Nobody's left. It's just me now," she sighed. "They let everybody go."

"What! Not with everything that happened?"

I asked about Jaquelle and all the people who worked in my old department.

"Oh, they're all gone, baby. They cut the whole department. Brought in some people from out of state to clean up and run things now, mmhmm." She clicked her tongue.

"I'm shocked." I genuinely was. How could they bring in people from out of state when people here needed jobs?

"Oh, they cleaned house, baby. Everybody's gone." There was no mistaking the bitterness this time.

I was shocked into silence.

She pulled a white handkerchief from the front pocket of her black polyester dress pants and wiped her nose.

It was one thing for me to lose my job—I was only a student worker—but all these people had families.

"But people need jobs...." I started.

"We're just the little people, baby. You know that. We're disposable to them." She started to cry and dabbed her eyes with the handkerchief.

"Oh, Miss Viv." My eyes got heavy with water. "Can I give you a hug?"

She laughed through her tears, "Of course you can, baby!"

I stepped around the book cart, and she put her arms out. I squeezed her as tight as I could, her head barely brushed against my chin. I could smell her familiar perfume, something musky and strong. When we parted I could still smell her on my chest.

"Who else came back?" I asked.

She named a few people I only vaguely knew. She paused and said, "You know who just came back? Miss Ginny over at her library. You should go over and say hello. I don't know that anyone's been over to visit with her yet."

"Okay, I'll do that," I stood and watched as she refolded her handkerchief and tucked it back in her pocket. I felt engulfed by an infinite sadness. "So, they've got you sorting all the books by yourself now?"

This seemed to spark her old complaints, and she piped up, "Baby! They got me running around doing everything in this place! It's just not right—look at all these books! They've been piled up since before the storm! And they have no concern. No concern at all."

"It's a lot of work, Miss Viv," I agreed.

"They have no concern at all," she sighed heavily. "When do you graduate, baby?"

"Hopefully in the summer."

"Well, you come back and visit us, hear?" She hugged me again and went back to the books.

Something about seeing this place empty, with Miss Viv alone in the books, made me start to choke. I could feel a torrent rise inside me, and I barely said, "I will," before I backed away and walked quickly out the sliding glass doors.

I started to sob the minute I was outside. I could still smell Miss Viv on my clothes. I was permeated with her, and all I could think was how disposable we were, indeed. All of us.

The department was gone. The Lifetime ladies were gone. I got into my truck and put the key in the ignition. Then I sat in silence and cried until I could drive the few blocks home. I couldn't bring myself to enter that library again.

* * *

I hadn't seen Marty or Jacob anywhere since we got back. All the porches were empty. The little house where the chunky drug dealer had lived with his grandma was boarded up and looked abandoned. Their yard was overgrown with wild grass and flowering weeds.

One afternoon I walked over to Kimee's house to see if she came back. As I walked down the center of our old street, I saw a ragged construction truck sat parked in front of Marty's old house. As I got closer, I saw a cat-shaped oven mitt and Marty's pink canvas tennis shoes tossed on the ground in front of her house. A man was surveying the backyard and walked through the space between her house and Miss Rebecca's.

"Hey, do you know what happened to the woman who lived here?" I called to him.

He shook his head, "*No comprendo.*"

"*¿La mujer—que vive aquí?*" I tried. He shook his head and got into his truck.

I raised my hand in a wave as he drove off, "Thanks."

I stepped into Miss Rebecca's yard. The grass was overgrown. Her garbage bins were empty and knocked over beside her front porch. I knocked, but no one answered.

Across the street was our old yellow Creole cottage. The door to Kimee's side of the house had a heavy black padlock over the doorknob. A white piece of paper was folded and taped to the front window. I walked over and unfolded the paper—an eviction notice. I wondered where she was and if she knew. I only had her landline phone number, which no longer worked.

I knocked anyway, and no one answered. The street was silent, so I stood on her porch and looked around. In front of our old stairs was a large pile of clothes and kitchen utensils and what looked like the contents of a college girl's apartment: summer shoes and colorful linens and cosmetics dumped in a cardboard box. Whoever was living there either got kicked out or never came back for her stuff. Whatever furniture she had was probably taken by the men in pickup trucks that roamed our neighborhood looking for things to sell.

I stepped over the pile and went up the steps to my old door and looked into one of the windows. A broom and can of paint sat in the middle of the kitchen. I could see some mattresses stacked in the back—probably for the construction workers now living there.

I walked home slowly, deflated. But I made a point of walking or driving down the street every week, looking for signs of life.

The abbreviated fall term passed quickly. By December, we were submitting our final papers and talking about plans for the New Year. We all agreed anything would be an improvement. There was no way to have a worse year than the one we'd just lived through.

On the final day of a literature class, the instructor stormed in red-eyed and furious. She practically threw her stack of papers on the front table.

"I have to tell you all what happened to us today," she collapsed in her chair, facing us.

Throughout that semester, she'd been sharing her story with us. Her home in Lakeview had been washed away. She was left with a concrete slab and a six-figure mortgage she was still paying every month. She'd spent the last two months barely avoiding bankruptcy, had spent all her savings, her kids' college funds, and she and her kids were living with her fiancé.

She had finally settled with her insurance company around Thanksgiving and received enough to pay off her mortgage, but not enough to rebuild.

It was a common story for nearly everyone in that class, so this was the main topic of discussion every week. She never saw a penny of the settlement. It was all on paper—transferred directly from the insurance company to the mortgage company. But at least she now owned the empty lot to put it on the market.

Through all the ordeals we had discussed over the last six weeks, she had been frustrated but stoic. Tired, but persevering. But the raw emotion radiating off her that night moved the whole class to silence. Our fifteen faces of all ages and shades focused on her as she started to cry.

Angrily, she started, "My father-in-law has been missing since the storm. We've been trying to track him down since the first of September."

It was a familiar opening. Half the people in that room had a similar story.

"We were told he was transferred to a hospital in Shreveport, then we were told he was transferred to a hospital in Texas, then Tennessee. No one had a paper trail on him, but everyone assured us that he was in one of the smaller hospitals that took in overflow. He was recovering from a minor surgery! It wasn't even life-threatening!"

Her breath choked her and stopped her voice. I believe the same thought went through all our minds: *They finally found her father-in-law.*

"We are going to sue every fucking hospital in this state," she said angrily. "And the entire fucking state itself. What the fuck were they doing with all this?"

The only sound was a few people crying.

"They told us to send a DNA sample to the morgue in Gonzales—just in case. Just in case! There's no way he would be there, they said. But just in case," she choked back a sob.

"They found him there—in the morgue! They can't tell us when he got there or how he died—but he's been there this entire time!" she yelled.

The last statement broke me. It broke all of us. We cried together for the rest of that final class. She wasn't alone, and we all knew it. So many people had spent months searching—hoping to find their loved ones—and so many searches had ended with a DNA test in a mass morgue in Gonzales.

I never saw that instructor again after that class was over. I heard she stayed. I'm sure she started a new life with her fiancé and kids. But I had no idea if they ever sued any hospitals, or how you could possibly sue the whole state for what happened in the aftermath of the flood.

There were many days where I wish we'd all tried.

* * *

The music scene had dried up with so many venues closed. One of Eliot's bandmates got married during his Katrina hiatus, and they sold their French Quarter condo and returned to his native Rome. We inherited half their furniture, a couple of bikes, and an old Apple computer. It joined the growing menagerie of things people gave us as they packed up and left the state. Nearly everyone we knew who wasn't born in New Orleans had packed up and left for their next adventure.

Our once spacious house was slowly closing in on us with our friends' furniture that was too difficult to move or too valuable to get rid of. We had more armoires and cabinets and dressers than we could ever use.

One afternoon I drove down our old street and saw Kimee's little red Civic—still completely keyed from front to back—parked in front of our old house. I pulled over and got out. Her front door was open.

"Kimee?" I called.

She poked her head out the doorway, "Oh, hey."

As I climbed the front stairs I saw she was sorting through papers and photos on her kitchen table. She didn't look up.

"That son of a bitch evicted me." She was going through a stack of photographs, putting some into a shoebox and others in a trash bag. "I've been calling that motherfucker since the day after the storm, asking him what to do about the rent. He told me there was roof damage and the house was ruined."

I looked around her apartment. The furniture was in disarray, but the house was fine. No damage. I looked back outside and noticed her TV was in the backseat of her car. She had just bought a new big-screen flat TV right before the storm.

She stopped and looked at me.

"He told me there was nothing left. Can you believe that? I've been in Florida this whole time with my mom, and I came back to see if I could salvage anything—I found an eviction notice on the door."

"Yeah, I saw it."

"He never said anything to me about it. I've talked to that son of a bitch a thousand times. If I hadn't come back to see if there was anything to salvage, he would've just tossed everything in the street!"

"What an asshole." I looked around—there was nothing wrong with the place.

"He just wants to double the rent, and he can't if I 'm back. I had just renewed my lease." She looked around. "Look at this. I can't take all this. I thought I was coming back to a fucking disaster, not to all my stuff still being here. How am I supposed to move all this? There's no trucks! I tried to find one yesterday, and there's not a goddamn one. I'll to have to leave all this shit."

"Do you need help moving? I've got a truck."

"To Florida?" She sighed and dropped the photos in her hands. "No. I appreciate it, though." We stood and looked around the kitchen in silence. Finally, she said, "You need a toaster?"

"Sure." We had two toasters so far, inherited in moments like this. I didn't want the toaster, but I thought it might make her feel better if not everything was thrown away.

"Hey, can you do me a favor? Can you take my desk?" She went in the bedroom and pulled a small black wooden desk into the kitchen. "It's not much of a desk, but my dad made it with me when I was a kid. I've had it since I was 10."

"No, take it with you!"

It was a child-sized desk. She could probably fit it in the Civic with the seats down.

"You know what? Even if I had the room, I wouldn't take it. I don't want to see anything from this fucking house again except my TV." She put her hands on her hips and looked at the desk. "I can't stand the thought of throwing it out, though. Take it, will you? I want it to go to a good home."

"Yeah, sure." I put the toaster down and helped her carry the little desk outside. It was small and light enough that only one of us needed to carry it, but we loaded it in the truck together.

"What else can I give you?" she asked.

"What else do you want me to take?"

"I don't know." She looked over at Marty's previously half-demolished house that was now nearly rebuilt.

"What happened to Marty?"

"I don't know," I said.

She sighed. "I should finish packing. I want to get back on the road before it's dark."

"Do you need any help?"

"Nah." She looked at me. "Are you staying?"

"I think so, yeah."

"Let me give you my address. I guess I'll be in Florida." We went back in her kitchen, and she wrote her address on the corner of an old bill. I picked up her toaster and gave her a hug.

"If you're ever in Florida," she said.

"Drive safe."

I left Kimee to pack what she could into her car, knowing I'd never see her again. She would become one of the many who started over somewhere new, never to return. I went home and added her desk and toaster to the menagerie in our apartment.

Not long after she left, a group of construction workers moved into her place.

Everything had become exorbitantly expensive. Our electricity bill had tripled on top of the astronomical expenses of gas and groceries. I needed to find some work.

When the campus reopened in January, I enrolled in another documentary production class. The instructor, Richard, was a producer from NYC that came down to make a film about the history of Mardi Gras. He hired me to do research at different archives around town. I also found a part-time job with a local producer—she was newly pregnant and needed an assistant to help her with corporate video productions.

While visiting a campus archive one morning, I finally walked over to see Ginny. I hadn't seen her since I covered her maternity leave a year earlier. As I opened the door to the little research archive where she worked, I was hit with the familiar cool, dusty air I remembered. It was immediately soothing.

I stood at the long wooden counter by the door. This little library was housed in one of the school's oldest buildings—beautifully furnished with heavy wooden shelves and ornate 19th century detailing in the crown molding.

Ginny was working at her desk next to a row of tall windows that lined the west wall. Bright light flooded in, and her dark brown pixie haircut was visible over a pile of file folders and books. She was leaning forward, writing in a notebook. Exactly as I remembered, and I took in the sight of her.

She looked up and her eyes and mouth went wide, "Hey! How are you?"

We laughed and I went around the counter to hug her. When she stood up, she pointed to her little belly bulge, "Look at this!" She was just starting to show a second pregnancy. "We're having another!"

"Look at you!" I laughed harder and hugged her. She was beautifully put together as always—soft brown corduroy skirt, cream cotton blouse, and burnt orange cardigan sweater. She was the living definition of anyone's favorite librarian.

"It's like I never left," I said. "How are you?"

"Oh," she sighed loudly, "you know. Our apartment's on the second floor of a house, so we're fine. But the first floor had some damage. They're redoing all the floors right now," she leaned on her desk for support.

"That's not too bad."

"I know. The owners might want us to leave so they can move into our place while they renovate the downstairs. I don't know, that's what they said, but I think they just want us out because..." she pointed to her belly and raised her eyebrows.

"What, the baby? That's crazy."

She rolled her eyes.

"When they rented to us they said they didn't want kids in the place. Now we'll have two. So, I don't know. We'll see what happens. What about you?"

"We're fine. No damage."

"That's great."

"Yeah. No complaints. I was just at the music archive doing some research for a documentary project. I remembered Miss Viv said you were here."

"I love Miss Viv! You heard they let everyone else go?"

"I did."

We looked at each other and widened our eyes.

I made a point of stopping by during Ginny's lunch break when I could. We fell into a natural rhythm of having lunch and drinking iced coffee under the trees in the quad.

In those first few months, Eliot and I tried to find a way back to who we were. We went to dinner on Saturday nights and had brunch on Sundays. For two meals every week we made small talk and supported neighborhood restaurants. We even went to movies at the little single-screen Prytania Theater when it reopened. It was a genuine attempt at finding a new normal.

There was an unspoken friction between us, and we slept in separate rooms, but we were committed to that city coming back. We were determined to do our part, even if we were trapped in a house with the ghosts of who we were.

I wanted desperately to feel home again, but my hands never stopped shaking. I woke up in a cold sweat, heart pounding, at least once or twice a night. I had an unending sense of dread every morning when I woke up.

Life is a Carnival (Reprise)

The first Mardi Gras rolled around, and the city was flush with journalists and film crews from around the world. This was the whole reason my instructor and new boss Richard was here. His production partner financed his six-month stay in New Orleans to film the first Carnival season after the flood.

He called me on the Friday morning before Fat Tuesday, "Hey, Nemesis is rolling on Sunday—you in?"

"For what?"

"Come on! You want to see St. Bernard?"

Nemesis was a Carnival parade in St. Bernard Parish. It rolled through the city of Chalmette, just east of New Orleans.

"You filming that?" I asked. I'd heard there was nothing left of Chalmette. Everything from the Ninth Ward east to Alabama had been wiped off the map along the coast—East Louisiana and Mississippi were a dead-zone the size of Great Britain.

"Filming is generally how it works. You in or not?" He sounded impatient.

I hadn't been out there, but I heard it was worse than anything in New Orleans. There weren't many FEMA trailers yet. Even six months after the storm there were very few people in St. Bernard Parish.

Apparently, that didn't stop them from putting on a parade.

"Yeah, what time?" I asked.

"Nine sharp," he hung up.

Displaced

That Sunday I woke up twenty minutes late. By the time I got on the road I was thirty minutes behind.

I should have known it would only go downhill from there.

A long line of sea-blue parade floats was turning onto Rampart Street just in front of me. They were making the long, slow trip from the float builder's storage warehouse in New Orleans to the parade staging ground in St. Bernard Parish.

I pulled up behind the last float and crawled along behind the line of floats, driving fifteen miles an hour. I was supposed to meet Richard in five minutes—there was no way I'd make it.

As I reached for my purse on the passenger seat to call Richard, it rang loudly. I fumbled with my coffee in one hand and dug into my purse with the other. I found my flip phone and popped it open on the fourth ring.

"Where are you?" Richard demanded.

"I'm behind the floats. We're almost at the bridge."

"Jesus." I could almost see his face scrunch. "Call me when you get here. I'll meet you where they're staging."

He hung up before I could answer.

It was about to be a very long day.

We crawled along St. Claude Avenue, passing through the Lower Ninth Ward and over the Industrial Canal Bridge into St. Bernard Parish.

Despite having seen reports and footage, I was completely unprepared for what I saw.

Block after block, for miles, brown muck-covered houses lined the streets. Windowless schools and abandoned businesses dotted the landscape. Fluorescent orange Xs were still spray-painted across buildings. Each one stood to mark the dead: one here, two there. It went on block after block.

Every side street was choked with the debris of broken lives. Debris and debris and more debris scattered across every vacant yard, blocking every vacant street.

Life is a Carnival (Reprise)

With every blink of my eyes, I was back on August 29. I was reliving the day the levees broke. I had to remind myself—it's been six months.

I moved my eyes quickly from place to place. I was afraid to look at any one thing for too long. At each makeshift four-way stop, where streetlights used to stand, I forced myself to focus only on the bright blue parade float in front of me. It was too difficult to stand still and face the destruction around us.

When our caravan finally arrived in Chalmette, the floats lined up in the staging area and I split off to park near a destroyed gas station. I didn't look around. I focused on the road in front of me. I focused on the job. I told myself to detach.

I left my Pathfinder next to the muddy walls of what used to be a convenience store and walked along the line of floats to find Richard. He wouldn't be hard to spot in this crowd—a gruff, middle-aged New Yorker with a loud bark and the confident build of someone who pays a lot of money for the best trainers in the city.

The morning was grey and cold for Louisiana. I pulled my long wool coat around me and watched men in flowing purple robes laugh and greet each other. They hugged with huge, slapping pats on the back. The float riders seemed joyous—they had survived to mount another parade.

Pickup trucks were parked beside the floats and women and children stood in the truck beds, rustling through massive bags of beads and t-shirts and cups. Hand-to-hand, they passed bags of throws and coolers filled with food and beer up into the floats.

I walked around small clusters of people who greeted each other with watery eyes and somber smiles. I imagined they held each other longer that morning than they did a year ago.

Richard was standing near the front of the line. He had a digital camcorder on a monopod and was filming the parade queen. She was probably a high school senior, if I had to guess. Her ladies in waiting looked younger in their glittery ball gowns.

They primped her hair and adjusted her crown. The girls giggled, trying to pin the crown to her hair, while the queen smiled and bowed her head.

As I took in the wider scene, I noticed there were probably more journalists and photographers than revelers. Network vans with tall antennae were lined up on the far end of the street.

A man in a navy wool cap tapped me on the shoulder. "Are you from here?" He had a thick German accent. A slight blonde man with a ponytail jogged up to us and stood next to the German. He carried a camera with a long telescopic lens.

"No. I'm with him—" I pointed to Richard, who was engaged in a shoving match with an ABC videographer. They were fighting to get the money shot of the king as he was crowned.

"Oh," the German looked disappointed.

"Looking for interviews?" I asked.

"We're covering the Mardi Gras, but we thought this might be a good special interest story."

"Yeah." So did everyone.

Richard ran over to us and introduced himself to the Germans.

"D'ja see that?" He asked me, referring to the shoving match. "Never be afraid to get in there." With contempt he added, "Network guys think they run everything. Don't let 'em push you around."

He glared at the network guy again before turning back to the Germans, "Where you guys from?"

"Berlin."

"Right. Where you staying?"

"Uhh...?" the reporter looked to the photographer.

The photographer squinted. "It's a little place. In the French Quarter, I think?"

"You're in a good place then," Richard said. He said everything as if he were illuminating you. "You're covering the parades? Here's my card." He pulled a card from his back pocket.

Life is a Carnival (Reprise)

"You get anything good, let me know. Maybe we'll see each other out there, get a beer."

The journalist pulled out his own card and passed it over.

"Excuse me," the German nodded his head toward the floats. The queen was about to be hoisted up into her throne. He and his photographer ran to get an interview before it was too late.

"You see that?" Richard asked me. "Always have cards."

"Uh-huh." I felt like I should take notes.

"You need to lose the coat," he nodded at the wool coat I'd worn. "I've got sweatshirts, come on."

We went to his black SUV with dirty New York plates, and he opened the back. It was filled to overflowing with lights, bags, papers, books, and all manner of dusty toolboxes and junk. He dug around for a sweatshirt and tossed it at me. "A coat's too formal. You need to blend in."

I took off my coat and pulled on the sweatshirt. It was about two sizes too big.

"Much better," he said. "You can leave your coat here." He dropped my coat on top of the pile. "Let's go to the bar. It'll be a while before they're ready to roll."

It couldn't have been 9:30 in the morning. But I never argued with a drink.

There was a dive-looking bar on a nearby corner. It looked to be the only business in Chalmette that was open.

We went in and I was momentarily blinded by the darkness. When my eyes adjusted, I could see it was a pool hall. It smelled like every neighborhood bar on earth—slightly woody and steeped in alcohol.

The room was packed to capacity. Float riders in purple robes mixed with people from town, everyone reconnecting with lost neighbors.

"What d'you want?" Richard asked as we dug out a space for ourselves at the far end of the bar. He set his camera and monopod against a barstool.

"Gin and tonic," I answered.

He looked at me as if I'd lost my mind.

"I don't like beer."

"Beer's the drink of the people," he said.

A middle-aged bartender came over to us. She looked a little haggard, like she hadn't slept in days.

Richard smiled broadly at her. "Honey, get us a Bud and a gin and tonic."

She gave him the same look he'd just given me, but she turned to get our drinks.

"You see what I'm saying? It's not even noon yet, you wanna look like a hard-core alcoholic?"

"I can't help what time it is," I said flatly.

He laughed, "Guess not."

I congratulated myself for amusing him. It was a tough trick to pull. In all the time I'd been taking his documentary film class, and working for him, he'd never cracked a smile. Everything was always business.

"Alright," he geared up to lecture. "You see what I've got?" He motioned to his camera. "Always use a monopod. More mobile. There's nothing worse than fucking with a tripod when you're trying to get a shot."

Monopod. Check. The bartender returned with our drinks.

"Thanks, hon." He tipped her a five.

She lingered a little. "What are you all filming? TV?"

"Yeah," Richard answered. "It's going to be on TV. How long you worked here?"

"Oh ... probably five, six years maybe."

"I bet you've seen a few things," his tone was flirtatious.

She half-smiled and laughed. Richard threw me a quick, sly "watch this" look.

"This is the first time it's been packed like this in a long time," she said, looking out at the crowd.

A man at the other end of the bar waved her over.

Life is a Carnival (Reprise)

"Come back around when you can," Richard smiled.

"Will do," she returned the flirty smile.

Richard turned back to me, "You want to get a story—you get in with everyone. Especially the bartenders, they know everyone's business ... and she'd make a good interview," he looked back over at her. "Pretty. Nice smile."

She was leaning over the bar to hug the man. He wasn't looking at her smile, and I laughed. I was already halfway through that G&T.

"Okay," he looked back to me. "Here's the game plan. We're going to shoot the start for maybe, I don't know, maybe 20 minutes, we'll see how it goes. Then we'll drive up to the main drag and get some crowd shots, get the beads, the kids, standard issue, then we'll drive around and get b-roll of the town."

"Okay."

"Your job is to learn. Keep an eye out for shots," he took a swig of beer. As an afterthought he said, "and get me a couple of t-shirts. That's your goal for the day. Don't let me down—I want one of those shirts."

"Right." Was he serious? He sounded serious, but it was a ridiculous goal.

T-shirts were the most sought-after Carnival throws, along with stuffed animals and limited-edition beads. To get a t-shirt or a premium throw, you had to go up to a float and beg for it.

There was no worse task I could imagine.

We drank in silence for a few minutes, and I took in the conversations around us—snippets of overlapping sound—lost property and insurance woes and future plans. And most of all, the stunning disbelief.

Finally, Richard broke the silence, "So, what do you want to get from all this?"

"What do you mean?"

"What do you want to learn, for your career? Where do you see yourself going?"

"I'd like to produce for PBS."

"God, PBS?" He sounded disgusted.

"Let me tell you something about them, they're fucking impossible. You know how many changes I had to make to my show to get them to air it? They're fucking impossible."

He took a long drag from his beer. I had drained my G&T and looked for the bartender.

"We'll talk about it another day." He made eye contact with a man across the room and raised his beer in salute.

As I gave up on getting the bartender's attention, I saw the man making his way through the crowd toward us. He was an older man, in his late sixties maybe. He was large and rough looking, and he wore one of the deep purple float rider robes.

When he finally reached us, he said, "I heard you all are making a TV show. You looking for local stories?"

Richard shot me an I-told-you-so look.

We all introduced ourselves. The man said his family had lived in the area for as long as anyone could remember. He had volunteered to stay for the storm as part of an emergency response team.

He was in Chalmette when the levees broke.

"Our house wasn't far from here," he said. "Just down the street there." He motioned toward the door with this hand.

His voice was husky and low. We leaned closer to hear him through the crowd.

"The water came in so fast, you wouldn't believe. We were all in a building up there, a strong one. Thought we were safe." He took a drink from his beer. "We stayed to help people, you understand. We were there to save other people's lives. And before we even knew what happened...."

He looked off, as if he expected the water to reappear.

"We were trapped just that quick." He looked at me as if he'd asked a question, as if he was waiting for a response. "I made it to the roof, but some guys were in the trees just holding on, you

Life is a Carnival (Reprise)

know? Everything, the entire city—we were underwater just that quick. Matter of minutes."

His eyes burned into me, as if to ask if I believed him.

"Minutes," he said again. His eyes were wet, and I could see fear, frustration.

Rage.

"Do you know who showed up to save us?"

"No," my voice barely cracked from my throat.

"The Royal Canadian Mounties," he said bitterly. Water rolled from his eyes then, freely, and made slick tracks down his face.

My own vision blurred.

"The Royal Canadian Mounties came and saved us before our own people did. Why?" He demanded angrily.

His voice rose to a shout over the crowd, "Why? Can someone tell me how in the hell the Royal Canadian Mounties got here before our own government did?"

I had the same question. The crowd was talking just as loudly around us. None of us had any answers.

He took a deep, staggered breath and continued proudly, "I will always carry a great love in my heart for those men who rode in and saved us...and until the day I die, I will always remember that they were Canadian."

I swallowed hard.

"Thank you for sharing your story with us," Richard said. He was straight-faced, emotionless, and held out his hand to the man. The man shook it.

"Thank you," Richard said again.

"I just want people to know what happened here." The man wiped his eyes with the side of his hand. Another float rider came over and patted him hard on the back, squeezed his shoulder. The second man leaned in and whispered something in his ear.

The man nodded and smiled at us, sadly, "The parade's going to start soon, are you all staying?"

"Wouldn't miss it," Richard said.

"Alright then, you all enjoy yourselves. You'll excuse me."

We all shook hands again and the man was enveloped by his fellow float riders. They talked loudly and held onto each other like brothers after battle. We watched them walk out the door together, beers in hand, as they cheered each other on.

Richard picked up his camera, "Let's get out there."

Outside, he wove through the crowd and got parade shots while I begged for t-shirts and made conversation with people in the crowd. I was on the lookout for potential interview subjects.

Within a few minutes I had two t-shirts tucked into the waistband of my jeans and I'd heard drunken stories from a merchant marine who tried to feel me up and a few incoherent drunk college kids. Not exactly compelling subject matter.

The parade passed in a blur. Masked men in tall blue floats threw beads at the crowd. Bright red convertibles rode by, topped with local dignitaries and weathermen and even one with Ronald McDonald—all waving at the crowd.

I heard Richard's voice boom out, "Come on, hurry!"

He was running toward me, "I want to catch the front of the parade before it gets to the main drag."

We cut through the parade to his SUV and climbed in—it suddenly felt like a heist, and we were on the run.

He drove down a side street toward the middle of the parade route. I tried not to notice the murky brown ghost town we drove through. I closed my eyes to the bombed-out buildings and broken storefronts and the toppled, rusting cars around us. I tried to ignore the skewed and scattered houses that were no longer aligned on the street. I tried not to see any of it, but it was impossible.

The entire town was covered in brown silt muck. The force of the water had blown out windows and doors and entire walls of houses. There was nothing but cracked, empty shells remaining in this place.

Life is a Carnival (Reprise)

We pulled alongside the parade route and saw families on lawn chairs and blankets spread out across the neutral ground, they ate and drank and laughed on the dead brown grass. New cars clogged every inch of curb space near the parade route. It appeared everyone and their brother, literally, had come home for this parade.

Richard huffed as we searched in vain for a parking spot.

"Jesus! Okay, look, I'm just going to pull over. We won't be in the way."

He pulled onto the sidewalk and parked.

"We've got to be fast!" He yelled as we jumped out of the car. "Come with me but keep an eye on the car. If you see a cop, it's your job to run back and handle it."

With that directive, he ran off to get the start of the parade as it rolled toward us. I followed him onto the neutral ground but slowed to a walk. I couldn't stop myself anymore: I had to take in the scene around me.

Strip mall storefronts were smashed and crumbled like buildings in war photos. Everything was caked in dried brown mud. Windows were shattered; broken bricks and ragged chunks of wood were thrown haphazardly across parking lots.

I walked among the families. They watched the parade approach as if the world hadn't been washed away around us.

Beyond the families I saw a bombed-out McDonald's across the street. The colors of the playground were muted by the dry, cracked muck that covered everything. The slides were packed with piles of earth and bricks and debris from the shattered building behind it.

It looked exactly like a movie set for the end of the world.

"Richard!" I yelled.

He was a block away, so I ran to catch up with him. I called out again, "Richard, the bombed-out McDonald's by the car, did you see?"

"What?" He stopped and turned.

I was panting when I reached him. "McDonald's. Ronald is riding in a convertible. He'll be coming around the corner soon."

Richard got what I was saying—film Ronald with the wreckage behind him.

"It might be overkill," he said, "but you never know. It's worth getting either way. Let's set it up."

We ran back, so he could set up a shot with the playground in the background. He got more crowd shots while we waited—kids in the street begging for throws. Laughing parents who cheered them on.

As we waited, I slipped further into myself. The reality of this empty town hit me, and the feeling of loss grew exponentially deeper the longer we stood there.

For every Chalmette there were hundreds of other towns just as damaged, or worse. Their loss was no longer an abstraction. It wasn't a picture on television or something I could safely view (or ignore) from afar.

I stood behind these families in the shell of their hometown. We filmed their broken city. I watched this terrible chapter in their lives unfold, and I watched them celebrate with a parade. I just couldn't square this circle. The dissonance felt too great.

I felt the gravity of what happened here, maybe for the first time, and it started choking me until a tight-throat suffocation overtook me. I couldn't catch my breath. I leaned over and held my knees as I started to hyperventilate.

"What's the matter with you?" Richard asked.

"I don't like parades." I tried to play it off as a joke, but I felt like I was dying.

"So, fake it," he snapped.

"I am." I had been faking it all day.

I stood up and leaned back like I'd just run a marathon.

He caught my eye, and when he spoke his voice was almost gentle, "You're going to fake it a lot in this business. Get used to it or find another line of work."

Life is a Carnival (Reprise)

For the slightest moment I felt his humanity through his eyes. I knew what he said was true.

His softness evaporated as quickly as it came. He looked back at the parade.

"Here we go," he shouted, giddily. "Money shot!"

I looked to the street just as Ronald McDonald rode into frame. He waved happily from his shiny red convertible and threw handfuls of candy to the screaming children. Behind him stood the remnants of a destroyed playground where they had played only six months earlier.

The kids raced around the car and grabbed for beads and candy. They screamed wildly, and to me they seemed genuinely happy. So did their parents. In fact, every face I saw looked overjoyed to be home again—to be back in their neighborhood.

Maybe this is what hope looks like. Maybe this is faith.

But I didn't feel hopeful, and I couldn't have faith.

Six months out, we stood in a bombed-out ghost town. We filmed a parade through the center of a hellscape. These children had no homes to return to, and it was unclear if they would ever come home again.

I felt a quiet, burning anger churn inside me. I couldn't quite place the source. It was everything.

Richard stopped the tape as Ronald passed and lifted the monopod. We took our time walking back to the car. It was obvious no one was giving out parking tickets today.

"Ready to get the b-roll?" Richard asked when we got back to the car.

I didn't say anything. *What were we doing in this place?*

He pulled into traffic and turned down a residential street. Every lawn had turned a chalky gray-brown color. A few houses had optimistic "For Sale by Owner" signs stuck in the ground. Personal objects were strewn across the road.

We turned down another street and saw a house that had half-fallen into a canal. Its front jutted up oddly against the sky.

Another house had broken open like a diorama, revealing ruined furniture and molded black walls inside. A kitchen was blown open in another house—the stove and refrigerator were toppled like blocks in the yard.

We turned again and came to a house that had slid halfway across the street. It blocked the road. A muddy radio control car and a Monopoly game were thrown like dice into the street, as if they'd slid right out of a child's bedroom as the house skid off its foundation.

Richard stopped the car, "We gotta get that."

He backed up and parked. I couldn't bring myself to follow him as he ran out to film the house.

I rolled down the window and leaned out to feel the breeze on my face. There was a pile of debris on the lawn next to me. Someone had started to gut their house, and they'd scraped their ruined belongings into a neat mound a few feet high. I saw chunks of black-green sheetrock mixed with muddy stuffed bears and ruined children's clothing. I saw a moldy VHS of Titanic and almost laughed.

In the house across the street, someone had hung a Confederate flag over a shattered window. I stared at it.

Richard returned to the car and got in. "What do you make of that?" He nodded at the flag.

"I don't know."

"You think if the South had seceded things would be different?"

"I have no idea."

He grunted, "Lemme tell you, that argument's coming."

I didn't want to tell him that argument had already started. I had been hearing it for months among Southern friends. The federal response had been as catastrophic as the storm itself in many people's eyes.

"I'm not proud to say this," he continued, "but I have a lot of family who say 'let 'em rot'. They think it's nothing but hillbilly

Life is a Carnival (Reprise)

redneck bullshit down here. And they don't like the welfare blacks any better."

He made a U-turn and went back the way we came. I couldn't get over the destruction. Miles in every direction. It was unlike anything I'd imagined.

"You think people are going to care about this place six months from now?" Richard asked. "Hell, six weeks? This is validation for people like that. They think the South should've been cut off a long time ago. Let 'em figure it out themselves."

His words hung between us. There was nothing I could say because I knew he was right. I heard the same sentiments in Denver and Boston and even from the West Coast: The South brought this on itself. It's a shit hole. Get the fuck out of this place, and let it rot.

I had no interest in those people's opinions, though. This was my home. Opinions and politics had done nothing to put our lives back together—it was meaningless noise to me.

Every house for hundreds of miles had broken apart. Every life inside was over, even if many of us went on breathing. Hundreds of thousands of lives ended in that storm, all at once, and I couldn't bear to see it.

"Every street is worse than the last," I said.

"This is nothing," he said plainly. "I was shooting in Virginia when I heard about the storm. My editor and I came out right after it passed. You know that road you came in on? Follow it out a few more miles. Go out to Plaquemines Parish. They've still got cattle in the trees. Not just cattle, either. Graveyards overturned, bodies up in the trees like Christmas lights."

I stared out the window at the endless rows of fractured houses. Every place was a graveyard now. We didn't need to film corpses in trees to know things were bad no matter which direction you looked.

"They're still there," he said. "Maybe not the bodies. But the cattle? That's still there, you can go today and see it."

I didn't have to go. I didn't want to. I knew it was true. I knew it from a classmate who drove out there every week to clean up their property. To see it firsthand would only push me further over the edge, and there wasn't much ground left to stand on.

We drove around for another half hour. We filmed houses in canals and cars in trees. We filmed the aftermath of the end of the world.

I retreated into silence. My grip on reality was slowly unwinding, and on each street I said a prayer for the dead and the living alike.

Richard drove me back to the gas station where I'd parked and stopped next to my Pathfinder. He went around to his trunk to get my coat.

I pulled off the sweatshirt he'd lent me and met him there.

"Your coat," he said and handed it to me. I handed his sweatshirt to him.

"Oh, hey," I pulled the t-shirts from my waistband. "Here's your shirt. I'm keeping the other one."

He smiled, "Hey, you got the shirts! Excellent job."

He held it up for a second then threw it onto the pile of junk. He closed the hatch and said seriously, "You did good today. Are you going downtown with us tomorrow?"

"I don't know yet."

"Call me if you want to come. We'll be out tomorrow and Tuesday." He seemed anxious to get on with his day, so we kissed cheeks quickly and said goodbye.

He raced off to somewhere else, and I sunk into the driver's seat of the Pathfinder. The unending pain in my chest had grown sharper and made it hard to breathe, so I sat and closed my eyes.

I cleared all thoughts of anything.

I had become a master at not feeling.

A few minutes later the pain subsided and I started the engine. The weight on my chest lifted slightly as I drove out of Chalmette, but as I crossed the bridge into the Lower Ninth

Life is a Carnival (Reprise)

Ward, I felt something crack inside me. I was not going to make it here. Not like this.

I picked up my phone and dialed friends in other cities. I needed to hear a voice from a far-away place. I needed to be reminded that there was another world out there, a world where "Katrina" and "FEMA" and "debris" didn't exist as they did here.

It was Sunday morning. No one was answering their phones. It was just as well—what could I possibly say? How could I explain this place?

I drove back through the streets of destruction, thinking about all the families scattered far from home. Six months had passed, and they were still in limbo, stretched out across the country and possibly starting new lives.

Which was worse—being gone or being here?

A vacuum had opened where there had once been a thriving community, and the pace of recovery was so slow it felt non-existent. By the time I got back to the relative normalcy of Uptown, I could barely move from the weight of what I'd seen. The pain in my chest blocked my airway again.

Escape was a necessity, not a desire.

I unlocked the door to our empty house. Eliot was still at church. For the hundredth time in as many days, I embraced the cold peace of a Xanax chased with alcohol. I crawled into Eliot's bed and gratefully closed my eyes.

I didn't hear him come home. Didn't hear him feed the dogs or take them out. Didn't feel him sleep next to me. I didn't hear or feel or see anything until I heard him call me from the kitchen the next morning.

One of my eyes opened at the sound of his voice.

I heard the clink of his spoon in his mug. He was making his morning tea. He had probably already walked the dogs. He was probably dressed for work. I focused on the sound of his spoon. It seemed to echo through the house.

"When should we go to the store?" he called.

Displaced

Going to the store in Post-Katrina New Orleans was an event. And during Carnival season it was worse. It required planning.

I did the mental calculus; The closest store was only open until 5:00. He got home at 6:30. This meant we usually drove to the Walmart half an hour away (open until 8:00) or we drove an hour to the market that was open until 10:00. And it seemed like were only four cashiers in all the New Orleans metro area, so we could expect to be in line at least 45 minutes.

As I thought through these details, he came into the bedroom carrying his tea. He was, indeed, dressed for work. The dogs jumped up on the bed with me and settled in.

"J, did you hear me?"

I watched his lips as he took a sip of tea. They were eclipsed as he pressed them against his mug. They tightened in slow motion as he swallowed. I was so focused on his lips I only vaguely heard his voice as he continued.

"It's Lundi Gras. They might not be open tomorrow. If I leave you some money, will you go for me today?"

I wanted to answer him, but my tongue was glued to the top of my mouth. It was caked with slime and tasted like something terrible and dead.

"Will you have time to go today?" he asked again.

I couldn't face the world. I closed my eyes.

I felt him stare at me another minute and he went back to the kitchen. I heard him rinse out his mug. He went to work, and I turned off my phone. I pulled the blankets over me and slept with the dogs.

That evening, I heard him come home. I heard him ask if I wanted to eat, but I didn't respond. He turned on the television, and I blocked out the sound. I felt his body as he slept next to me, but I couldn't touch him. I could only sleep.

On Mardi Gras morning I rolled over and turned on the television to watch the news coverage. I stayed in bed, eyes half-

Life is a Carnival (Reprise)

closed, and hit the mute button. I watched the silent, costumed families on St. Charles move their lips excitedly.

Eliot came into the bedroom dressed for a run and sat on the edge of the bed to put his shoes on. He had the dog's leashes in his hand and they were jumping excitedly around him.

"Are you going to get up today?" he asked.

I stared at the television. My mind had turned to cotton, all white and soft and no longer living. I may not have been dead yet, but I surely wasn't alive.

"You can't just lie there." He tied his shoes and looked at me. "Why don't you come for a run with us?"

I stared at the television screen, silent and sideways.

The mayor, Ray Nagin, come on the screen. He wore a military costume and rode a big, white horse up to Gallier Hall. *Our hero.* He puffed a fat brown cigar and shouted something to the crowd. They cheered.

Cut to close-up of Nagin triumphant. Cut to wide shot of laughing, dancing families. Cut to medium shot of genuine Zulu dancers in the street. Cut to close-up of Governor Kathleen Blanco toasting the crowd and drinking champagne.

Cut to the crowd shot: *We still love to party, America!*

Eliot stared at me. I couldn't think of anything to say.

We lived in a cesspool, and we threw a parade to celebrate.

Something in my mind had ripped open in St. Bernard Parish. I knew it, and I felt myself come sliding out of the schism. I could no longer reconcile my world.

Eliot stood up and took the dogs and left me there. I heard the front door slam a few seconds later.

It was Ash Wednesday before I could scrape myself together and go back out among the living.

The New Normal

I needed another job after Mardi Gras because Richard drove back to New York, and I had a hole in my schedule. The more I worked, the more normal I could pretend to feel. Eliot went back to work at his old day job and spent most weeknights rehearsing with other musicians, waiting for the chance to perform again. Things were starting to settle into a kind of normalcy.

A nonprofit production group needed a researcher and editor for a documentary about rebuilding. I fit the bill.

Day in and day out, I edited footage—hours of raw footage of people who had lost everything. People who were gutting houses. People who were trying to find a way home. All of us trying to forge a path to a new normal.

On most days I'd grab two slices of quiche from a bakery near the office and head over to Ginny's library for lunch. Her baby bump was growing alongside her angst about their shaky apartment situation.

"We're definitely going to have to move," she sighed one day as we stood in line for iced coffees at the campus coffee shop. "My uncle's got a basement apartment, but it won't be finished for another month. I don't know. It's so far out from the city."

She and James only had one car. She held her belly.

"I bet you could make it work," I said. It's not like they had other options.

"I admire your Pollyanna spirit."

She didn't admire it, but I didn't blame her for being sarcastic. There were no rentals in town.

"Touro needs to reopen," she continued. "I'm not delivering this baby in Jefferson Parish."

Touro Hospital was just down the street. It was one of the oldest hospitals in the city and had sustained a lot of damage. It was still being renovated.

"There's time," I said.

"I was born there, my mother was born there, my grandmother was born there, I gave birth to our first baby there—I'm not giving birth anywhere else. They need to reopen. It's bad enough I have to drive to Metairie for appointments."

"They will." I had no idea if they would or not, given how slow things were moving, but I wanted to reassure her. Things were crazy enough without worrying about where to give birth.

We got our coffees and sat on a bench under the trees. It wasn't yet hot. It was a perfect spring day where everything's in bloom and there's no wilting heat.

"How's your job?" She asked, unpacking snacks from her lunch bag.

"Which one?" I laughed. I had the internship with the nonprofit and three days a week I still worked for the other pregnant lady in my life—the corporate film producer who had hired me as her assistant a few months back.

Ginny smiled. "All of them. I want to hear what people are talking about out there."

"Everything's good. The lady I work for is on bed rest with her baby, so she sends me out with her videographer. We're doing comeback videos to promote tourism. It's fun. I get to interview people."

"Oh, that sounds fun! I wish we could go to Jazz Fest this year, but it's too crazy with everything," she handed me a bag of carrot sticks, and I took one.

"We're supposed to show how great it is to be back. Get people here, all that. We're going to cover a convention. I think they only have one booked this year."

The New Normal

"That makes sense," she looked out across the quad. There was a soft breeze blowing through the trees.

We ate in silence, taking in the view of the old stone buildings and quiet campus.

"You know what we should do?" she asked. "We should have a craft night. You should come over after we put the baby to bed and we can bake cookies and have a lady's craft circle, what do you think?"

"I love it!"

"Me, too! Let's do it!"

Thus began the Sunday evening Lady's Craft Night at Ginny's house while James, a musician, was out at band practice. We baked cookies and made wax paper stencils and knit or crocheted or pulled out her old sewing machine and worked on quilts while Gray's Anatomy played on the TV in the background.

For two hours every Sunday night, there was no Katrina, no heartache, and the only drama in our lives was who Meredith was sleeping with on TV between her shifts at the hospital.

For the first time, I started to feel like maybe things could be okay. Maybe we could all find our way out of this. It was a shaky hope, but I wanted to believe.

At the nonprofit job, I was piecing together the rough edit of a documentary. One of the interview subjects was a local filmmaker. Although I'd never met him, I had been editing his interview footage, and I became invested in his story. He and his partner had lost everything, and they were rebuilding their house with their own hands. They had two dogs, like we did, and I wanted so badly to see them succeed.

One day he came into the office, and my mouth fell open. "Hey! How's your house going?"

He looked confused.

"Sorry!" I laughed. "I'm editing your interview. I'm sorry! I feel like I know you."

He laughed, "Oh! It's all good. I do that all the time. Eh, everything's going. It's better than not going, I guess."

"Yeah."

"I stopped by to see if you guys want to see When the Levees Broke? We got some extra tickets to the premiere."

"Heck, yes, thank you!"

It was Spike Lee's documentary for HBO. We had all been excitedly waiting for the release, and they were doing a screening at the arena next to the Superdome. It was the most anticipated Katrina project of the year—maybe of the entire ordeal. We were all ready for some kind of cohesive narrative.

On the night of the screening, I met our group at the stadium. We piled into our nosebleed seats at the top of the arena, and the place was packed to capacity. I'm not sure any of us blinked or breathed or moved for the entire four hours of the film.

We all sat in that packed arena, transfixed.

We sat with thousands of other New Orleanians and collectively relived the heat and the sorrow and disbelief we were still living with every day. The energy in the arena that night was electric. We were breathing as one.

I watched the crowd as much as I watched the screen. So many of us had been in that fog of confusion. Yet, here we were, together. We made it home. I felt the closest thing to happiness I'd felt in the many months since we'd come back. It felt like a first spark of healing. We were all in this together.

After the film I got into my truck and started toward home. I was in a daze. It wasn't until I stopped at the red light on Lee Circle that I realized I was driving on St. Charles Avenue. I realized I hadn't driven, or even walked, on this street the entire seven months I'd been back.

I rolled down the window and felt a light breeze rush in and brush my face. It was late and there was no one on the street. I was stopped under the freeway—to my right was the high-rise building I had lived in when I first arrived.

The New Normal

My avoidance of this area had been completely unconscious. I didn't even realize I was avoiding these memories—this place. But it all flooded in at me at once. Water filled my eyes and the world went blurry. A sharp, deep pain stabbed through my chest—the silence hit me.

The storefronts were all dark. The bars were empty. There were no people walking the street. No lights. The pain in my chest choked me as I looked around. The street was silent. Even the freeway overhead was quiet. The less I heard, the more I choked on the tears that flooded from me—the sound of my tears filled the void I felt. It welled up and became hard crying. Ugly crying. Sobbing. My face was soaked and my vision blurred to block out the sadness of what I saw.

There were no tourists. No stumbling students. No ragged panhandlers laughing in the circle. No musicians carrying instruments to gigs. No service workers in the neutral ground with cigarettes in hand. No rumble-pop of an oncoming streetcar.

It was just past midnight and there was nothing—no one—on that street. I choked on the absence of it all, even after the light turned green.

Everyone was gone.

I drove slowly down the avenue, past the apartment I had loved, past the boarded La Madeline's restaurant that never reopened. Had Eliot really brought me breakfast from there in another life? I drove past the bagel shop I used to visit on Saturdays—now an empty storefront. Each block was more silent than the last. The sound of the streetcar never came, because it still wasn't back in service.

Everything was gone.

I got home to a dark house but I couldn't bring myself to sleep alone. I went into the bedroom and stood in the doorway. Eliot was lying down; I could make out his Roman profile in the dim light from the window.

"I was worried," he said. "How was it?"

"It was four hours."

I kicked off my shoes and crawled into bed with him, fully dressed. I felt tears still draining from my eyes, but there was no emotion left. I was too tired. I found my familiar spot in the crook of his arm and closed my eyes against his chest.

"I drove down St. Charles without meaning to," I whispered into his chest.

"Uh-huh," he said in an offhand way that made me think he was already falling asleep.

"It was sad."

"I know." His arms relaxed slightly around me. "Go to sleep."

"My heart is too broken," I whispered.

He squeezed me and rubbed his chin against my forehead. "Go to sleep."

I waited until his breathing slowed to a steady sleeping rhythm, and then I let myself slip in after him.

One Sunday I showed up for lady's craft night and found cardboard boxes stacked along a wall in Ginny's kitchen.

"What's going on?"

She sighed, looked exhausted, and held her belly. "They finally kicked us out."

"No way! You're practically about to give birth!"

"I know." She sat at the kitchen table and let out a big, audible breath. "You want to make the cookies?"

"They could've at least waited until the baby came."

"I know. It's crazy. My uncle's got his basement apartment pretty much remodeled. We've got to move by next week."

"That's so quick!" I turned on the oven and got a tube of cookie dough from the refrigerator. She had a sheet pan out.

"Right? We knew it was coming. It's not like we didn't know."

"Do you guys need help?"

"No. James's brother has a trailer; they'll move all the furniture out this week. We'll be out by the weekend."

The New Normal

"Oh my gosh, that's fast!" I felt a twinge in my chest. "How far out is your uncle's place?"

"It's out by Lakeview, so it's not too bad. Not close! But not too bad. I'll be on maternity leave soon anyway. We'll make it work with one car."

I put the cookies in the oven and sat at the table. "I'm sorry this is happening. I'll really miss seeing you."

"I know!" She started to cry. "I wish we could've stayed at least a few more months. It's bad enough...all this happened."

"I know. It'll be okay, though."

"Oh, I know. At least we have a place to go. This just isn't how we imagined..." she trailed off, but "this isn't how we imagined" summed up everything we all felt every day.

"Let's have a really good craft night," I said, pulling out a knitting project from my bag. She poured tea into cups and took out the cookies. We carried everything into the living room and sat together on the couch. Gray's Anatomy was starting, and the drama was about to unfold.

"This baby is going wild tonight. You want to feel?"

I put a hand on her belly and felt a little arm or leg wave past. I smiled, "That baby is definitely having a time of it."

"Right! This child knows I'm stressed out."

"That baby will be the most mellow child that ever lived. Nothing's going to phase it after all this."

I left that night with a hug and told her I'd come by the library before she went on maternity leave.

"Touro will be open by the time this baby comes," I said.

"We can do anything for a year," she replied. "Everything will be so much better a year from now."

Would it? I wasn't convinced. It had been almost a year and I was a wreck. But it sounded nice, so I agreed.

On the drive home, I started to cry. It was more than just Ginny moving away and going on leave. It was everything. It was the gutted houses and dark streets. It was the constant reminders of what happened and the nonstop slog of putting this place back together.

A year hadn't been long enough for me to put myself back together. It was hard to imagine another year having an impact one way or another.

A few days later Eliot came in from a run and rushed into the kitchen looking like a kid at Christmas.

"Hey, guess who's back?"

"Who?" I was making a cup of tea.

"You'll never guess!"

"I didn't—who came back?"

"Pete and Andrew!" he said excitedly.

"No way!" I got excited, too. "Oh my god, what happened to them? They've been gone forever!"

"I just saw Pete on my run! I don't know, we didn't have time to talk. They're having a pool party at Francesco's next weekend—you want to go?"

"Uhh, yes! Of course!"

Pete and Andrew were as iconic to me as the Mississippi River, and we hadn't heard a word from or about them since we got back. They had seven golden retrievers—which had also disappeared—and their house was empty. No one knew where they'd been all these months. They didn't have cell phones, and we didn't know how to find them.

The following Sunday we went down to the Marigny—a neighborhood near the Quarter. I'd never met Francesco, but he was a native New Orleanian who inherited the beautiful old home we were visiting. It was one of the few homes with a pool at the center of its lush courtyard.

When he met us at the door, the word that came to mind was "dandy." In another time and place, he most definitely would've been described that way.

He led us to the courtyard, where Pete was swimming laps in his American flag Speedo and Andrew was lounging on a chaise

The New Normal

fanning himself. The minute he saw us he yelled, "I can't believe we made it home!"

I knew there was going to be a story. I saddled up to Andrew, ready to listen.

"Where have you been? We couldn't figure out how to find you," Eliot said.

Pete pulled himself out of the water as Francesco brought out a tray of drinks—luscious cocktails with fresh mint.

"Honey! You would not believe the ordeal we went through," Andrew fanned himself faster.

Pete took a drink, "For once, he's not exaggerating."

Eliot and I took our glasses and we all sat in pool chairs, ready for Andrew to hold court.

"You would not believe what we went through. We were held hostage," he started.

"What?" I shouted.

Eliot looked to Pete for confirmation, and Pete raised his eyebrows and took a drink.

"You remember after the flood how all those troops were going door to door through the neighborhood?" Andrew started. "They were putting people on busses to God knows where? You remember how it was! It was terrifying. So, I said to Pete—Peter, we are going to have to leave with these dogs before things get any more serious."

"It's true, he did say that," Pete confirmed.

"Well, I don't know if you remember," Andrew continued, "but there were some volunteers going around and helping people get out."

"I don't remember that," I said.

"There were! There were people in vans going around the neighborhood, offering to give people rides. And you know we have all our puppies. We didn't have any way to transport all the babies, and we sure weren't going to leave them here!"

"No, we definitely wouldn't do that," Pete said.

"This is insane," Eliot said. "Where did they take you?"

"Let me get there! You're jumping ahead."

"So, we met this wonderful, sweet lady, she was going door to door. Just the kindest lady you'd ever want to meet. And she says to us, 'we've got this big van, why don't you let us take you and the dogs to safety?' And I said, 'where would you take us?' Because I was trying to get in touch with my nephew, and we were going to stay with him."

"That would've been a good idea," Pete chimed in.

"Oh, Pete! You know it's not my fault that didn't happen!"

"So, what happened?" I asked. I wondered how many times Francesco had already heard this story—he was gazing out over the pool, sipping his drink, unfazed.

"Well, we let this lady talk us into going with her," Andrew continued. "She said they were a nonprofit with a beautiful property in Pennsylvania and we could stay there rent free until we figured things out. There would be plenty of open space for the dogs to play…"

Pete snorted. "There wasn't."

"Peter!"

"You went to Pennsylvania?" I couldn't believe it.

"They took us to Pennsylvania," Pete deadpanned.

I covered my mouth in shock. Eliot said, "Why didn't you just come home?"

"Child!" Andrew shouted. "They wouldn't let us go!"

"No!" I yelled. I was feeling drunk and animated.

"They would not let us go," he repeated.

"We had no way to leave," Pete said.

"How did that even happen?" I asked.

Pete took over the story as Andrew fanned himself in a fit.

"When we got there, everything was fine. We were trying to get in touch with Andrew's nephew, but we couldn't make the connection. And we had the dogs, so we weren't sure who to call to transport them…"

The New Normal

"They held us hostage!" Andrew said.

"Well, hostage is a bit extreme," Pete said, "but they refused to help us arrange any kind of transport back. Frankly, we never should've gone with them." He eyed Andrew.

"How was I supposed to know they'd kidnap us?" Andrew shot back.

"This is crazy," I said. "How long were you up there?"

"Oh, months."

We sat in silence for a beat. Eliot and I exchanged a look.

"So, wait," I said, "how did you end up getting home?"

"We were finally able to get in touch with Andrew's nephew, and he found a place that helped us move the dogs," Pete said. "But those people were no help at all. That dump they stuck us in had no phone service, no internet. It was a dumpy little cabin in the middle of nowhere. We were practically in the wilderness. And we had no car. We had to rely on them for everything. It was like being in an abusive relationship."

"We were kidnapped," Andrew said.

"I mean, if you had no phone or internet or car..." I agreed.

"It was a horrible experience," Pete said. "I felt like a prisoner. That kind of thing should be illegal. They acted as if we had no life to come back to! Like they were doing us a favor keeping us trapped there."

"That is so messed up," Eliot said.

Francesco finally looked at us, "Who wants another drink?"

We all put our glasses on the tray as he held it out to us.

On the drive home, Eliot turned to me, "What'd you think about their story?"

"Just when you think things can't get any more fucked up."

"Right. Can you even imagine?"

"No."

"I'm glad they got home," he said.

"I cannot imagine that nightmare."

232

Convention Returns

New Orleans is a convention town, and unfortunately the convention center was the epicenter of some of the worst tragedies broadcast around the world. Every scheduled conference in 2006, the year after the flood, had been canceled. Well, all except one: the American Library Association. I was proud of my library people for standing strong that year.

The loss of the other conventions, however, was a huge blow to the local economy. To get shows back on the books, a local tourism group commissioned a series of videos to show national convention planners that it was safe to return to New Orleans.

We're back in business! Please forget what you saw here.

The woman I worked for was producing all these videos. By the time the ALA conference rolled around, I had already been sent on several promotional shoots with her videographer, Luke. We'd covered Jazz Fest, French Quarter Fest, Satchmo Fest, the Tennessee Williams Fest and every other festival that had been held that spring and summer.

Tourism needed to come back to the city, and I understood that. We needed to put a shine on the facility that had been burned into people's minds in such a negative light. I knew it had to be done, but my anxiety rose every time I had to put on a happy face and put a glossy spin on things.

There were many days that ended with me sitting in a dark room and drinking until I couldn't feel. My hands always shook. I didn't sleep. I had to stop taking Xanax because the temptation was too great to never wake up.

The one bright spot on these jobs was Luke. He didn't say much and wore the same flannel and jeans the entire time we worked together, and he had a warm disposition. I liked working with him because we were the same age, and he had a gift for capturing light. He made everything look cinematic and more striking than real life. He knew exactly how to shoot around ugly, unpleasant realities.

Lining up shots and watching the playback made me feel peaceful inside. He knew how to capture that dream we all longed for.

In another life, I would've fallen in love with Luke. But things being what they were, I only felt empty inside. I could appreciate his talent and enjoy his company. We were creating something beautiful. That was enough.

Like nearly everyone, Luke's house had completely flooded. He and his girlfriend lived in a tent on their property for the first few months they were back. They were still deep in rebuilding that house themselves because they couldn't keep a contractor. No one could. There weren't enough.

On the first day of the shoot, I drove out to pick up the sound guy. He was a friend of Luke's. He said this guy was the best sound guy in NOLA. I pulled up, but all I saw was a lanky teenage kid standing in the distance with a bag of equipment. And that kid looked confused.

I waved tentatively. The kid waved back confidently and smiled and bounded over. I leaned over to pop open the passenger door.

"Hey, sweet ride!" he said and nodded admiringly at the Pathfinder.

"Yeah, it's awesome, thanks. You can put your gear in the back." It was a seventeen-year-old 4x4 Pathfinder with blown alignment, chipped paint, and 47 dents. The truck was probably older than he was.

"Seriously, I bet you could do some damage in this thing!" He yelled as he loaded his gear into the backseat.

"It gets me out of potholes," I said. That was true. The flood had ruined nearly every street in the city, but this baby could drive through anything.

Most cars in post-Katrina New Orleans had cracked at least one axel and lost more than one tire, but none of my tires had fallen off. I'd never broken an axle, either.

"Sweet. I don't have a car yet, but I would totally get something like this." He climbed in the front seat and ran his hand along the cracked leather trim.

I laughed. I liked this kid.

We picked up Luke and his equipment and set off to the convention center.

I carried our notes as we walked in. "We need to pick up our passes at the next concourse," I told them. We rushed through the main hall. Everything was shiny and new. The air reeked of fresh paint and new carpet.

"Is it just me or is this really weird?" the kid asked.

"It's not just you," I replied.

He sniffed the air, "Fresh carpet?"

Luke spoke, "Fresh carpet, fresh paint, all of it."

"Nice way to cover it up," the kid snorted. "You think people are thinking about the dead bodies?"

I looked around. A standard-issue crowd of conventioneers rushed through the concourse and ducked in and out of wide, open doors. I peeked through the doors and watched them shuffle from booth to booth on the exhibition floor.

"Hard to tell," I said.

"Well, I'm thinking about it," the kid replied.

"Me, too." I looked at Luke, who was noticeably quiet. "Have you been in here before?"

"Not since," he says, "but before, yeah, tons of times."

We arrived at the press station to pick up our passes, and Luke and the kid went up to the catwalks to get overhead shots.

"You have a lot of press coming through?" I asked the girl at the desk.

"A fair amount," she said. "We appreciate all the coverage."

"Yeah." I couldn't think of anything to say, but I wanted to be encouraging. "The place looks great."

She brightened. "It does, doesn't it? They did a lot of work to get it ready. Right up to the night before."

"It looks good." It did look good. Everything was brand new.

We both looked around. I didn't know about her, but my mind was replaying CNN footage of sheet-covered bodies, and I was trying hard not to think about what they found when they cleaned this place out.

"We've had a great turnout!" She smiled brightly.

"Good. That's great," I smiled.

"We needed it."

"Yes."

"So, we're glad."

"Indeed." I was trying not to be awkward with her, but it couldn't be avoided.

No one could've predicted how people would feel coming back to the Convention Center. Next year's bookings hinged on this event. At least it seemed like things were going well.

Luke and the kid came back from the catwalks. I thumbed through the production packet, felt a sharp pain in my chest, and faked a smile, "Let's start going down the list."

The highlight of the event, for me, was Madeline Albright's keynote speech. Not for what she said, although it was a fine speech, but for what happened just before it began.

We got to the auditorium an hour before the speech to set up. Luke and the kid went to stake their ground, and I took a seat in front of a platform filled with videographers and event crew. They were setting up to record the day's speeches.

A woman with a clipboard rushed down from the stage and ran to the platform behind me.

"Speaker order changed," she panted.

A man behind me answered, "What?" I heard him roll his chair to the edge of the platform to get closer to where she stood. I wanted to turn around so badly but didn't want them to see I was eavesdropping.

She laughed, "Landrieu stormed off."

"Oh, yeah?" The guy said. I could tell by his voice he was smiling even though I couldn't see his face.

I said a prayer of thanks that I'd landed in the middle of such sweet gossip. Landrieu was Mitch Landrieu, the Lieutenant Governor at the time. He had recently lost a bitter mayoral race against incumbent C. Ray Nagin.

"He thought he was introducing Albright," the woman said.

The man laughed, "Who told him that?"

"I don't know, but he was pissed," she laughed.

The man snorted.

"They're going to put him on first."

"It's all the same to me," the guy said. I heard him roll his chair back to the center of the platform.

She walked past me on her way back to the stage and yelled back, "Just letting you know!"

I could tell they loved the political gossip as much as I did. Luke came over to sit next to me while the kid stayed with the camera. Just as the woman had said, Landrieu went on first. Whether that was always the plan or not, who knows, but it gave me a laugh after all the political fallout we'd been dealing with in the months leading to the convention.

In the first months after the storm, Ray Nagin had been called many things. He was either incompetent or heroic depending on how you viewed his actions after the storm. In the days after the flood, he gave an impassioned interview with radio host Garland Robinette that had moved all of us to tears. It was the infamous interview where he told President Bush to *get off his ass and send in the troops, man.*

At that conference in 2006, I wanted to believe Ray Nagin could bring New Orleans back. I wanted him to be the man of the people he claimed to be. I wanted the city returned to what it was, and to me that meant bringing home every New Orleanian who wanted to come home, whether they were rich, poor, or in between. I wanted affordable housing and public transportation better than we had before.

I still clung to the idea that affordable living was possible, even if Nagin was embroiled in allegations of corruption and taking heat for the insanely slow pace of rebuilding.

After many months of nearly no progress, we had just gone through a mayoral race that featured heavy race baiting. New Orleans had been a black-run city for as long as anyone could remember, but Landrieu, a white Democrat, was running against him. That wasn't going to fly. Nagin gave a speech where he declared New Orleans a *Chocolate City*.

It worked; he won the election.

When it was all said and done, he ended up in prison for wire fraud and money laundering...but at that keynote in 2006, I still wanted to believe Ray Nagin could bring everyone home.

As the keynote address began that day, many suits paraded across the stage. Suit after suit stood at the podium and delivered speeches of hope, renewal, and faith. New Orleans had become ground zero for national politicians desperate for publicity and photo ops, and it seemed like they were all there that day.

When Ray Nagin was introduced, he casually strode out in a YMCA polo shirt and casual Friday pants. *I loved it.*

I loved the theater of the swagger. Luke and I exchanged dropped jaws and laughed. The most shocking moment was yet to come.

Nagin performed his man-of-the-people speech—one we'd heard a hundred times that year—only this time he added a twist for the benefit of the conventioneers. He added a line about walking out of his French Quarter home that morning.

"Since when does Nagin have a place in the Quarter?" I whispered to Luke.

He rolled his eyes, "He doesn't as far as I know."

In fact, it had been widely discussed for months that Nagin had moved his family to Dallas after the flood. I didn't know if it was true, I had no interest in fact checking his personal life, but that was the widely accepted rumor around town. People were saying he spent as much time in Texas as he did in New Orleans.

That speech was the first time I questioned his sincerity—including the interview with Robinette that had galvanized so many people like me in his favor.

Of course, I knew politicians lie. That's what they do. Politics is a hustle on a global scale. The city had seen a second flood of national politicians using us as fodder for their campaigns all year. I had been watching the political jockeying for months and found the whole thing obscene and disgusting.

But somehow, up until that speech, I wanted to believe our local politicians were sincere about equitable rebuilding. Things were supposed to change for the better. People were supposed to come home. We were supposed to get our lives back. The more time passed, the more it all seemed like lies.

It was another crack in my ability to fight this fight. If none of these people cared about improving this city for everyday people, if everyone was just grifting, then why was I putting myself through this shit?

There had been a whole lot of political finger pointing in the last year, but this place was still *fucked*.

It struck me we'd been doing this almost a year. Putting a glossy spin on things while developers bought up all the land didn't seem to be helping anyone.

For the entire week of the convention, we shuttled around the city capturing events. On the third day, my phone buzzed.

It was a text message from Ginny: *Healthy baby girl! Please visit as soon as you have a break!*

She had delivered at Touro Hospital.

I was over the moon. Whatever the city's problems, I was thankful the hospital reopened in time. Grateful everything had gone well. Ready to meet that little girl.

Our last scheduled shoot was at the Monteleone Hotel, one of the oldest and most beautiful hotels in New Orleans, best known for a rotating carousel bar off the lobby.

Luke and I went straight to the roof to get sunset shots of the Crescent City Connection, that famous bridge that defines the New Orleans landscape. He set up the shot while I took in the late afternoon view.

Standing on the roof of the Monteleone, looking down on the rooftops of the French Quarter, watching the long black and orange barges float by on the river—I remembered why I loved New Orleans.

She was a stunning city, straddling both banks of that blue-gray river, especially at dusk when the sky shifted from bright gold to purple to black. I could've stood there all night, but we had one last event to cover in the hotel. It started in an hour.

"Carousel bar?" Luke asked.

We went downstairs and sat at the bar to start a slow, circular trip around the room. The bar was made to look like a carnival carousel with ornate gilded details and bright yellow lightbulbs. We took two seats at the bar.

"Jack and Coke," Luke told the bartender.

"Same," I said. "How's your house?"

"We're putting up some sheetrock ourselves, but we still can't find an electrician. One guy we talked to won't be free for a couple of months."

"Jeez."

The bartender brought our drinks.

He took a long drink. "How about you?"

"Same old. I wish one of us could find another place."

"Good luck with that." He took another drink.

"I know."

I drank about half my drink in one swallow. I was waiting for the warmth in my throat to spread to my brain.

In another reality, I would've flirted with Luke. In this one, I just wanted to get the hell through this day. It had gotten too difficult to navigate the gulf between public relations and how I really felt about "recovery."

I checked my watch. The event was in one of the ballrooms. "Should we go?"

He pulled his camera bag onto his shoulder and picked up the tripod. I jumped off the carousel with a hop.

The reception went by quickly, so I asked, "Do you mind if we stop for another?"

"I was hoping you'd say that."

We took another round on the carousel, and he tipped his glass to me in a toast, "To a very long shoot."

"The very longest." I clinked his glass and started drinking. We complained and laughed about the assignment, and I stopped counting after our third round. At some point I heard myself asking, "But don't you want kids?"

"Not really."

"Don't lie, I've seen you—you love kids," I laughed.

He smiled, "Maybe, but I don't think it's in the cards."

"Anything is in the cards if you want it."

He took a drink and looked out across the bar.

"Not with how things are now."

I knew he was in a similar predicament—trapped in a house. It seemed like so many of us were trapped in a house with nowhere to go.

"Have you noticed how everyone either got married, got divorced, or got pregnant after the flood?" he asked.

I laughed. "Now that you mention it. Everyone."

"Right?" He ordered another round. "It's funny. How people deal with things."

"Who would've thought—any of this?"

I felt like I was slowly sinking into the barstool. I was sinking and slowly turning around this room, at a snail's pace, on this ridiculously beautiful carrousel, asking myself what the hell I was doing here.

"Do you ever think about leaving?" I asked.

"No."

"Not even once?"

"I have a house to rebuild." He put his glass down and looked at me. "You ready?"

He put an arm around my waist to help me off the carousel. My legs were jelly, ready to collapse under my weight.

We walked to Luke's truck on a nearby street. Luckily my truck was at our producer's house—he had driven that day.

I called to let her know we were on our way to drop off the day's tapes. Luke loaded the equipment behind the seats and helped me into the passenger seat.

"Why don't I drive you home? I can drop off the tapes and you can pick up your truck tomorrow," he said.

"No, I'm fine. I'll deliver the tapes. It's late, you can go home."

We pulled up to the producer's house and the front door opened. Our heavily pregnant boss waddled out onto the porch, "How'd it go?"

I stumbled toward the steps, "Great."

Luke waved and drove away.

"I would offer you a drink..." she said as I entered the house. It was a double-wide shotgun with a studio built off the side.

"What do you have?"

"Really? I've got some wine if you want."

"Please."

I walked into her office and sat on a green vinyl couch. She followed a few minutes later with a glass of wine. I recounted the details of the day, forgetting I was drunk and rambling on about the interviews. I handed her the tapes and didn't even notice if she was listening; I was lost in my own mind.

What time was it?

I stood up to leave but my knees buckled, and I plopped back down on the couch.

"Why don't you let my husband take you home?"

"No, I'm fine. I just need a second."

I genuinely believed I was fine, until I realized I wasn't. My legs were made of jelly. I couldn't see straight. The alcohols were creating a dangerous brew in my stomach.

"You know what? If he could drive me home, that'd be great."

I had to accept defeat.

I was beyond drunk. I was damn near blind drunk. Her husband drove me home with my face pressed against the cold glass of the window.

I was very much not okay. The last year was crashing down on me, and I didn't know whether to scream or cry.

At home, I stumbled up the stairs and barely got my key into the lock. As I turned the knob my stomach exploded, and I knew I was about to throw up. I crashed my way through the house, cursing every piece of furniture I ran into along the way.

Eliot sat up in bed, "Is that you?"

I hated him, lying there in that pitch-black house. I hated *myself* as I tripped on a dog toy or a shoe, I didn't know what, but I kicked something, and it careened off the dresser. I hated us both and who we'd become in this fucking house with this fucking furniture. Living in the detritus of our old life that we had loved so much.

I barely made it through the bathroom door before puking into the claw foot tub and throwing up buckets of orange vomit. It felt like projectile vomit from my soul that would never end.

I hated the sound of him behind me, closing the bathroom door to keep the dogs out. Pulling a washcloth from the dryer, turning on the sink, and wringing it out. I hated the sound of my own puke landing in that fucking claw foot tub, the one that had sold us on this place.

I hated all of us in this hellhole of a city, my hair full of puke—and there he was beside me—pulling my hair back, saying, "What happened to you?"

I was blacking out. I had never been so drunk that I blacked out, but I knew my eyes were open, yet I couldn't see.

I have to hold on to my sight.

It was an irrational thought, and I started to cry. I was crying big drunk sobs with clots of snot falling from my nose, mixing with the puke. I was not going to black out in this god-awful claw foot tub.

When my stomach was empty, and my sobs died down, I slid off the tub and pressed my face against the cold slate floor.

Eliot slid down the wall and sat next to me. He tried to wipe my face with the washcloth, but I shooed him with my hand. He tried again. I was too tired to stop him a second time. I let him wipe the snot from my face.

"I hate to see you this way."

The disappointment in his voice cut through my chest. I pressed my face harder into the slate.

"I can't live like this anymore."

He got up and stepped over me to wash my puke down the drain. "You've had too much to drink, that's all."

"*I can't do this anymore.*" The voice that came out of me was small. I didn't recognize that voice, breathing out against the slate. "I can't do this anymore. I'm going to die here."

He rinsed out the washcloth and squatted next to me. "Don't talk like that. You just need to get cleaned up."

He put the washcloth on my limp hand.

I pulled myself up on my elbow; the room was spinning. It was spinning fast, not like the carousel. It was out of control and threatened to throw me. My stomach lurched, but there was nothing left inside me. I looked at his body in front of me, tanned and too thin these days, naked except for his old blue running shorts.

"Why can't you see what this is doing to me?" My voice was harsh from vomiting.

"What do you want me to say?" He went from squatting to kneeling, his face concerned.

"I want you to leave with me," I started to cry again. "I want you to say we'll go someplace new."

"Why would I say that? Our life is here." His face went placid.

"What life?" I demanded. "What life is here?"

"OUR life." His brows tightened.

"We have no life! We have no life anymore!" I started to sob again, desperate for air.

"You just need to give it more time." He got up and went to the sink.

"It's been a year!" I shouted.

"Then give it another year!" he yelled back.

Standing with his back to me, he washed his hands and said quietly, "You had too much to drink tonight. You'll feel better in the morning."

I stopped crying. I sat up and leaned against the tub to keep from falling over. Bent my knees to brace myself.

I looked up and watched his shoulder blades contract as he dried his hands; they spread slightly as he rubbed his eyes. He looked exhausted. He looked as tired as I felt.

He glanced in the mirror above the sink then turned around to face me. He put out his hands and said softly, "Let me put you to bed. Please."

I let him pull me up.

I braced myself on the sink to rinse my mouth. My hands shook so hard the water splashed from them. I leaned down and put my mouth into the stream. The ice-cold water soothed my lips, washed out the inside of my mouth.

Displaced

It was true, I had too much to drink that night. But I had never felt more sober in my life. I was going to die in that place if I didn't leave. I was coming untethered in this house, in a city where everything had changed.

In the bedroom, I flopped onto the mattress like a corpse. I let him pull off my shoes and jeans. He covered me with blankets in what was formerly our bed. That night he slept in the living room, and I fell into a dreamless sleep.

At some point, I heard his voice through a fog.

"Hey, get up."

I opened an eye. The sun was burning especially bright through the window.

"What time is it?"

"Quarter to 8. We're going to get your car," he patted my leg, already dressed in his running gear. "Come on, I don't want to be late for work. Put your shoes on, we're going for a run."

For the first time in a year, I didn't complain. I didn't argue. I was hung over, head splitting, puffy eyed, but I got up, got dressed, pulled on my running shoes, and followed him out the door. He handed me his sunglasses and Navy baseball cap. Thank God—because that sun was brutal.

It was seven blocks to where my truck was parked.

That morning was as hot, humid and beautiful as any morning had ever been in New Orleans. We ran past Audubon Park, and I was already covered with sweat.

It was Saturday morning, and the streets were empty. There were no clouds in the perfect blue sky. I smelled freshly cut grass in the distance, and wet air filled my lungs every two strides. I smelled all those distinctly New Orleans smells: the steamed earth and sweet olive trees, the river water and the sweat. I could smell every memory in that dense air as we ran, as we had for years, down these same streets.

"Feels good to be out, doesn't it?" Eliot said when we got to my car.

I didn't feel anything except maybe nostalgic. I felt the sun was very bright, and the air was thick and heavy. I felt like he was trying to reach me for the first time in a long time, but I was too exhausted to reach back.

Still, I agreed, "It feels great."

In my heart, I made up my mind to leave. Not because I didn't love New Orleans, or even because I didn't love this man, but because I was drowning. I would die here if I didn't step away.

* * *

I hadn't yet seen Ginny's basement apartment, so I was excited to drive out to see the baby.

It was a modest house on a modest block, and a family was living in the main house upstairs. In New Orleans, the "basement" is the ground floor, usually an apartment sitting under the main house. I knocked on the door with a gift basket. Ginny answered with a tiny baby swaddled at her chest.

"Hey!" she beamed, "Come in! We're about to have a bottle."

"Look at that little sweetheart!" I rubbed the baby's tiny back—she looked at me with the most peaceful expression I'd ever seen. Just chilling on her mama's chest, looking at me with big cloudy blue eyes.

We went into the kitchen, where a glass bottle was sitting in a pan of water on the stove. "I'm breastfeeding, but thought you might want to feed her?"

"Absolutely!"

"James took big sister out for snowballs—it's been a little overstimulating with them both together."

"Sure, that makes sense."

I took the baby and the bottle. "How are you doing?"

"Oh, you know." She pointed to the floor, "Polished concrete floors."

She said it with a slight glare.

"It looks nice."

"All I can think about is the girls cracking their heads open. There aren't enough rugs in the world."

"Oh...yeah, that could be a problem."

"Come look at this," she led me to the window over the sink. "What do you see?"

I looked out and saw a fence. "The fence?" It was a wooden plank fence, maybe eight or ten feet high.

"Look at the fence."

I did, but I wasn't picking up the problem.

"The water line," she said.

"Oh." This property had flooded, and a dark brown water line skimmed the top of the fence.

"Jocelyn, this basement was entirely underwater."

"Oh...."

"Every time I look out that window, I think about how we had to wade out during Katrina with the baby in chest-high water. James had to carry her out over his head to a boat. If it happens again this year, that water would be over our heads in a minute."

"I see what you're saying."

"I can't live here."

"There would be time to evacuate, though. You wouldn't get caught in a flood again."

"It was up to our chest within a few minutes! How could we get two babies out in time if something happened?" She was getting upset.

"No, I understand what you're saying. I get it."

"I told James we have to leave. I don't know where we go, but I can't live in this place with two babies."

"I completely understand."

"There's a farmhouse in Hattiesburg that I found online. I have a brother out near there. I think we could probably buy it."

"Oh, wow. Hattiesburg. That seems far away."

"I could get a job at an archive there. I already reached out. They said I could come talk to them when we see the house."

I looked down at the baby drinking from her bottle, peaceful as a baby Buddha.

"That sounds very doable...you've got to do what's right for your family."

She started to cry.

"This isn't how anything was supposed to go."

"I know."

"We were supposed to raise our kids in the city and spend summers at the museum, and we could've been neighbors and had craft nights..."

"I know." The baby was sleeping soundly. I removed the bottle from her mouth. "She's so perfect," I whispered.

Ginny smiled at the baby and took the bottle. "I swear this baby never cries. She's been so easy."

"She's a sweet little angel," I whispered to the baby.

Ginny led me to a Moses basket in their bedroom where the baby slept. I placed her in, and she barely stirred.

"We should all sleep that well," I said.

I knew, without saying it, that circumstances were about to take us far from each other's lives. As I left their house that day I started to cry. It wasn't sadness. It was the weight of a year of grieving and feeling too damn exhausted to grieve anymore.

It was knowing that Eliot and I would never be on the same page about leaving. He was never going to want children—and I didn't blame him for not wanting to be a father, given what happened with his family. I couldn't hate him for wanting to stay there, even if I said I did when I was angry. I couldn't be angry anymore, even if I wanted to leave.

This city would never be a place I could have a family. I couldn't imagine going through this again.

I wanted all of us to find a better way forward.

There were only three classes left to complete my degree, and I'd be finished that summer. After that, there was no reason to be there anymore.

It had only been a year. It felt like several lifetimes.

"What do you want to do about the house?" I asked Eliot as our lease was coming to an end. I was feeding the dogs while he finished making dinner.

"Do you want to stay? We can renew."

"No. I really don't. I want to leave."

"I see." He served two plates and put them on the table.

"Why don't we both leave? We could go together."

He sat down to eat. "My life is here."

"You can't have a life somewhere else?" I sat and looked at him. He had made a carbonara; it looked delicious.

"My contacts are here. My connections are here. You think I can just pick up in a new city? I've been here 20 years."

"You can't do something else?"

He looked at me. "What would I do? I'm a drummer. It's the only thing I ever wanted to do—the only thing I've done. Would you stop writing?"

"You can be a musician anywhere. It doesn't have to be here."

He went back to eating, and I joined him. It was a pointless discussion. I understood what he was saying about his contacts, his gigs. He wasn't going to leave. He'd invested a lifetime here.

We ate in silence. It was an exceptional carbonara.

"What do you want to do about the dogs?" I asked.

"You should take them." He didn't look at me.

"Are you sure? Where will you go?"

"I'll stay at the church. There's an empty apartment upstairs."

"I see."

For the second time in my life, there was no argument about leaving. We divided everything equally. We packed our things without a scene. I took the dogs and a trailer of boxes to Houston to sort myself out. My mom and stepdad had relocated there for work, and it seemed like a solid place to regroup.

Postscript: 2009

I hadn't seen Eliot in the two and a half years since I left, even though I still traveled back to New Orleans every few months for work projects. Most of my contacts were still in NOLA, so I'd put thousands of miles on the old 4x4 Pathfinder I was still driving in the summer of 2009.

To help me process the flood, I'd been writing essays about the city and applied to a nonfiction MFA program in Boston. I didn't tell Eliot that I'd been writing about our life together. I didn't tell him I was accepted into the program or that I planned to move to Boston. But somehow, a month before I was planning to move, I got an email from him:

hey j, i'm leaving new orleans. i'm moving home to boston. give me a call if you want. love you, e

It was unbelievable. I felt like NOLA was giving me one last bit of luck on this adventure. What were the chances we independently decided to move to Boston at the same time? I called him, and over the course of a few weeks we made plans to drive up together. Maybe we could try again, or at the very least, we could share a rental truck.

It could be a new start for us. I was open to that possibility. And wouldn't that create an incredible ending to the book I started drafting?

I sold the old 4x4 and rented a moving truck bound for New England. The dogs would stay with my mom. Eliot and I would have one last weekend in NOLA before heading north. He was still living in one of the upstairs apartments in the church.

As I drove the moving truck into our old neighborhood, I passed Pharez's building and imagined his S.O.S. comforter still hanging off the third-floor balcony. He had never come back to New Orleans, and the building had been repainted and looked brand new, but I half expected to see him up in that balcony waving down at me.

Big white film production trucks were blocking the road by Audubon Park. It must've been a major production, judging by the number of trucks blocking traffic. There was nothing but red taillights the entire length of the park.

The city was no longer smiling on me. I couldn't get around the traffic. I drove over the median to bypass the mayhem and found parking a block away from the church.

I called Eliot as I stretched my legs and started walking over. When I saw him walking toward me, it was as if I was seeing him for the first time. He was walking fast, wearing his old khaki shorts and a blue striped t-shirt. He smiled and yelled, "Jaaaayy!"

"Hey," I gave him a hug, his shirt was damp with perspiration.

"How was your drive?" He held onto my arm for a second and looked at me. "You look great. Come to the church, there's a film crew staging there, so we need to stick around until John gets here. Then we can go get dinner."

He rushed me the remainder of the block to the church. I couldn't tell if he was rushed because of the chaos of the film crew, or if he was nervous that I was there. We'd been talking every day, sometimes two or three times a day. I thought we'd slipped into a warm familiarity, but something felt off to me. I told myself it was because he was wrangling the crew at the church and there was a lot going on.

Cars and production trucks lined the street. People with headsets and clipboards fluttered about, shepherding actors from the church lobby to the park and pacing around the side entrance of the church. We passed them and climbed the stairs to the fellowship hall. Folding chairs were strewn everywhere.

Postscript: 2009

"The extras just left," he explained.

I looked around. Nothing had changed in four years.

I hadn't stepped in that space since our week in hell, but everything smelled the same: a familiar scent of old wood and mildew. The fluorescent lights were still too harsh. The air was still too heavy. There was still a brown stain in the ceiling where the water had leaked during Katrina.

On a bulletin board near the door, I saw the weekly schedule for the holy trinity of Anonymous groups: Alcoholics, Narcotics, and Gamblers. The flyers hadn't changed in the years I'd been gone. *Only the dates change*, I thought.

"You've got a lot of Gamblers Anonymous meetings now?"

Eliot started folding and stacking chairs against the wall. "Uh-huh. Lots of gamblers now, you'd be surprised."

I walked to the back of the hall, toward the kitchen, to wash my hands. Two signs were propped on the ledge of the window above the sink. One said: *Angel Food*. The other: *God is Good*.

Angel Food was a program that gave low-cost groceries to people in the neighborhood. Eliot had been helping them distribute food for years.

I went back into the fellowship hall to help him put chairs away. It was getting dark, and the frosted windows were turning charcoal gray.

"Where do you want to eat dinner?" I asked.

"I don't know. Anything's fine," he sounded almost shy. I got the sense again that something was off between us.

A guy with a clipboard came in and needed help, so Eliot left me to finish with the chairs. I put them away and sat at an old wooden desk by the door. After a few minutes I got bored and went outside.

John was standing by the door with Eliot and two production assistants. It was the first time I'd seen John since the day we left after the flood. I felt a surge of something irritating—a mix of anger and disgust.

"Hey, Jocelyn. How are you?" He smiled at me—a flat, placid smile that made me uneasy. I walked toward them.

"Fine, John. How are you?"

"I heard you drove a moving truck. Are you moving back?"

Eliot was staring at us like it was a Mexican standoff. I felt surreally out of my body.

"No. I'm on my way to Boston."

"Well, that's too bad."

"I stopped by to pick up Eliot."

"Good luck to you then."

I realized it was his preternatural calmness that made me uneasy. I felt like there was something just below the surface waiting to strike.

John resumed his conversation with the production assistants. Eliot and I walked toward St. Charles.

"I can't stand that guy. He gives me the creeps," I said.

"What do you mean? He's a good guy."

I sighed. It wasn't worth arguing about.

By the end of dinner my mood improved, and I forgot about John and the church and even the entire city of New Orleans. Everything felt fresh with hope. I was excited for a new life. We sat in the restaurant and talked about the trip. We'd take our time and sightsee for four days. We talked about the little studio apartment I'd found in Mission Hill and how convenient it was to the train line.

On our way back to the church we laughed about the old times and shouted our goodbyes to the old neighborhood.

Since I was only in town for two nights, I was able to stay in the church's vacant upstairs apartment. Eliot was living in the guest studio, but the pastor's unit was empty. The church was between pastors...as it often was. Eliot and I climbed a dark, narrow staircase behind the fellowship hall stage.

"Sorry, there's no light," he said as we felt our way up the narrow path.

Postscript: 2009

"It's fine. I'm just glad I didn't have to pay for a hotel."

I followed him into a small two-room apartment, and he snapped on a bare lightbulb hanging from the center of the room. I put my overnight bag on the floor near a twin bed that was hastily covered with a stained comforter. It was musty and dark. The place looked dirty, like it had never been cleaned. The hardwood floors were scratched and battered. The walls, a faded cream color, were scuffed. It gave me the creeps.

He turned on an ancient air conditioner in the window. "It takes a few minutes to cool down in here," he apologized.

There were piles of kids' toys and clothes and plastic bags of junk stacked along one of the walls.

"Are you sure it's okay I'm staying here? I'm not putting anyone out?"

"No, the pastor's family left months ago. I think his wife got tired of living here, they had two little kids. They haven't been back in a long time."

"But they left all this stuff?"

"They'll come back and get it sometime."

"Oh." A shudder went down my spine imagining a young family trying to live in this claustrophobic space.

"They were young. I think the wife was only 25 or 26 and they already had two kids." He was standing in the doorway. "They weren't from here. I think she had a rough time with the kids and wanted to go home."

"Makes sense." I bent down to rifle through my overnight bag for my camera.

"You want to go downstairs while the room's getting cold?"

"Sure." I took my camera from the bag and followed him downstairs. There were three doors at the landing: one to the fellowship hall, another to the altar, and a third went down to the basement. I let him lead the way through the altar door. "How do you keep from getting lost in here? It's like a maze."

He shrugged. "Go sit in the pews and I'll bring drinks."

I took it all in knowing I would never come back. I would never again be in this phase of my life. I never wanted to walk through these doorways again. I lifted my camera and took three photographs of the stairwell.

Eliot pushed through a squeaking door to the kitchen. The same door that blew open and closed on the night of the storm. I heard glasses clink in the distance.

I stepped through the door that led to the altar. The chapel was dark except for a streetlight shining through the wall of windows.

Behind me, Eliot entered and flipped on a switch. Yellow light washed over us, illuminating a large room of pews and doors leading to the main church entrance. I walked out toward the pews. To me, it didn't feel like a sacred space. It was a crumbling, empty church. The threadbare red carpet was shiny and tattered from decades of wear. A window was cracked and looked ready to shatter. There was scaffolding set up along one wall where Eliot and the maintenance man were trying to patch over structural cracks.

Eliot spoke behind me. "I've got something for you. You're never going to believe what I found."

"What?" I turned to see him set two glasses on the altar table.

"Close your eyes first," he laughed. "Hold out your hands."

I obeyed and smiled and held out my hands.

"Keep them closed!"

"They're closed!" I laughed. I heard him approach and felt him stand in front of me. He laid something flat and heavy on my hands, but I could tell he didn't let go.

"You ready? Open them!"

I opened my eyes and saw an annotated copy of the Bhagavad-Gita in my hands. It was the book he'd borrowed all those years ago. He let go of it as soon as I saw it.

"Oh my God," I yelled. "I thought you lost this!"

"I know! I thought I left it on the streetcar!"

Postscript: 2009

He started laughing. "I was packing last week, and I found it in a box. Isn't that funny? I must've forgot I brought it here."

My heart sank, but I was laughing. I had completely forgotten about that book. Before we even moved in together, he told me he accidentally left it on the streetcar. I never expected to see it again, but this felt like a sign. Every loose end had been tied.

Is this a good omen or a bad one?

"Are you surprised?"

"Yeah, of course. I thought it was gone." I flipped through it. "Did you ever read it?"

"No. Maybe a little...no, I didn't. I thought I left it on the streetcar." He handed me a glass of grape juice.

"Is this communion juice?" I looked at the glass.

"It's not blessed yet." He sat cross-legged on the altar and watched me stare at the glass. "Don't worry, there's plenty for the service."

I sat next to him and took a drink. He stretched out on his back and folded his hands behind his head and crossed his feet. I put the book down and swiveled around to face him. He closed his eyes, and I squeezed one of his bare feet and shook it. "Hey, are you ready for this move?"

"Uh-huh." He didn't open his eyes or move a muscle.

"This is a pretty big move for you."

"Not really. I'm just going home."

"Are you sure you're ready to leave this place?"

"Uh-huh."

"Uh-huh." I repeated. I ran my hand over his ankle and patted it. "I'm glad you're coming. It's good to see you again."

He sat up. "Are you still thirsty? Do you want more juice?"

"I'm okay."

"I'm going to get some more," he got up and walked toward the kitchen.

I tucked the book under my arm and picked up my camera to follow him.

"I've been thinking about taking up piano again," he said.

"You play piano?"

"It helps you be a more melodic drummer."

"Since when do you play piano?" I chuckled but felt disconnected. I lifted my camera and snapped a few photos of the space.

"Since always. I learned when I was a kid."

Another swish-click of my camera. "Why didn't you ever tell me that before?"

He snapped off the light switch and the room went dark. "I don't know. It never came up. You want more juice?"

"No. I'm going to bed."

"Okay. My room is across the hall if you need anything."

The next morning, Eliot went to his last day at work, and I jogged around Audubon Park for a final time. The sweat ran down my spine in the old familiar way. It wasn't even noon yet and I was soaked. I cleaned up and made my way to Whole Foods to meet Ginny for lunch. Their time in Hattiesburg was brief. They just moved back to a house by the lakeshore.

When I walked up to the store, I barely recognized her. Her hair was longer and blonde, completely opposite the dark brown pixie cut I'd always known. She looked relaxed and casual and not pregnant—again, the opposite of my most vivid memories of her. It took me a few minutes to adjust to this vision, this new Ginny in the making.

Heavy sheets of rain started to fall as we hugged in the store's entrance.

"Look at you!" I laughed.

"James is bringing the girls from the car—you're not going to believe how big they are!"

The last time I'd seen them was a trip I took to Hattiesburg two years earlier. Their oldest was three or four then. In my memory, she still had her baby face and little blonde ringlets. The baby was as mellow as the day she was born.

Postscript: 2009

"When are you coming home?" Ginny asked.

"I haven't even gone to Boston yet!" I laughed.

"I know, but you need to come home! We can be neighbors now and have craft night like the old days!"

"I love you," I hugged her again.

Two little girls came bounding toward us from around the corner: the oldest maybe five and the baby almost three. They had matching freckles and wavy dark blonde hair with choppy bangs. They were pure energy and life with shining blue eyes, even in the wilting August heat.

James had brought my going away present: a framed black and white photograph Ginny had created in their lush backyard. It was a long exposure that created a ghostly image of a woman walking from a rocking chair. She titled it "The New Life" and had carefully framed and signed it.

That bright August day in 2009 was too beautiful to spend indoors, so we drove to the French Quarter. The Satchmo Summer Music Festival was happening around the Old Mint building on Esplanade Boulevard.

It was a perfect New Orleans summer day. Live music pounded from every corner of the block. Snowball vendors sold sticky phosphorescent ice cones from rolling metal carts. Every imaginable sort of person mingled and lounged, slowly making the rounds from one pulsating stage to the next.

The sweat on our bodies flowed as freely as the cold Abita beer in frosted plastic cups. Square paper fans advertised local radio stations—and flapped at the end of every person's arms.

We made our way through the crowd to the Old Mint, where the girls could make art projects. I photographed them as they painted Zulu coconuts with other children in the craft room.

When we'd cooled down enough, we made our way back out to the grassy stage area and staked out a patch of grass. James brought us bright red and blue snowballs covered with cherry, bubblegum, and watermelon syrups.

Displaced

The girls and I were covered in Technicolor stains by the time we drank the last of our icy syrups. We danced to the throbbing brass sounds of a local jazz band, and I photographed the charismatic singer as he riled up the crowd and surfed over their heads between trombone solos.

On the way back to the car, baby girl reached out and took my hand and told me about all her favorite things: the new litter of kittens that lived in their backyard and bath time and stories at bedtime. Her hand was so small and feathery soft. I hunched over to hear her while holding her little hand tight.

I prayed that only peace and happiness would ever visit these sweet babies of New Orleans. May they never experience what we went through before they arrived.

That night I met Eliot after work, and we walked to the streetcar. We rode down to the Quarter for one last date night and reminisced about the past. It was a perfect day of my favorite things with some of my favorite people.

I was ready to say goodbye.

On Sunday morning we packed Eliot's drum kit and a few boxes into the truck and made the uneventful drive to Boston. We passed four days like siblings, talking about the scenery and ranking our favorite cities and playing music by the bands we listened to in our youth.

We stayed a night with his brother at their family house, and it had changed dramatically since 2005. The antiques had been replaced by piles of toys and a playpen—Eliot's niece just had a baby. The old family photos had been swapped with new color snapshots of his brother and his brother's granddaughter. It was a happier space filled with new life.

We unloaded the drum kit and Eliot's boxes into his childhood bedroom, and the next day we moved everything else into my new apartment. He helped me unload and return the truck and we filled the fridge with groceries. I couldn't contain my excitement to be settling down in a new place.

Postscript: 2009

We started unpacking boxes in the kitchen.

"Hey, I'm going to go back to New Orleans for a drum clinic," he announced.

"I'm sorry, what?" I knew I hadn't heard him right.

"I've got a drum clinic. I booked a flight back."

I stood there with plates in my hands, staring, as he unpacked a box of silverware and linens.

"You're going back to New Orleans?"

"Only for a week. Maybe two at the most."

"Wait, I'm confused. You just drove all the way up here..."

"Yeah, well I scheduled this drum clinic. So, I need to go back for a week or two. Then I'll come back. I'm going to stay at my brother's tomorrow to see my mom, then I'm flying out."

"When were you going to tell me this?"

"I just did."

"You came all this way up here..."

"Well, you were coming up anyway. It's just a couple of weeks tops, and I'll come back."

I had no words. I mean, there were literally no words for the rush of panic and fear flooding through me.

"You aren't coming back, are you?"

"Of course I am!"

"Don't lie to me! You came all this way, and you knew you were going back!" I put everything down and went to the living room. I was starting to shake. I had expected a completely different outcome than this, but I realized this was the only outcome we would ever have.

"I told you it's just a couple of weeks and I'll be back," he followed me into the room.

"You won't. But I know you're telling yourself that."

He rolled his eyes. "You don't know that."

I wasn't going to fight with him. I let him believe he would come back, even if I knew he wouldn't. The next day he took the train to his brother's house, and I didn't say a word.

He called me that night, "I saw my mom after I left you."

"Yeah? How'd it go?" I could hear in his voice it didn't go well.

"They moved her to the hospice floor. She can't remember me anymore."

His voice carried a heaviness I hadn't heard before.

"I'm sorry to hear that." I genuinely was. I liked Aurora.

There was a brief static-filled silence. "My flight's at 6 in the morning. I'll probably schedule the cab tonight."

"That's a good idea. Have a safe trip."

"Uh-huh. Thank you." He hung up.

I wasn't going to fight with him when I knew he was struggling with his mother's illness. If I was in his shoes, I wouldn't want to come back either.

A few days later he called to tell me he was home—in New Orleans. He sounded lighter, happier, but he complained he was miserable in the blight of the city. He swore he couldn't wait to be back in Boston.

I just agreed with him. There was no point in arguing.

Months went by, and I knew he would stay in New Orleans. Whether he admitted it to himself or not, he was happy there in a way he would never be happy anywhere else.

He was *home*.

Sometime later I made a disc of the Satchmo Summer Fest photos for Ginny. I realized with shock (but not surprise) that I recognized that charismatic trombone player we'd seen crowd surfing that day. I checked the black and white prints on my Boston wall: I had photographed the same handsome trombone player during my first visit to the city just before I'd met El Diablo. There he was, hanging on my wall. I'd captured him twice. Of course, he was incredibly talented, and New Orleans is a small town writ large.

His photo hung next to the signed print from Ginny.

Postscript: 2009

I settled into Boston to write and make sense of the last eight years of my life. Despite how things went with Eliot, I was relieved and excited for a new beginning.

As I began sorting through the notebooks and photographs and videos that I made during those years, I found a passage I wrote in 2006, just before I moved out of our house:

Nothing is the same, but at one time this was the best part of me. I was the sound of the streetcar. When it rained, I was the fog we traveled through. It never occurred to me that in one morning it would all be swept away. Had I known, I would have savored it. I would have preserved every second in my mind.

Acknowledgments

To me, New Orleans is a place that defies logic. Someone once told me it's like being in love with an alcoholic. You know it's toxic and dysfunctional, but you just can't leave it alone. I know a lot about alcoholics, being in recovery myself, and that perfectly sums up how I feel about that beautiful city.

A few notes about the writing of this book: A section of the manuscript was originally published in the anthology, *New Orleans by New Orleans*. People's names have been changed and some of the chronology during and after the flood may be slightly off—some of my notes and timelines may have been out of order. Any inaccuracies are unintentional.

The first draft of this manuscript was completed as part of the creative nonfiction MFA program at Emerson College. I owe a debt of gratitude to the 2009-2011 cohort, particularly Sebastian Stockman and Jodie Noelle Vinson, whose thoughtful feedback and edits helped turn a collection of essays into a cohesive story.

There have been too many people to list who helped me beyond the writing and publishing of this book. Many were there during the Katrina years but weren't named in the narrative, and I want to thank a few here.

I am forever grateful to my mom and stepdad, Susan and Rod Koertner, for providing scaffolding for us after the flood, and for giving me a safe place to land when I needed to sort things out.

I'm deeply grateful to the friends and family who provided support and helped me through that period, especially the Lee-

Tsao family, the Peters family, K.C. Crill, Paul A. Greenberg, Ethel Matshiya, and the Windham family. Grateful isn't the word. They were lifelines in a dark time, and words can't express how much I appreciate their support.

I am especially grateful to people who took a chance on hiring me in New Orleans at that time, especially those who taught me skills and gave me the opportunity to build the career I've been blessed to carry forward.

It was difficult to pick up this book again after putting it down in 2011, but I hope it presents a small slice of the story's history—a story of everyday people trying to put our lives back together. "Eliot" is still one of my closest friends, and he still lives in New Orleans. No matter what happens in life, we are always going to be family.

Finally, I am grateful to Tom, who saw me sitting in a Boston coffee shop on a frozen January morning. He sat down next to me, struck up a conversation, and made me laugh, truly laugh, for the first time in a long time. We talked for four hours straight, then met again the following day to talk for several hours more. I regained hope that I could be happy again.

No one has ever understood me more deeply or challenged me more completely to become the person I wanted to be. He was the first person to see this book's plot points taped across my Boston apartment wall, and he sat with me in a New Orleans pub on the ten-year anniversary of this event and listened to me talk through that horrible week. We drove through Louisiana and ate the best damn fried chicken ever prepared, and I finally had better memories to overwrite the bad ones. Through knowing him, I learned to lighten my load and trust that everything will always be okay.

www.ingramcontent.com/pod-product-compliance
Lightning Source LLC
Chambersburg PA
CBHW060554080526
44585CB00013B/558